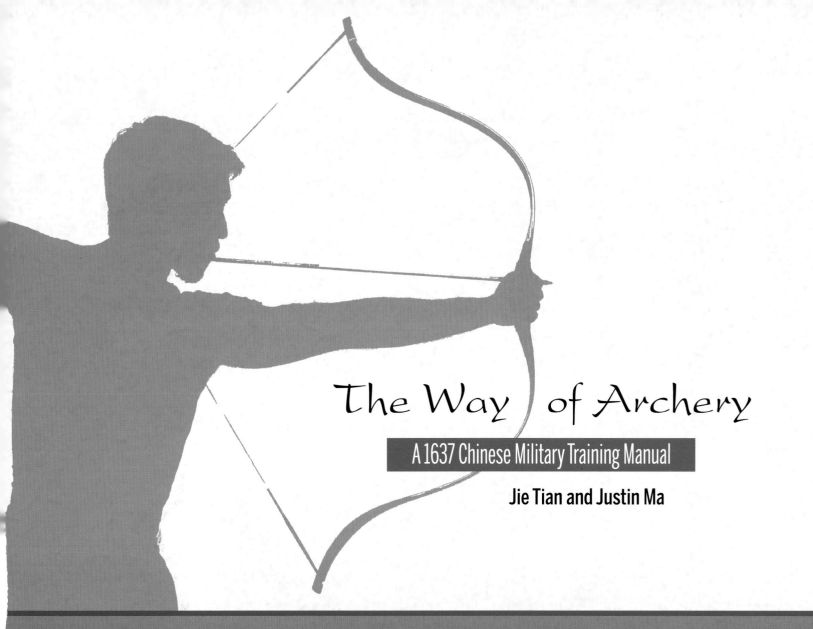

The Way of Archery

A 1637 Chinese Military Training Manual

Jie Tian and Justin Ma

Schiffer Publishing Ltd

4880 Lower Valley Road • Atglen, PA 19310

Other Schiffer Books on Related Subjects:

Weapons of Warriors: Famous Antique Swords of the Near East by Vic Diehl & Hermann Hampe et al., 978-0-7643-4116-8

Legends in Archery: Adventurers with Bow and Arrow by Peter O. Stecher, 978-0-7643-3575-4

The Armies of Warlord China 1911–1928 by Philip Jowett, 978-0-7643-4345-2

Photographs courtesy of Chang Pengfei (常朋飛 先生); Jaap Koppedrayer of Yumi Archery; Mike Loades; Glenn Murray, Esq.; Lukas Novotny of Saluki Bow Company; and Stephen Selby.

Front cover: shedao (射道, *"The Way of Archery"*) calligraphy by Zhang Chen (章晨 先生), member of the Chinese Calligraphers' Association (中國書法家協會會員). The calligraphy is in the style of the Zhou Dynasty (1046–256 BCE) bronze script (金文). As this is an earlier style of writing, we can see the character for "archery/shooting" (射) resembles an archer shooting an arrow from a bow. The ancient character for "way" (道) shows people (人) on the left and right walking on the path towards the truth as a destination (首) — this is how a path becomes a way. These two words written in bronze script are a testament to the importance archery has played in Chinese culture at least 3,000 years ago and earlier.

Disclaimer: Archery, like any other sport, carries with it inherent risks. Practicing archery requires strenuous exertion of certain muscle groups. In rare cases, practicing could lead to serious sports injury. Equipment such as bows, arrows, and other archery accessories carry the risk of failing or breaking, which could in turn injure the archer seriously. Although archery is generally a safe sport, it is always good to exercise caution. Always inspect your equipment for safety and stop using it if you detect defects. Do not overexert yourself. Stop practicing when you feel unusual discomfort or pain.

Published by Schiffer Publishing, Ltd.
4880 Lower Valley Road
Atglen, PA 19310
Phone: (610) 593-1777; Fax: (610) 593-2002
E-mail: Info@schifferbooks.com

For our complete selection of fine books on this and related subjects, please visit our website at www.schifferbooks.com. You may also write for a free catalog.

This book may be purchased from the publisher. Please try your bookstore first.

We are always looking for people to write books on new and related subjects. If you have an idea for a book, please contact us at proposals@schifferbooks.com.

Schiffer Publishing's titles are available at special discounts for bulk purchases for sales promotions or premiums. Special editions, including personalized covers, corporate imprints, and excerpts can be created in large quantities for special needs. For more information, contact the publisher.

Designed by RoS
Type set in President/ZapfEllipt BT/KaiTi

ISBN: 978-0-7643-4791-7
Printed in China

In memory of Ma Shaochen

馬紹楨

(1922–2002)

Contents

Foreword

Kay Koppedrayer

Voices from the past call to us all the time, but mostly we pay little attention. An emperor may build a grand tomb to celebrate a life in its passing and while we feel wonder as we survey his army of terra cotta warriors, how much of his life do we really understand? With each stitch, the embroidery that brings a dragon robe, a *jifu*, to life proclaims a state of being, its artistry whispering the wonders of its craft. But are our senses sharp enough to recognize its beauty? Of this body of knowing and doing, what do we comprehend?

An inscription on a calligrapher's brush rest, can we gauge its intention? How much of that meaning is now lost to us? A scholar will toil to leave a legacy behind. Yet how much heed do we pay to that labor? Some manuscripts survive; others are lost or forgotten. Or neglected or destroyed according to the dictates of time. Or worse, held captive by an agenda other than its own.

The separation of then and now, this distance is but part of the many obstacles you face as you turn to listen to a voice calling us from the past. Language can stand in the way, as can your ability to attend to what is being relayed. Preserved only in a written form, its comprehension presents so many challenges. The text speaks, but you have to learn how to listen. The clarifications you demand of the writer are there — maybe. Or maybe not. It is up to you to figure it out, for though it has not stopped speaking, the voice will say no more. The rest is up to you. You need to be able to discern meaning, appreciate nuance, and sense inflection, and also decide if the voice is worth listening to in the first place. And most of all you need to be there, to be ready to hear what is being said.

Justin Ma and Jie Tian did just that in their preparation of this translation. They took the time to listen to an old man offering to share some hard-won understanding about a topic dear to his heart. What he had to say related to form and focus and also to physical capacity, in a practice where the equanimity of body and mind is of the utmost importance. Emphasizing the need of careful self-examination, he spoke of rigorous training and never giving up. He didn't, possessed of a character trait he sought to impart to others. That same trait is perhaps what compelled him to put his perceptions into words.

Long gone from this world, the old man was once known as Gao Ying or sometimes as Gao Shuying; the discipline he wrote about so many centuries ago is archery. He talks about the simple act of picking up a bow and letting an arrow fly, but for this master, it is not just a simple matter. What he wishes to impart is a way of archery. He knows it is a simple matter — so long as you are doing it right. He will tell us how, so long as we are willing to listen. That is what Justin Ma and Jie Tian did, they listened, and in homage to the spirit of the old man who spoke to them, they in turn pass his words on to others in this translation.

The practice of archery has a long history in China. Copious documentation both in artifact and written form testifies to its development and transmission. Facility with the bow was the hallmark of a cultivated individual. Demonstration of that proficiency featured in court ritual and also in war. Strategies determining its use contributed to the rise and fall of various dynasties. And over the centuries, placement in certain highly sought-after government positions came only to those candidates proving their skills with the bow. From the Confucian *Analects* to the later compendia of teachers like Li Chengfen and Wang Ju, there are hundreds of works that expound upon archery.

Yet, among the many Chinese texts extolling the virtues of archery, our translators chose this one. Of this large legacy, why turn to Gao Ying? Why would these two men, one software engineer, the other an economist, dedicate themselves to this work? Although it is better left to them to lay out their reasons, every time they pick up their bows they bear witness to their motivations. Somehow, in some way across space and time, Gao Ying spoke to them.

Indeed, it shows whenever they take up their bows.

The first time I saw Jie shoot, the beauty of his form almost took my breath away. No formal demonstration, the moment was casual. A small group had come together for a Chinese archery training program. Jie wanted to explain something and the best way to do so was to show it. Without the encumbrance of words, he drew his bow and released an arrow. Just like that. No hesitation, eyes to the straw bale, he raised his bow and in one fluid motion, drew his arrow. A nearly imperceptible moment passed; in that was the paradox of full draw, the moment of full tension, yet the archer was at ease. And then almost without knowing came the release. The sound of the arrow conveyed what Gao Ying had been expressing, something that we could acknowledge only after watching the form being brought to life.

I had met Justin earlier, in Qinghai, China, at the 2012 gathering of traditional archers from all corners of the world. The proving grounds of cross-cultural exchange, the event brought archers face-to-face with their own and with others' traditions. Part spectacle, part theater, part real, the gathering was a showcase of performance and display, and a wonderful arena of exchange. So many traditions were present, each with their different roots and trajectories, so many directions, so many pathways. So many conversations to have all at the same time. Within the folds of the many histories present were signs of what archery had once meant to China, and what tradition means now in this new era of appreciation. This was an arena where one's own tradition mingled and mixed with so many others.

For many traditional archers and bow-makers of a new generation in China, the bows of the Qing dynasty call, their attraction reminding them of their own roots. For Justin, however, the unspoken question about one's own had already found its answer in Gao Ying's introduction to martial archery. It was in the Ming, and not Qing, dynasty that he found the key to what he was looking for. Perhaps his own martial arts background was a factor, perhaps his recognition of the value of Gao Ying's writings, perhaps his interest in an earlier era of Chinese history, whatever the factors, Justin found Gao Ying's teachings pushed him to the ideal he sought.

On the competition grounds in Qinghai, he drew his bow in accordance with what he learned from Gao Ying. In doing that, Justin managed something extraordinary. He had brought back to China a living expression of its own archery history. While much of that history has been nearly forgotten, Justin and Jie have made a commitment to ensure that the teachings of one master will be better known. Through demonstrations, talks, programs and competitions, they have revived the spirit of the archery master they have taken for their own. Now, with this translation, they have made his teachings accessible to others. What better way to meet this master than by his own words?

Born in the latter half of the 16th century, Gao Ying must have been quite a character. By the time he took up the task of compiling his insights, he'd seen it all. He lived at a time when the Ming Dynasty was experiencing its decline. Internal corruption matched with troubles on its northern and southern frontiers weakened the empire. Its military strength was waning; even the emperor knew that. Recognizing that his soldiers were no match for the Manchu armies gathering in the north, Chongzhen ordered his bureaucrats to bolster their preparedness.

Gao Ying's response was to prepare his training manual, completed in 1637. His approach was not to speak of military strategy, but rather turn to the very basis of military strength, namely the martial capacity of the individual soldier. In that way, his voice is that of a coach, explaining what constitutes the right technique to anyone who will listen, and admonishing them if they think otherwise. So convinced he is of the proper way to hold the shoulders that he returns again and again to the basics. Knowing the limitations of words, he tries his best to be as clear as possible, resorting to imagery when he thinks it will help us grasp what he is saying. He knows he is writing for posterity.

In spite of it all, Gao Ying is no easy teacher. He expects you to get it right and has no qualms about telling you so. You can almost imagine him shouting out his instructions. This coach takes no flak from anyone — not from his students, and certainly not from any other self-appointed master. He has no qualms about telling others they are wrong.

At other times Gao Ying's voice is cajoling. He encourages us to take our practice seriously and indeed take ourselves seriously. He tells us to strive after an ideal, and settle for nothing less. Interestingly enough, Gao Ying's manual dates about a century later than Roger Ascham's *Toxophilus*. Despite their many differences, they seem to echo each other when it comes to practice. Like Ascham, Gao Ying seeks perfection. When he senses we might give in to mediocrity, he scolds. His rebukes are relentless. For him there is nothing worse than amplifying bad technique through repetition. Get it right from the get-go is his advice.

His coaching warrants attention, and not just because he shouts so. He has a lot to say about the importance of coming to full draw. No matter what style of archery you do, his observations ring true. He has seen enough to caution against faulty technique. He can point out how certain forms of draw and release are empty and lacking in energy. And better yet, he doesn't just point out the flaws, he lays out the how and why of doing it right.

Gao Ying can be pretty funny, too. In one place, he makes mention of the different venues of strength we have. He cites leg strength, hip strength, arm strength, and just when you settle in to hear about how they work together, he clobbers you with a simple observation. Leg strength is good for walking, hip strength is great if you need to carry something heavy, but neither of these will help with archery. Even as important as arm strength is, what matters is matching your equipment to your capacity. His counsel, don't over-bow yourself, you'll be doing yourself no favors, is worthy advice aspiring archers need to hear even today.

For his timeless advice Gao Ying's writings are worth reading, and not just for archers. Bow-makers can also pick up some useful tips. In the middle of his first text Gao Ying provides a very useful synopsis of everything to be considered when building a horn composite bow. He starts at the beginning with choice of materials, and walks his readers through all the steps, right up to the qualities a good bowyer seeks in a finished bow. Ever the coach, Gao Ying helps the novice bowyer learn to recognize what those qualities are. On bamboo he offers sound guidance, knowledge experienced bow-makers have gained only through experience. Talk with bow-makers today who work with bamboo and you'll find they echo Gao Ying's observations.

For the historian Gao Ying provides insights into archery of the late Ming Dynasty. His remarks the wind having an effect only when you're aiming at making a hit at more than 200 feet gives you a sense of the distance they were shooting. Likewise, his recommendations of changing to a bow string with shorter loops is a reminder of the differences between western recurves and the Chinese bows of his time.

The classically trained scholar that he is, he draws upon oft-repeated examples of the past — to become like a wooden chicken or the tale of the louse (which he considers an exaggeration) — and turns them back to his own style of teaching. In the second volume of his manual, he turns to the aphorisms archery teachers of his period studied in search of the wisdom of the past. With his commentary Gao Ying makes meaning out of these elusive statements. Often correctives of what other commentators have said, his pronouncements serve to demonstrate the validity of his teachings. If they so clearly accord with what the ancients have said, who then will have the audacity to question them? Put another way, who else besides Gao Ying can so boldly proclaim this truth? Still, when he speaks of the qualities to be cultivated in order to be a good archer, virtues such as equanimity, harmony, and discipline, he gives us a taste of Confucian ideals. How you conduct yourself matters. Like handwriting analysis, your draw and release tell it all. The process needs no mystification, all you need to do is pay attention to the basics. As he repeats so often, no matter what seductions are out there, do not fall prey to them.

Underneath it all, you find traces of his own life. Here and there in comments almost in passing, he details some of his journey, particularly the times he went wrong. You sense you're hearing true confessions, tinged with his feelings of shame. With that his urgency not to allow others to fall into the same traps makes more sense. Towards the end of his second volume, he ties it all together:

> WHEN YOU ARE ABOUT TO SHOOT AND WANT TO SETTLE YOUR BODY, YOU ARE FOLLOWING THE WAY OF ESTABLISHING A SOLID ROOT. WHEN YOU PULL THE BOW VIGOROUSLY TO REACH FULL DRAW, YOU ARE FOLLOWING THE WAY OF BEING MOTIVATED AND DISCIPLINED. WHEN YOU GATHER YOUR MIND AND STRENGTH TO HOLD FULL DRAW STEADILY, THEN YOU ARE FOLLOWING THE WAY OF DILIGENCE AND SELF-IMPROVEMENT. WHEN YOU RELEASE, IF YOUR MIND AND FORM ARE SHARP, THEN YOU CAN ACHIEVE INTERNAL PEACE WITHOUT ANY ANGER: YOU ARE FOLLOWING THE WAY OF PURSUING PERFECTION, STAYING MOTIVATED, BEING SIMULTANEOUSLY HARD AND SOFT, AND CATCHING THE RIGHT MOMENT! AFTER THE ARROW RELEASES, IF YOU KEEP YOUR FORM AND SPIRIT CALM AND COLLECTED, THEN YOU ARE FOLLOWING THE WAY OF TRANQUILITY.

Such is Gao Ying's way of archery, and so our translators invite you to experience it for yourselves.

Kay Koppedrayer *(BA, MA, PhD) is a retired professor from the Department of Religion and Culture at Wilfrid Laurier University, Ontario, Canada. She is a writer and archery historian, widely published in American and European magazines such as* Primitive Archer, Instinctive Archery, TradWorld, Traditionell Bogenschiessen, Journal of the Society of Archer-Antiquaries, *and* US and International Archer. *She is also an Associate Editor of the magazine* Primitive Archer, *as well as coorganizer of the Fort Dodge International Horse Archery Festival (the first large-scale international gathering of traditional archers).*

Acknowledgments

This book would not have been possible without the efforts, contributions, discussions, feedback, encouragement, and moral support of many. Some of these individuals were responsible for reviving entire movements of Chinese and Asian archery. Some of them wrote influential books that we read as beginners, and which launched us into this Asian archery odyssey. Some of them were pioneering researchers in Chinese and other forms of military archery. Some of them gave us invaluable technical advice as beginners. Some of them gave us a venue to practice and hone our skills, as well as to teach newcomers the basics of the art. Some of them steered us right when we started to veer off course. Some taught us how to assemble arrows and strings, and how to take care of equipment. Some of them provided the bows, arrows, and other equipment we use in practice and competition. Some of them explained to us the nuances of bow making. Some of them were photographers who provided us outstanding pictures to use in our book. Some of them provided us a forum to talk about our research. Some of them gave us helpful advice on how to publish our book. We are grateful to all of you. We have listed the names in alphabetical order by surname. We apologize profusely to anybody we have omitted. 由衷感謝朋友們對我們的支持與幫助，以下姓名以英文字母順序排列.

Nadeem Ahmad; Adnan Akgun; Gokmen Altinkulp; Larry Andrews; Torin Andrews; Sebastian Bae; Howard Haotian Bai; Rick Beal; Deborah Berube; the Borton Family (Greg, Grace, Alix); Marcus Bossett; Devon Brinner; Professor Lee Brown of the Center for Sport Performance at California State University, Fullerton; Duke Bhuphaibool; Jhoneil Centeno; Chang Pengfei (常朋飛 先生); Hing Chao (趙式慶 先生); Steven Chau; Brian Chew; Daniel Chung; Peter Dekker of Manchuarchery.org, dedicated Qing/Manchu archery researcher; Zack Djurica of Nomadic Arts Archery; traditional archers at the Double T Archery Club in Amherst, New York; Bede Dwyer; Enrique Escudero; Nicholas Freer; Dee Dee Furler; Joe Gibbs of the English War Bow Society; Michael Gilbert; Peter Gillis; Hilary Greenland of the Society for the Promotion of Traditional Archery; Gui Shunxing (歸順興 先生), bowmaker known as Mariner (水手); Larry Hatfield; Angelika Hornig of Verlag Angelika Hornig; Richard Hornsby, experienced traditional archer and coach, former UK NFAS 3D Primitive Champion; Hsin-Hsin Hu; Kathy Hua; Ramin Izadi; the Kalinovski Family (Evguenia, Yann); Heon Ku Kim; Jaap Koppedrayer of Yumi Archery; Kay Koppedrayer, archery historian and retired university professor; Christopher Chi Lee; Li Tieyou (李鐵友 先生); Professor Dennis Lieu and the archers of the Cal Archery Club at University of California, Berkeley; Yu-te Odin Lin (林育德 先生) of the Taiwan Traditional Archery Alliance; Fong Liu; Mike Loades of the California Centaurs, historical weapons expert; Professor Scott Lynn of the Center for Sport Performance at Cal State University, Fullerton; Wendy Mao; Dan McGehee; Mike McIntyre; Hilary Merrill of the California Centaurs; Robert Molineaux; Tanawat Muninnimit, graphic designer; Glenn Murray, Esq.; Lukas Novotny of Saluki Bow Company; the Niu Family (Adrian, Sophia, Ethan, Jade); Murat Ozveri; Jungmin (James) Park; Reed Peck-Chris; Chiao-Yun Peng (彭巧芸 女士) of the Taiwan Traditional Archery Alliance; Cesar Perez of Legionnaire Archery; Thomas Vu Pham; Raph Rambur; Mike Retodo; Stephen Selby (謝肅方 先生), founder of the Asian Traditional Archery Research Network (ATARN) and pioneer in reviving traditional Chinese archery; Hugh Soar of the English War Bow Society; Sonoma Coastal EquesTraining Center; Mark Stretton of the English War Bow Society; Wayne Suhrbier; Philip Tom; Jeffrey Tsao; Nils Visser; Wang Gang (王剛 先生) of the Traditional Chinese Archery Commission of the Chinese Archery Association; Dan Winheld; Anne Xiao; Xu Kaicai (徐開才 先生), former Chinese National Archery Team coach and athlete, committed pioneer and leader of the traditional archery revival in China; Yeochang Yun; Dan Zeltwanger; Zhang Chen (章晨 先生), member of the Chinese Calligraphers' Association; Zhang Li (張利 先生) of Ali Archery (阿利弓箭); Zhenghu CKTA (正鵠社的伙伴們); the Zipser Family (Karl, Hanneke, Nino); Michael Zou.

Thanks to Schiffer Publishing for the very generous opportunity to work with them.

Lastly but most importantly, we are grateful for the love and support of our wives and families, who somehow managed to put up with us during the entire book writing process!

Introduction to *The Way of Archery*

Chinese Archery

We (the authors) started practicing Chinese archery because we wanted to develop a connection with our heritage. Archery has played a prominent role in Chinese culture and history. The Chinese had long considered the bow and arrow the most prestigious weapon on the battlefield. Archery was likewise held in the highest regard in the civil arena. In the Zhou Dynasty (1046–256 BCE) archery was one of the Six Noble Arts and archery rituals were used to select rulers and officials. Moreover, archery had strong connections with the pillars of Chinese philosophy: Daoism and Confucianism. In fact, Confucius himself was an archery teacher. Generation after generation had acknowledged archery's significance up until the 20th century, when practical considerations (as the bow and arrow had become obsolete as a military weapon) and complicated political/economic circumstances caused Chinese archery to fall into obscurity.

Fast forward to the 21st century, and traditional Chinese archery has been revived as a cultural pastime thanks to the pioneering efforts of a handful of individuals inside and outside of China. Their efforts have paid off, and traditional Chinese archery seminars, tournaments, and festivals are thriving. But when it comes to learning the **technique** for Chinese archery, where do we begin?

China has a large geography and a long history. As a result, many variations in archery technique emerged over time, including those described in a handful of Chinese military manuals. Ideally, any archery technique you practice should be **practical** (with a clear blueprint for improving your skill in hitting the target) and **ergonomic** (helping you avoid injury in the process). Unfortunately, with the diversity of Chinese styles we found ourselves trying everything in the beginning. Some styles were uncomfortable and caused injury, while others contained flowery and extraneous movements that did not help with shooting accuracy. We only regained a foundation for a practical and ergonomic archery after stumbling upon the 1637 Chinese manual written by Gao Ying, whose no-nonsense military style we have dedicated ourselves to reconstructing.

Gao Ying（高穎）

The twilight of China's Ming Dynasty (the dynasty ruled from 1368–1644 CE) was a turbulent time. At the end of the 16th century, the Ming empire achieved taxing victories against the Japanese (who twice attempted to conquer Korea), the Mongolians, and rebels in the Southwest. However, that feeling of accomplishment was short-lived, as the beginning of the 17th century saw the accumulation of stressors that would lead to the Ming Dynasty's ultimate demise. These included food shortages, a complacent and declining military, further internal rebellions, decades of systemic government corruption, and the emergence of the new Manchu nation (which would eventually found the Qing Dynasty, 1644–1911 CE). But it was in these challenging times that one of the most unconventional and innovative archery thinkers would emerge. His name was Gao Ying.

Gao Ying was born in 1570 in the Southern Chinese city of Jiading, which is now a district in modern-day Shanghai that borders Suzhou. He was well-educated in the classics and he was well-versed in the military art of archery, what the Chinese call *wenwushuangquan* 文武雙全 (excelling in both scholarly and military affairs). This background made him especially qualified to compile his 40-plus years of archery experience into two books, *An Orthodox Introduction to Martial Archery* (*Wujing*

Shexue Rumen Zhengzong 武經射學入門正宗) and *An Orthodox Guide to Martial Archery* (*Wujing Shexue Zhengzong Zhimiji* 武經射學正宗指迷集), which he published in 1637. At that time, the Ming Dynasty was crumbling and Gao was a very old man at 66 years of age. When you read Gao's books you can feel a sense of urgency, which stems from his sincere desire to help his country and help real archery enthusiasts in his twilight years. Thus, he did not have time to mince words, to care about prestige, or to worry about hurting other people's feelings. As a result, he wrote with unprecedented detail, clarity, and bluntness.

The Process of Writing This Book

Gao Ying was the ultimate archery enthusiast. His love for archery permeated his entire existence: even when he was not practicing, he was thinking about the nuances of archery at all hours of the day. His dedication to the subject shows in the great amount of detail he put into his books, which is what made researching Gao's work all the more compelling for us. Our first glimpse of Gao Ying was from the excerpts that Stephen Selby translated in his book *Chinese Archery* (Hong Kong University Press, 2000), namely Book 1, Chapters 1.1–1.5 and Book 2, Chapters 5.7–5.10. Those excerpts inspired us to research our own original translations of Gao's entire work (2 volumes with 8 extensive chapters).

Although the original Classical Chinese text of Gao Ying's work has been in the public domain for quite some time, until now there has not been a translation of the full work into English. This was far from an easy task because we had to spend many hours over many months collaborating across multiple time zones. The process involved reading Gao's teachings, practicing Gao's teachings, reflecting on our practice (at times debating the meaning of Gao's words), and repeating the cycle again and again until we converged on our final interpretation.

Reading Gao's teachings was the first challenge. Classical Chinese is not the easiest language to translate. It has a terse grammar that can be difficult to parse even for modern-day native Chinese speakers. We spent extra time studying to refamiliarize ourselves with the conventions of classical grammar. Even then, knowing the grammar and the literal meaning of the words was not enough because the context was just as important. There was the historical context for which we had to cross-reference the various people, places, and events that Gao mentioned in his text. Then there was the vitally important context provided by actually practicing the form.

We would not have progressed as far as we did without putting Gao's writings into practice. With each new passage we encountered came a new hypothesis about archery technique, which we would take to the practice field to test and verify objectively. Did we shoot stably? Did the arrow land straight or in a funny orientation? Did it allow the arrow to fly without oscillation? Was shooting comfortable? Did we strain any muscles unnecessarily? Afterwards, we would discuss the effectiveness of the concept, reread the passage, and readjust our understanding.

For example, the expression *pingzhiruheng* 平直如衡 appears a lot in Gao's text. We actually vehemently disagreed with each other about the meaning of this expression in the beginning. One of us initially advocated the simple translation of that phrase meaning "straight as a beam." But as we would later discover, aligning your shoulders and arms in a perfectly straight line actually yields a tense posture that engages peripheral arm muscles unnecessarily and has the potential to injure you. From reading, re-reading, and consulting with actual traditional archers from other cultures, we finalized the translation of that expression as "well-aligned," which characterizes the more organic, triangular posture that we eventually settled on. This was a good example of when our collaboration would have moments of strong disagreement. The same sorts of debates would happen again in other cases: we disagreed on whether to make the draw-side elbow drop slightly (*shaochui* 稍垂) before the release or after the release; we disagreed on what optimal draw length would allow us to more easily achieve a clean release and put the bulk of the effort in the back muscles; we disagreed about the timing of the draw motion; we disagreed on the finger placement and release motion of the draw hand, as well as various other technical elements. But in each case, we would take a step back, put aside our egos (oftentimes conceding that the senior archer had a lot to learn from the junior archer), and realize that the objective result (straight, controlled arrow flight) and whether we could shoot comfortably (in an injury-free way with moderate-to-heavy draw weights) was what mattered in the end. Our motivation for a deep understanding of Gao's form was so strong that we also sought the help of Professors Lee Brown and Scott Lynn at the Cal State Fullerton Center for Sport Performance to conduct biomechanics testing (complete with electromyography and motion capture sensors). They helped us understand in a scientific way the roles the rhomboids, deltoids, lats, and other muscle groups played in our shooting, and also helped us with prescribing a strength training regimen. The desire to learn and the willingness to keep an open mind (regardless of whether it was in scientific testing, or our reading of the text, or our practice, or our debates) helped us converge to a common understanding of Gao Ying's form.

In the end, working on this book changed us. It gave us confidence, which came from Gao giving us a clear blueprint for improving our technique, as well as from verifying that other styles shared the same principles. It opened our eyes, as we began to see the commonalities in other archery traditions and developed an appreciation for them as a result (whereas before we saw traditional archery as a collection of different discrete styles). Finally, it made us more patient. Our efforts spanned many months, and finding the spare time to commit to this project was challenging because of other obligations (such as career and family). Nevertheless, we persevered and we are happy to share the results of our labor.

The Way of Archery 射道

In his work, Gao Ying frequently refers to the **Way of Archery** (*shedao* 射道 or *shezhidao* 射之道), which has both a technical side and a philosophical side.

The technical side of the Way of Archery describes Gao Ying's archery form, which is a synthesis of military archery styles that he encountered and adopted in his 40-plus years of archery experience. He sought good advice from experts around the country, including Qian Shizhen (the general from Jiading who helped lead the Ming to victory against the Japanese samurai in the first Imjin War). Gao also calls his technique the Five-Step Method (we adopt Selby's less verbose translation of what is originally 審彀勻輕注法: the "Estimation, Full Draw, Balance, Lightness, Focus" or *Shengouyunqingzhu* Method) and the Inchworm Method (尺蠖勢). It is a technique for shooting with military-style bows using the thumb ring, as the thumb release was the predominant method for drawing the bow in Asian archery. The form encourages aligning the joints properly and using the correct muscles groups efficiently, which in turn makes it easier to develop consistency, avoid injury, and extend the archer's shooting career.

Because of the form's utility and the clarity of Gao's writing, his Way of Archery would go on to influence other traditions of East Asia. However, in interpreting the Gao's form we relied primarily on Gao's direct writings, our direct practice, and our discussions with military/hunting-style traditional archers. Looking through the periscope of particular archery styles which do not have a military emphasis (such as the popular and widely-practiced Olympic archery or the modern, standardized Japanese archery form of Federation Kyudo) would not have allowed us to understand the military-style elements of posture that were crucial to Gao's technique. Looking through the periscope of Chinese melee martial arts (which evolved in the last few centuries without practitioners ever handling an actual bow, arrow, or thumb ring) would have ignored the fundamentals of archery (such as how to get the arrow to fly straight without wobbling).

Only through our discussions with archers from a variety of military/hunting traditions would we find that Gao's form actually bears a striking resemblance to other forms around the world: these include English warbow archery, Ottoman Turkish archery, American traditional archery (Howard Hill being a prime example), the archery of the Liangulu "elephant hunters," the archery of the uncontacted Amazonian tribes, certain genres of Korean traditional archery, Japanese military styles such as Heki-ryu Bishu Chikurin-ha, and many others. Observe them closely and you will notice they share many (if not all) of these elements in common: how they cant the bow, how they incline their torso, how they keep their draw-side elbow closed, how they keep their bow-side shoulder completely settled down, and how they raise their bow hand and their draw shoulder a little higher to reinforce the bow shoulder's lowered position in a triangular arm/shoulder alignment. Ray Axford's *Archery Anatomy* (Souvenir Press, 1995), with its computer modeling and mechanical analysis of the body, helps us explain why the posture and technique of these traditional styles seemed to converge. Traditional military/hunting posture allows archers to make more symmetric use of the back muscles on both sides of their body to bring both shoulder blades together and lower both upper arms into full draw position. As a result, shooting heavier bows becomes more feasible, and shooting with light-to-moderate weight bows becomes more comfortable.

The philosophy of the Way of Archery is one of continual self-improvement. You need to be self-aware, with a willingness to examine every element of what you do during your practice. You strive to make these elements more natural and comfortable, eventually developing them into a cohesive whole. You cannot deceive yourself, because the arrow does not lie. No amount of mystical energy can substitute for diligent, thoughtful practice. You put in hard work to seek the right path early on, and it makes your journey easier later. But the journey never ends, because we are continually working towards refinement.

How to Read This Book

This book is a translation and commentary of Gao Ying's original text, thus we place our English next to the original text written by Gao Ying in Classical Chinese (which is included as a quotation). In the English text, the translation of Gao Ying's words is in normal text, and we place our inline annotations and commentary in square brackets like so: "[▶ …]" (" ▶ " indicates "translator's note"). In other instances, we will place lengthier annotations in a separate text box.

At times Gao Ying will make his own parenthetical remarks, and these will be in angled brackets like so: "<…>" (in Gao's original text his parenthetical remarks appear as small-font double-column annotations inline with the main text).

In Book 2, Chapter 1–4, Gao begins his critique of other contemporary Chinese archery texts where he quotes the original source and then follows with his own commentary. We have formatted those quotes of other sources (and our translations of them) by placing them between " 『…』 " markers to distinguish those quotes from Gao's own commentary.

Now, let's begin!

Book 1

An Orthodox Introduction
to Martial Archery

Introduction to Book 1

Archery has principles, just as craftsmanship has rules. A craftsman can show people measurements and data, but he cannot show people the art behind his craft [▶ as if to materialize some abstract concept for people to see]. Rules have form, whereas art is formless. You can discuss things with form, whereas things without form are difficult to articulate. That said, although art is hard to describe, we can make an effort to methodically describe a path to comprehending the nuances of the art while avoiding any pitfalls. In this way, we can begin to understand the art and science of archery.

From past to present, many people have written commentaries on archery saying what is good shooting and what is bad shooting. But when it comes to good shooting, they do not explain how to cultivate it; when it comes to bad shooting, they do not explain how to correct it. Thus, although some teachers will teach day after day, they do not have a solid basis for their guidance. They are leading students to a blocked gate. Students who do not know how to develop good technique or correct bad technique end up developing bad habits. They are unable to find the gate.

In this book, "The Shortcut" (Book 1, Chapter 1) provides a basis for archers to learn the art and science of archery. "Common Mistakes" (Book 1, Chapter 2) discusses ways to correct various bad habits that can emerge while learning to shoot. "Choosing Equipment" (Book 1, Chapter 3) provides advice on how to select appropriate archery tackle. Learning correct technique, knowing how to correct bad technique, and understanding how to select suitable equipment: these are the pillars of the Way of Archery. Learning these things will surely lead you to the right gate and help you avoid being led astray to the side door. This approach is my Orthodox Introduction, based on many years of personal archery experience.

People who read this book should set aside any prejudice or complacency, and they should not skim through carelessly. Otherwise, you will learn little from it and quickly toss it away. Studying technique requires your utmost attention. Doing so will allow you to continue progressing as you gain experience. Only this way can you deeply comprehend the nuances of shooting and achieve the kinds of archery feats the ancients did.

The wheel maker might make constructing a wood wheel look easy, but doing so is only possible because he dedicates blood, sweat, and tears to gain the necessary experience. Even his son cannot simply "inherit" that experience without putting in effort. Archery is much the same way.

武經射學入門正宗　前序

夫射之有法　猶匠之有規矩也　匠能與人以規矩　不能與人以巧者　以規矩有形而巧無形　有形者可言　無形者不可言也　巧雖不可言　而所以適於巧之路　與害巧之弊　以助其巧之具　未始不可言

古今言射者眾矣　第言如何而善　如何而不善　言善而不言所以適於善之路　言不善而不言所以去其不善之根　則雖終日教人射　總屬浮言　是欲其入而閉之門也　學射而不得其所以適於善之路　與去其不善之根　則雖終日習射　而茫無畔岸　是不得其門而入也

愚帳中所云捷徑門者　所以適於巧之路也　辨惑門者　所以去其不善之根也　擇物門者　所以助其巧之具也　由其徑　去其惑　執其物而射之道昭如也　學者由此而進　庶乎得其門而入　不爲旁門別徑所惑　故名爲射學入門正宗云　此皆得之歲年廣稽博採　歷試屢驗而成　覽斯帳者　勿偏心以自是　勿隘心以自足　勿粗心浮意淺嘗之　而遂謂道終不可得而自棄　惟凝神體認　深造不已　乃能入其門而居其室　漸臻巧妙之域　以追古人善射之踪　皆始於此　雖然斷輪小技也　甘苦疾徐之妙　父不能傳子　而況射乎

其機緘動於意色之微 變化據於
形神之際 意也 神也 非奉臂諄
諄 耳提面語 不能盡也 然不得其
人而授之 而穎年已老 又不及待 不
得已而托之簡編 以寄其懷 淺言之
而不能盡其詳 深言之而不能闡其
幻 雖微辭婉轉極意摩研 而筆墨限
量 僅可達其皮膚骨節之粗 其間隱
如躍如之態 時迅時緩 時行時止 一
種先後天成自然之節 不能寫也

在敏悟者 因言以契其意 因意
以會其神 庶幾服習之久 形與神
通 揣摩之深 機與道洽 <骨節相
對 體勢堅完 之謂形 熟而生巧 莫
知其然而然 之謂神 疾徐甘苦 適
相湊泊 之謂機 行乎其所 不得不
行 止乎其所 不得不止 是之謂道
> 而予欲吐不能吐之苦心 或得藉
是以宜暢 而夫人巧力 欲發而未能
發者 亦因是以奮揚 乃可謂曠世同
符 千里神合者矣 若而人者 予雖
不及見其面也 較之見予面而不知
予之法 習予法而不能窮其奧者 相
去遠矣 悲夫

　　　　　　　—崇禎丁丑仲春
　　　　　　　　高穎 自述

The timing of archery all rests in your familiarity and understanding. The details of the movements correspond with the coordination of your body and spirit. Understanding. Spirit. These concepts are difficult to articulate and teach to others. Plus, I am old. I do not have a lot of time left. That is why I prepared this compilation so that I can convey my ideas to future readers. A superficial explanation will not be able to cover the details. Yet a thorough explanation will not be able to explain some of the intangible aspects. Although explaining things concisely helps, pen and paper have their limits. They can only give you a rough idea of what your skin and bones need to do. All the while there is this interplay between hidden and obvious, between fast and slow, between moving and stopping. It is that special feeling that allows your joints to move naturally day after day. You cannot put that on paper.

Savvy folks will study until they understand the meaning behind the words. From understanding the meaning, they can internalize it and harmonize it with their own spirit. When you have practiced a lot, form and spirit are linked. As you dig deeper, you acquire the sense of timing and are on the Way. <When the joints are straight and the body is solid: we call this "form." When familiarity turns into mastery, you can achieve things without even having to think: this is "spirit." Finding the balance between going fast vs. slow, soft vs. hard: that is called "timing." Stopping and going when the moment is right: this is the Way.> All these years, I have been dying to tell everything, and I would feel much more relieved knowing it could reach a savvy audience.

When it comes to people's mastery, I have seen all different kinds of outcomes. There are those who have not yet shot but really want to learn. Once they commit themselves enthusiastically to practice, they achieve exactly that intangible mastery over the art. These people understand what I am talking about even though they have never met me.

Then there are those who know me but do not want to learn from me, as well as those who practice with me but still do not understand what I am saying. These kinds of people are just so far behind. How tragic.

— Chongzhen Era, Ding Chou Year, Second Month, Sixteenth Day
(1637 CE, March 12th): Gao Ying

Book 1, **Chapter 1:** The Shortcut
by Gao Ying (style name Gao Shuying), Liu City, Ming Dynasty

1.0 *Introduction*

   The Way of Archery is like a highway. Traveling on this highway requires you take a step-by-step approach. If you take the true path, you will be able to enter the main gates of the city and reach the inner chambers of city hall. You can count the days it takes to reach your goal.

   But if you decide to take the wrong path, then the moment you enter the side gates will be like trying to chase a swallow: you will be lost and stuck in a rut. The further you go, the further you will diverge from your true goal.

   Suppose you take the wrong path. When you are starting archery as a youth, your joints are free of problems, your muscles are strong, your concentration is sharp, and you can reach full draw. You become settled with your technique and have no problems hitting the target. But when you have practiced this way for a while, your joints will develop deep-seated problems. Even before you have reached old age and have become decrepit, you will suddenly lose the ability to reach full draw. The more you shoot, the more your arrows veer away from the target. You compare your current shooting with how you used to shoot, and it is like looking at two completely different people. But people do not know the reason why. In the Sanwu region, I have seen a lot of people with these problems. Year after year, they gradually lose their ability to reach full draw. When you ask them the reason for this decline, they have no clue. I do not see many people who reach old age and are able to understand and resolve problems in their archery form.

   There is no other explanation: it happens because in the beginning they pull the bow haphazardly, making every kind of mistake, entering the side gate, and veering from the true Way. If you want to follow the true Way, you should practice the technique that lets you improve as you practice more, not the technique that makes you worse as you practice more! This is the true Way: first is estimation, second is full draw, third is balance, fourth is lightness, and fifth is focus.

武經射學入門正宗 （卷上）
捷徑門
　　明嘐城 高頴叔英父著

　　捷徑門 序

　　夫射之道 若大路 然入路自有
次序 得其路而由之 始而入門 既
而升堂 又既而入室 計日可到 不
得其路而由之 一入旁門 猶適燕越
轍 愈趨愈遠

　　當其年少初習時 病（骨節不直
之病）未入骨 筋力強 神氣銳 引
弓可彀 機勢一熟 便可中的
　　習射既久 病（骨節不直之病）
根一深 不過數年 精神未及衰老 引
弓遽爾難彀 射逾久而矢離的逾
遠 回視昔年中的時 若兩截人物 今
人莫曉其故 竊見三吳 彎弓之士 以
善射名者比比 數年後俱坐不滿之
病 中數漸減 問其故茫然不解 既
至暮年而能解此病者 不及見也

　　此無他 只因習射之初 妄自引
弓 或為拙射所誤 偶入旁門 不得
正路而由耳 若果循正路 則射愈
久 法愈熟 烏有射久而愈不如前者
乎 所謂正路者何 一曰審 二曰
彀 三曰勻 四曰輕 五曰注

穎請 以法詳著於篇 使人得循
途而進 不為邪徑所迷 近不過百
日 遠不過期年 命中可幾矣 其功
最捷 故名其門曰捷徑云 世人只欲
旦夕期效 一聞期年之說 便爾駭
然 詎知 無法之射 愈趨愈遠 白首
而無成

　　穎所云期年者 合法之射 計日
可到 期年之期 豈不為捷徑乎 期
年之間 必須時時講究明通其理 又
須日日演習 百病皆知 使弓手相
親 以身使臂 臂使指 則弓與手相
通若一體 指揮操縱無不如意 方可
云期年耳 若一作輟 前功盡廢 即
終身演射 白首無成者 比比皆是
也 安可望期年命中乎

論審法 〈第一〉

　　發矢必先定一主意 意在心而發
於目 故審為先 審之工夫直貫到
底 與後注字相照應 俱以目為主 故
欲射先以目審定 而後肩臂眾力 從
之而發

　　然審法不同 有審鏃於臨發時
者 有審於弓左者 皆非也 審於臨
發時者 固已倉猝 且專審於箭鏃 恐
鏃對而箭桿不對 發矢亦斜 若審於
弓左者 箭在弓右 目不見鏃 注的
不清 矢之遠近 何從分別 總之 以
意度之耳

I have written the details of the method in this book so readers can have a clear path to improvement and avoid getting lost on strange detours. Within a hundred days to about a year, you will be able to master the whole form. The practice you apply here will be the most efficient kind. That is why I call this "The Shortcut." These days people want to improve overnight, so when they hear they have to dedicate a year before achieving results, they get scared. Little to do they know. If they practice without technique, they will get further and further away from achieving good results. By the time they reach old age, they have failed to learn anything.

As for what I said about practicing for a year, if you use proper technique to practice, you can actually count the days that it takes to improve. After a year you will have reached a high level of shooting. How is this not a shortcut? Within that year, you must constantly contemplate every aspect of technique. You must practice on a daily basis and be able to identify all the different technical faults. Your hands must develop an intimate familiarity with the bow. Just like your body is linked to your arms and your arms are linked to your fingers, the bow becomes a part of your body. You can control and manipulate it as you wish. And this is all within a year! If you give up too soon, your efforts will go to waste. Even with a lifetime of practice, you will not be able to match the results you can achieve with a year of proper form!

1.1 Estimation

Before shooting an arrow, you must first focus your intent and use your eyes to estimate the target before releasing. That is why "estimation" comes first. Estimation encompasses all aspects of shooting and is linked to "focus" at the very end. Both have to do with where your eyes are looking. Thus, before you shoot you have to use your eyes to concentrate on the target, and then summon the strength of your arms and shoulders. From this foundation, you release the arrow.

However, there are different techniques for estimation. There are people who aim with the arrowhead just before releasing. There are people who aim with the left edge of the bow. Both of these are wrong! If you only aim at the moment of release, then you are in too much of a rush. If you only aim using the arrowhead, you might place the arrowhead correctly but the arrow shaft might be pointed in the wrong direction, which will cause the arrow to fly off course. If you aim over the left edge of the bow, you will not be able to see the arrowhead on the right side of the bow [▶ for a right-handed archer], and you will not be able to focus clearly. You will have difficulty controlling the elevation of the arrow because you are aiming solely by feel.

Here is the true way to aim. First, fix your eyes on the target at pre-draw, then start drawing the bow. As you are about to reach full draw, use the corner of your eye [▶ your peripheral vision] to look along the arrow shaft to the arrowhead, and trace an imaginary (parabolic) trajectory to the target. You have precise control over the distance and left-right position of where your arrow lands. This is estimation.

But using this method for aiming is only appropriate for shooting far away. If you shoot a target within 50 paces (87.5 yd, 80 m), you are looking exclusively over the left edge of your bow. [▶ Gao Ying teaches canting/tilting the bow, which explains why you look over the left edge of the bow for closeby targets.] The same applies for horseback archery, for which you do not shoot unless the target is within 10–20 paces (17.5–35 yd, 16–32 m). If you use the aiming method from the previous paragraph to shoot nearby targets, you will shoot too high! That happens because shooting at nearby targets requires you to lower the bow hand below the draw hand. You will not be able to aim along the right edge of the bow, that is for sure.

[▶ The exact distance at which you switch between using the method for aiming faraway or aiming nearby highly depends on the poundage of your bow and the mass of your arrows. It will vary from archer to archer, so Gao Ying's 80-meter recommendation is not rigid.]

1.2 *Full Draw*

"Full draw" means drawing the arrow until the arrowhead is touching the bow handle. It is the basis for shooting, and all the skill you develop stems with this part. Full draw is connected with the aforementioned estimation, as well as the subsequent balance and focus phases of the draw. If you do not reach full draw, your joints will not properly extend, and your arms and shoulders will be loose like a tree without roots: how can you have the energy to release? People who cannot reach full draw will not be able to accomplish anything. Even if they know the form in their heart, how can they apply it without reaching full draw? People like to talk a lot about different shooting styles, but they do not talk about how to reach full draw. They ignore the foundation and focus too much on superficial things. They will shoot for a while but fail to improve. Thus, to establish a foundation for archery, you must first reach full draw.

故審之正法　惟於開弓時　先以目視的　而後引弓　將彀時　以目稍自箭桿至鏃　直達於的　而大小東西了然　是之謂審

然此審法　射遠乃爾　若五十步以內者　俱視在弓左　與騎射同　騎射非十步二十步之內不發　射近而亦用前審法　則矢揚而大矣　故射近者　前手須低於後手　安能審在弓右乎　此又不可不知

論彀法〈第二〉

彀者　引箭鏃至弓弝中間之謂　乃射之根本　巧妙之所從出也　惟彀　則前段審的工夫有所托　以用其明　後勻注之功有所托　以收中之效　儻引弓不彀　骨段節未盡　肩臂俱鬆　猶不根之木　生意何由發　喪心之人　百務必不集　縱有巧法　安從施哉　世人講射法者紛紛　但不講所以彀之法　是舍本逐末　老而不精　故射之根本　必先於彀

然彀法不同 有鹵莽彀 有氣虛
彀 有氣泄彀
　夫鹵莽彀者 引弓將彀時 將
射 鏃露半寸許於弓弣外 臨發時 急
抽箭鏃至弓弣中間而出 是全以氣
實用事 急於小彀 激動前臂 大發
必不準 名曰鹵莽彀

　氣虛彀者 引弓迅速 急抽箭鏃
至弓弣中間 不及審的 後手力量已
竭 膽氣俱虛 曾不能少留 隨旣發
出 矢亦不準 名氣虛彀 以形彀而
氣不彀也 此皆非彀之正法

　夫正法者 只有一條大路 世人
不知 偶合其一二者有之 然非心知
其善 亦未必能守也 及習射旣久 病
〈骨節不直之病〉根漸增 始之偶合
者〈偶然骨節稍直〉亦稍消減〈久射
筋疲 始之骨稍直者 漸歸不直〉原
歸不彀矣

　彀之大路云何 彀法根本 全在
前肩下捲 前肩旣下 然後前臂及後
肩臂 一齊舉起 與前肩平直如衡 後
肘屈極向背 體勢反覺朝後 骨節盡
處 堅持不動 箭鏃猶能浸進 方可
言彀

However, people have come up with various wrong ways to reach full draw: the Reckless Draw, the Empty Draw, and the Leaky Draw.

In the Reckless Draw, you draw until the arrowhead is within about half a cun (0.63 in, 1.6 cm) of the handle. When it comes time to release, you jerk the arrow back suddenly until the arrowhead reaches the handle, and then release immediately. It is a very hurried way of reaching full draw, where you let the arrow go in a moment of excitement. There is no way your release can be consistent. That is why it is called the Reckless Draw.

In the Empty Draw, you draw rapidly until the arrowhead reaches the bow handle. You have not had time to aim, but your draw hand is already exhausted. You lack the energy reserves to hold the full draw, and as a result you let go of the arrow immediately. The arrow cannot fly accurately. That is why it is called the Empty Draw: you look like you are at full draw but you do not have the energy to support it! These are not the ways you want to reach full draw. [▶ Oddly, Gao Ying's text omits a detailed description of the Leaky Draw.]

There is only one true path to reaching full draw, but a lot of people are not aware of it. Some people can reach full draw by chance. But because they do not understand how they were able to achieve it, they are not able to maintain it. After practicing a while, the problem of misaligning their joints creeps in. At first the problems are not severe because their joints are occasionally aligned. But then over time, their muscles get strained, and the joints that were almost aligned eventually become completely misaligned. In the end they cannot reach full draw at all!

What is the right way to reach full draw? The basis of reaching full draw rests entirely in the bow shoulder settling down and rotating clockwise [▶ for a right-handed archer]. Once the bow shoulder settles down, the bow-side and draw-side arms and the draw-side shoulder lift together and assume proper alignment with respect to the bow shoulder. The draw-side elbow bends all the way and points towards your back. You feel your back exerting most of the effort and your joints have reached their limit. You can hold the draw without moving. The arrowhead has a little room until it reaches the handle. This is what you can call full draw.

Although people have different arm spans, they all should consider full draw as the moment their joints feel like they are at their limit. Strong folks should not overdraw. Weak folks should not underdraw. That is the proper way to do things.

Nowadays, people do not know how to reach full draw. They rely entirely on muscle strength to draw the bow and think that it is enough for the arrowhead to reach the handle to call it full draw. They do not account for joint alignment at all. However, within a given day a person's strength will change. From morning to night, your strength diminishes gradually. If you rely exclusively on strength and try to measure your full draw length, then you would be able to reach full draw in the morning but fail to reach full draw by the end of the day! With multiple draw lengths, the distances which you are able to shoot will change accordingly. How can you achieve consistency? Only when your joints are at their limit can you consider it full draw. That is why people with long arms should use long arrows, and people with short arms should use short arrows. Strong people should use heavier bows, and weak people should use lighter bows. In all cases, the arrowheads of these properly-sized arrows will reach the bow handle, and only then will they be able to draw to a consistent length.

Now the method for aligning the joints all rests in making sure the bow shoulder is settled down. People today do not talk about how to lower the bow shoulder. There is a lot of useless chatter going about that misses the point. Any of these methods that ignore lowering the bow shoulder will not let you achieve a steady full draw! The details for lowering the bow shoulder are in the "Pulling the Bow Carelessly" section of "Common Mistakes" (Book 1, Chapter 2.1). Please read it carefully. With this technique, you will be able to lower the shoulder effortlessly, and you can reach full draw without even trying. This is how you work on reaching full draw! <I also talk about this in *An Orthodox Guide*, "Miscellaneous Questions and Answers" in Book 2, Chapter 4.7.>

人之長短不齊 各以其骨節盡處
為彀 則力大者 不能太過 力小者
不能不及 此天造地設之理

今人不知彀法 專恃力以引弓 鏃
至弓弝為彀 骨節平直之法 置而不
講 則就一人之身 一日之間 力亦
有衰旺 夫人朝氣銳 晝氣惰 暮氣
歸 氣銳時 則力旺而彀 氣衰則不
彀矣 彀不彀分 而矢之遠近亦因
之 安有定衡乎 惟以骨節盡處為
彀 則長人用長箭 短人用短箭 力
大用勁弓 力小用軟弓 矢鏃俱引至
弓弝中間為彀 方有定準

然骨節平直工夫 全在前肩下
捲 下前肩法 今人絕不講 問有言
及者 俱出耳聞 不得其竅 此所以
前肩不得下 欲彀而未能耳 下肩
法 詳於辨惑門潦草引弓章內 宜細
求之 則肩不期下而自下 弓不期彀
而自彀矣 此下手入彀工夫也〈此
段宜與指迷集四卷中 或問十發章
合看〉

Settling down the bow shoulder to its lowest point. *Courtesy of Glenn Murray, Esq.*

23

〈大抵引弓 前後肩臂俱有相因
之勢 後手引弓極彀時 至體勢反覺
朝後 方為彀弓之妙境 然體勢朝後
者 前肩必前突出 則有括臂之病 故
又須前拳斜側 向肩前航出一寸許 與
肩齊 但前拳過航 則前肩必然退
縮 故又須將前肩極力向前番下捲
實 令肩上潭窩前向 同臂番直向地
則前拳雖航 而肩不退縮矣 然
肩之根在於背 欲肩窩前向 又須將
前肩背骨（飯超骨）向前番下 送
前肩番出 則肩窩方得向前 此皆相
因之勢 不可缺一 不然背骨不番 則
肩窩必不能向前 肩窩不向前 則前
拳必不能前航 而免括臂之病 可以
收體勢朝後彀弓之功乎〉

Left: improper bow shoulder position from hyperextending the entire bow arm backwards. The bow and the body are too crowded together. Right: proper bow arm and shoulder position accompanied with canting. The bow hand is slightly in front of the body, thereby creating a triangular space in the horizontal dimension between the bow and the body. *Courtesy of Chang Pengfei.*

Note: Applying Back Tension

When you are drawing the bow, the bow-side and draw-side shoulders and arms coordinate with each other. When your draw hand has pulled to full draw, your back is exerting the greatest amount of tension. That is the skill involved in full draw. But when you are applying back tension, the bow shoulder will have a tendency to bulge forward of the body, which indicates that you are exposing your bowside forearm [▶ as a result of hyperextending your entire bow arm backwards]. To fix this, you need to cant/tilt your bow hand clockwise and position your bow hand about 2 cun (2.5 in, 6.4 cm) in front of your body. [▶ Your bow shoulder joint will angle the bow arm forward of your body a bit.] There is still a straight line from the bow fist to the bow shoulder. However, if your fist is angled too far forward, it may cause your shoulder to hunch up. Thus, at pre-draw you have to make doubly sure that your bow shoulder is settled and rotated down, so that the top of your shoulder is facing in front of your body. Start with the bow arm extended towards the ground at pre-draw.

A proper triangular space in the horizontal dimension at full draw. The spacing helps minimize the body's interference with the bow. The force from the bow helps keep the bow shoulder blade settled down and towards your back. *Courtesy of Chang Pengfei.*

Although the bow fist is positioned up and forward of your body, the shoulder will not hunch up. The support for the shoulder comes from the back. If you want the top of your shoulder to rotate forward, then you must rotate your shoulder blade to send your bow arm angled a bit in front of your body. That is the way to do it. You cannot afford to ignore any one of these interconnected posture elements.

Otherwise, if you do not position your shoulder blade properly, the top of the shoulder will not rotate forward. If the top of the shoulder does not rotate forward, then you will not be able to position the fist in front of your body. As a result, you will not be able to avoid exposing your arm [▶ due to hyperextending the entire bow arm backwards]. How can you apply back tension properly under these circumstances?

"Top of the shoulder pointing forward" and "rotating the shoulder blade to send the bow arm angled a bit in front of the body" are the key for "lowering the shoulder" in Gao Ying's form. Gao Ying says "the top of the shoulder points forward," but this is the symptom of lowering the shoulder properly, not the cause. If a beginner mistakenly tries to achieve this by contracting his neck muscles, he may risk injuring himself. Instead, he should think about using the back muscles below the shoulder to bring the shoulder blade down to its lowest point. Rather than contracting with the neck muscles, instead the neck muscles stretch and follow the lead of the back muscles below the shoulder, which "lock" the shoulder down at pre-draw. Once you do this at pre-draw, the force of the bow loads from the bow hand directly to the back and shoulder, because the fully lowered and retracted shoulder blade is fully connected with your rib cage (and therefore the rest of your body). At this point you are able to avoid injury because the position allows you to readily apply back tension.

Opposite: (1) Start with the bow and arrow pointed to the ground and the draw-side shoulder hunched. (2) Draw the string back as you lift your bow arm, making sure the bow shoulder blade is settled down the whole time. (3) Use your back and shoulders to push down your arms to reach the end of the draw. (4) Now you are at full draw and ready to release.
Courtesy of Mike Loades.

論勻法 〈第三〉

勻者 前後肩臂 分勻而開之
謂 所以終彀之功 而啟後輕注之巧
妙者也 勻之時矢猶浸進未發 今人
當引弓旣彀時 骨節盡而筋力竭 信
手便發 何暇浸進而加勻之功 勻開
之功不加 發矢時斟酌不清 所以矢
之大小左右 俱顧不暇 發矢一偏 則
彀之工夫 總爲無用 此彀之後 當
繼之以勻 而勻開之功爲最急

1.3 *Balance*

"Balance" means dividing the force of the draw between the both sides of the shoulders and back. This is the final aspect of full draw, and is linked to the lightness and focus that follow. In the balance phase, the arrowhead is still approaching the handle and you have not yet released. Nowadays, when people reach full draw their joints and muscles are already exhausted, so they have no time to look at the target and just release immediately. Without dividing the force of the draw between the shoulders and back, they do not give themselves enough time to hold the draw and aim at the target. Their view of the target becomes blurry and the arrow could go off in any direction. Once the arrow veers off course like this, they have wasted all the work they put into reaching full draw. That is why after full draw you must balance the force of the draw. During the balance phase, your shoulder and back muscles are putting in the greatest effort.

然勻之法 莫妙於用肩 而勿用
臂 何也 臂之力小而肩之力厚也 引
弓既彀時 筋力已竭 欲使兩臂分勻
而開 勢必不能 惟肩力厚 則能施
運而悠長 弓彀之時 臂力將盡 以
肩力繼之 前肩低力下捲 <向前面
下爲捲> 後肩堅持瀉開 則箭鏃從
弓弝中間 徐徐而進 如水之浸漬
然 豈非勻之正法乎

今人當彀之後 只用臂力分開 臂
之力小 如何能開 必將彈力一抽 箭
鏃急進 激動前臂 發矢必斜 前功
盡棄 故曰 勻之法莫妙於用肩 而
勿用臂 <古云 胸前肉開 背後肉緊
者此也> 此勻之下手工夫也 今人
講勻 不講下手工夫 則說得 行不
得 說之何益 下手工夫 獨得之
祕 當爲智者道也

To achieve balance, there is nothing better than using the shoulders. Avoid using your arms. Why? Because your shoulders are much stronger than your arms! By the time you reach full draw, you have already maxed out your arm strength. If you continue to use your arms to divide the force, you will not have any stability. But because your shoulders are much stronger, you will be able to hold the full draw longer if you use them. Thus, when you have reached full draw and your arm strength is about to dissipate, you should transfer the force to your shoulders: you press and rotate the bow shoulder all the way down while you continue to revolve the draw shoulder open. This way, the arrowhead will draw ever closer to the handle (like submerging something deeper and deeper in water). This is the true way to achieve balance!

People these days only use arm strength to divide the force when nearing full draw. But arm strength is weak: how can they draw this way? They will have a tendency to pump the arrowhead towards the handle to reach full draw just before release, which disturbs the bow arm before release and causes the arrow to fly off course. All the previous effort they invested goes to waste. That is why I say nothing beats using your shoulders and back for balance. Do not use your arms. The ancients had a saying: the chest muscles should open, and the back muscles should be tight. This is exactly what I have been talking about. This is the basis for balance!

People these days talk about balance, but will not tell you how to achieve it. Instead, they keep it a secret to themselves. Is that any way to do things?

Applying back tension requires bringing the shoulder blades together and using less effort in the arms. *Courtesy of Mike Loades.*

"Lightness" comes from coordinating the bow-side and draw-side hands to achieve a light, relaxed release. But the key to lightness is very subtle. During the release, if you try to be light and do not use any force at all, the arrowhead will creep forward before you let go. And even if you prevent it from creeping forward, the arrow will lack energy when it releases and will fall short of its mark. Now if you are afraid of the arrow falling short, then you start to use some force to release. But you do not want to draw the arrow back any further because you are already at full draw. Yet by using extra force, you inadvertently pump back the arrow, an action which is nervous and inconsistent. Your arrows will veer far off course!

To avoid these problems, after reaching balance (when the draw shoulder has revolved open and the arrowhead has reached the handle), the way to hit the target is as follows. You clench the draw fist firmly and coordinate it with the bow hand palm. The strength of your bow-side and draw-side arms and shoulders are at their limit, but they are holding solidly together as a unit. Then, you very lightly move the draw hand backwards in opposition to the bow hand so that the draw hand exits straight back. At the same time, the draw elbow will drop down and towards the back. If you do not drop the elbow during the release, the draw hand will not be able to release straight back and the release will be dirty. But if you drop the elbow during the release, which allows the draw fist to exit straight back, the release will be much more calm. Like a dragonfly landing on the water and barely making a splash, or like ripened fruit dropping from a tree, the action has to be entirely natural. When the release is relaxed and crisp, the arrow will fly in a straight line to the target [▶ without any unnecessary oscillation]. This is the method for applying lightness. Just like the old saying: "the draw hand releases the arrow and the bow hand does not react."

論輕法 〈第四〉

輕者 後拳與前拳相應 輕鬆而
發矢也 然輕之功極細 發矢時 若
欲輕而不敢用力 矢鏃必然吐出 卽
使不吐而定 發矢亦覺無氣 氣怯則
矢發必傷於小 懼其小也 而稍用
力 則力微而矢不能進 懼其不進
也 而極力求進 必然一抽而出 就
著氣質 機神衝動 不能凝注 矢不
能少偏矣 故旣勻之後 後肩瀉開
時 箭鏃已至弓弣中間 決機命中 全
在於此 後拳必將筋力緊收 與前掌
相應 前後肩臂殫力 并實堅凝一
片 輕輕運開後拳 與前掌約勻 平
脫 後肘又須垂下向背 若拳平脫 後
肘不垂 發矢無勢 如此肘垂而拳平
脫 氣質煙火之性 泯然不露 如蜻
蜓點水 輕揚活潑 如瓜熟蒂落 全
出天然 鬆而且脆 矢出如葟 細衝
至的 此下手用輕之工夫 古云「後
手發矢 前手不知」者也

Left: releasing the draw hand sideways away from your body will cause the arrow to oscillate as it leaves the bow. Right: releasing the draw hand straight back is necessary for the arrow to fly straight and land straight.
Courtesy of Chang Pengfei.

論注法〈第五〉

注者 目力凝注一處 精神聚而
不分之謂 與前審字相應 夫人一身
之精神皆萃於目 目之所注 神必至
焉 神至而四體百骸 筋力情氣俱
赴矣

李將軍射石 一發沒鏃者 以虎
視石也 神之至也 故發矢時 目力
必凝注一塊 目注而心到 意到手
到 發無不中矣 古云「認的如仇」
者此也此下手用注工夫也

然注與審不可分爲二事 引弓之
初 以目視的 是之謂審 發矢時 以
目注的 亦謂之審 總之皆用目力 原
非二事 何爲分審與注之名也

只爲世人引弓時 雖能目視的 及
旣彀之後 筋力已竭 信手便發 無
暇認的 精神散漫 發矢俱偏 故于
勻輕之後 復立一注之名 以提醒世
人 使發矢時 目認的間一塊〈見後
面註釋〉或認的之心 或認的之足
與首 精神手法 俱向此一塊而發

故注之名 原爲世之拙射而設
者 善射之人 手一擧弓 目力便
審 精神便凝注一塊 自始至終 神
氣精專 弓一彀而勻輕以出矣 何待
勻輕之後而注哉 善學者不可不察

1.5 *Focus*

"Focus" means your eyes are focused on one spot, and your mind is paying full attention without any distraction. It is related to the aforementioned estimation step. A person's spirit is concentrated in his eyes. For anything he focuses his eyes on, he will be able to project his spirit towards the target. And wherever the spirit projects, the rest of his limbs, bones, and muscles will act accordingly to help reach the goal.

General Li Guang was able to penetrate a stone with an arrow because when he shot at it, he thought it was a tiger! That is the power of projecting your spirit! Thus, when you are about to release, your eyes should be focused intensely on a single spot. Where you focus your eyes is where your willpower can project. Wherever you project your willpower, the rest of your body will follow suit. You are sure to hit. There is the old saying: "Look at the target as if you had a grudge against it." That is the method for achieving focus.

General Li Guang (李廣) was a general from the Western Han Dynasty (206 BCE–9 CE). He was particularly well known for his archery skills and his long arm span. He earned his reputation as "The Flying General" from his battles against the Xiongnu.

However, you cannot actually separate focus and estimation into two separate tasks. Before you draw the bow, your eyes are looking at the target: that is estimation. When you are releasing the arrow, your eyes are focused on the target: that is also estimation. Ultimately they both involve using your eyes. In reality, they are not two separate steps. But why do we give estimation and focus separate names?

It is only for the following reason. Most people are able to look at the target when they start to draw the bow, but they exhaust their strength by the time they reach full draw. As a result, they release carelessly without taking time to identify the target. Their spirit is undisciplined, and all their arrows will not fly straight. That is why after applying balance and lightness, telling people to focus is a way to remind those people to focus intently on a spot on the target <see the following note>. They might choose to focus on the center, bottom, or the top of the target. Regardless, their spirit should guide their hand technique, focusing on that single spot and releasing the arrow to hit it.

In reality, the word "focus" is a crutch to help archers with less skill. For skilled archers, the moment they take up the bow, their eyes estimate the target and their spirit focuses at a single spot on the target. From start to finish, they maintain a high degree of focus even as they are pulling to full draw, achieving balance, and applying lightness. Why should you only wait to focus until after you have reached the balance/lightness stage? Good students cannot afford to ignore this point.

Note: Focusing at a Spot on the Target

<Although you have to pick a spot to shoot on the target, the method for choosing that spot will depend on the situation. This is not one-size-fits-all deal. Sometimes the wind changes direction, or the draw weight of your bow may vary. If the bow is light, aim for the top of the target. If the bow is heavy, aim for the bottom of the target. In the extreme case where the bow is heavy and you have a tailwind, you are not going to aim for a spot on the target, but rather a spot below it. If the bow is light and you have a headwind, you can position your bow hand above the target as you aim. If a wind is coming from the left, you should aim to the left. If a wind is coming from the right, you should aim to the right. In the extreme case where your bow is light and the sideways winds are very strong, then you may have to aim as much as one zhang (3.5 yd, 3.2 m) left or right of the target. If the bow is strong and the wind is light, then you can decrease the amount of left-right adjustment you have to make. This is how you deal with wind regardless of the direction. When it comes to spotting the target according to the wind, you must realize that conditions can change at any moment. You cannot just spot things one way. Ultimately, you have to use your discretion to find what works for you.>

1.6 *Conclusion*

Estimation, full draw, balance, lightness, and focus. Although I describe them in five steps, they are actually one process. Estimation and focus are the start and finish of the process, and ultimately both involve the eyes. Estimation occurs as you are pulling the bow, and focus occurs as you release the arrow. During this process there is full draw, which forms the basis for the archery technique.

Balance provides the strength for you to hold full draw, which in turn provides the foundation for you to fully control when you want to release. But people who talk about archery only pay lip service to "full draw," because the moment they reach their "full draw" they release immediately. They have no time to make any adjustments in

注释：目認的間一塊
<目認的之法極活　不可執一　或隨風而變　或隨弓之軟勁而變　弓軟則認的之首　弓勁則認的之足　甚者　弓勁風順　則不及認的　而以鏃頂半路者有之　或弓軟風逆　或頂的于左手掌下者有之　若東風　則頂之左　西風　則頂之右　甚者　弓軟風大　則認的之左右丈餘者有之　弓勁風微　則頂的之左右尺寸亦漸減　東西南北皆然　故頂風認的　隨時而變　不可執一　斟酌在人也>

捷徑門　總結

　審彀勻輕注　雖爲五段　其實一貫　審與注　首尾相應　總之皆用目力　審於開弓之時　注於發矢之頃也　中間彀字　乃開弓之根本
　勻者　乃所以終彀之力量　而斟酌發矢之機宜也　世人言射　只言彀字　一彀便發　大小左右俱不暇顧　詎知彀者　乃發矢遠到之本　非中的之本也　彀而不勻　發矢皆偏　何取於

彀 惟於彀之後 復引箭鏃 勻調浸
進分許 斟酌既定 而預爲出矢輕鬆
之地 故有勻之功 而彀力始不虛

　　輕者 乃竟勻之機 而發必中節
者也 上文勻之時 矢猶未發 而斟
酌定矣 輕者 承勻之後 而輕鬆以
出 發矢以準 故有輕之功 而後勻
之妙始著

　　注者 又合衆法之精神 萃而歸
之的 以終審彀勻輕之大成也
　　自審而彀 而勻 而輕 而注 相
通一氣 一審便彀 一彀便勻 輕而
注 發以達於的 捷於呼吸 猶人一
身 自頂至足 疾痛相關 不隔一
縷 而射之道盡矣

　　然有終身習之 而不得其門者 亦
是爲拙射所惑 偶入斜路 白首難
改 猶學文者 一入惡套 揮之不
去 又猶學書者 把筆一差 到老仍
誤習矣 若一更改 反覺不便 此初
射者 斜正之門 不可不辨 而下文
辨惑之門所由作也

their aim. Little do they know: full draw only helps you shoot far, but it does not help you hit the target!

If you reach full draw without balance, your arrows will all fly skewed. Then what is the proper way to reach full draw? After you have reached full draw, continue to pull the arrowhead back a little bit so your back muscles can divide the force of the draw. Getting this part right is the prerequisite for being able to release in a light and relaxed manner. When you apply balance, then the effort you put into full draw will not go to waste.

Lightness, which follows balance, is a crucial step for achieving accuracy. When you have obtained the aforementioned balance, you have not yet released the arrow but are able to hold full draw steadily and take a look at the target. Afterwards, you apply lightness to release in a light and natural way. That is how you get the arrow to fly accurately. Thus, if you have lightness, then you will be able to take full advantage of the work you put into balance.

Focus is closely linked with your spirit, which you collect and project towards the target. It is the crucial conclusion to the sequence you have performed up to this point.

Estimation, full draw, balance, lightness, focus: you should strive to make these steps part of a cohesive whole. Drawing the bow and releasing the arrow become as natural as breathing. Just like with the human body, everything from head to toe is fully connected. Then you will have fully realized the Way of Archery!

Yet, there are people who shoot their entire life and still cannot reach a decent level. That happens because they develop bad shooting habits. Once these problems start to develop, they become very difficult to correct. Just like when learning to write articles: the moment you resort to cliches, it becomes difficult to eliminate them. Or like when you are learning calligraphy: if your pen holding technique is even slightly off, then after some time you will have learned the wrong brushwork entirely. Although you might be able to correct your mistakes, the corrections themselves will feel very unfamiliar. Thus, beginners must be able to recognize the difference between good and bad habits. I cover these topics in the following chapter, "Common Mistakes" (Book 1, Chapter 2).

2.0 *Introduction*

When beginners go to the range, they will observe archer after archer shooting in all manner of styles. They will see good and bad shooting, but will not be able to tell them apart. It is as if you were a child in a marketplace looking at the vast arrays of merchandise for sale: you cannot distinguish jade from plain rocks, or pearls from fish eyes. Among the different archers, you might see one who scores hit after hit. You think that archer is good and want to imitate his shooting style. But you do not know any better. Just because he hits does not mean his technique is proper.

Maybe the archer is strong, so he can grasp the handle very tightly and is able to hit the target. Maybe the bow is heavy, so he can nonchalantly point the bow towards the target and scores by coincidence. Maybe he just practices everyday, and through repetition he is able to hit. Maybe he is an oblivious youth with a lot of energy: he does not care whether or not he hits. Or maybe he thinks he is smart and makes up some new technique that lets him score. These are all ways of hitting the target by accident. These are not proper techniques!

These tricks might help you hit today, but you cannot count on them to help you later. People who use these tricks may score, but if you yourself try to copy them you will not be able to hit. It is luck! You cannot call this control. However, with good technique you will be able to properly control your shooting.

For those who have orthodox technique, when they draw the bow their joints will work in a coordinated fashion. They will have a solid hold of the bow and a stance as solid as a mountain. You will not see them shaking. Their focus and vision are as clear as the sun and the moon: they can pay attention to the minutiae of what they are aiming at and can see through the haze. They have full control of their grip and can draw smoothly without pause. Their release is light, crisp, and relaxed, with no trace of sluggishness. When they go shooting, their spirit is directed towards the target, and their intent is tenacious. They having nothing to fear and can avoid being distracted.

Their path is steady and smooth, like traveling on a highway. Teachers can observe rules and techniques to explain to others. Students can deepen their understanding by following a sequence. This is the proper way to do things. Other ways are useless. There is only one highway and it is the natural way: if you take it, you will avoid many problems down the road.

武經射學入門正宗 （卷中） 辨惑門

辨惑門 序

初習射之人 挾弓矢升場 見彎弓角射者紛紛 人自多其能 賢否莫辨 眞贋混淆 何異小兒入市 百貨具陳 燕石混玉 魚目混珠 烏知其非 見紛紛角射中 有一人中的多者 就以爲善而學之 不知 若人之中 未必合正法

或者其人多力 前手能強持而中 或弓力勁銳 偶然對的而中 或日逐習射 機熟而中 或年少得意 神揚氣旺 得失不介懷而中 或其人少有小慧 獨創一見而中 此總屬偶然 非正法也

今日用之而中 他日守之未必中也 此人用之而中 他人學之而未必中也 偶也 非可爲訓也 可訓者 正法也

夫正法者 其引弓也 骨節相對 堅持岳立 不可搖也 其審視也 明如日月 大小左右 錙珠不爽 不可涸也 其持盈也 浸進有節 無停機也 其發矢也 輕鬆脆裂 無凝滯也 其欲射物也 精神畢赴 意思精專 利害不惕 不可紛也

其道坦夷 如大路然 教人者 可以循規按法 昭告於人 學法者 可以由淺入深 循序而進 如此則是 舍此則非 只有一條大路 皆出自然 絕無勉強矯拂之艱

如天之生人 只有仁義爲正路 舍此卽爲旁門惡徑 禍端百出矣 雖其學法旣成之後 巧拙由人殊 而初學入門 必須按法 安可舍此正路而妄趨哉

若初學之人 一見其人偶然中
的 不辨眞贋 遽爾學之 舉其陋態
惡習 盡皆學習 相習旣久 病入骨
髓 當初學時 病根未深 或年少力
強 引弓可彀 猶可中的 習射稍
久 病根一深 年力未及衰老 引弓
必漸不滿 〈年力未衰而引弓不滿
者 乃俗云毛病 非力衰也 年老力
衰而引弓不滿者 空引亦不滿 對的
發矢亦不滿也 若犯毛病而不滿
者 空引則滿 對的發矢則不能滿 此
爲毛病 極難去 今人坐此病者最
多〉 中數必不能如前之多

It is just like with people: being righteous is the only true path. Otherwise, you end up taking the side door of treachery and vice, through which endless misfortune awaits. Although you finish learning proper technique, whether you shoot well depends on you as an individual. However, all beginners must follow the process of learning good form. How can you abandon the true way and veer off in some other direction?

So when a beginner sees people hitting the target accidently, he cannot identify whether bad technique is being used. Instead, he haphazardly imitates what he sees. He picks up ugly habits and strains himself during practice. After training this way for a while, the problems embed themselves deep into the marrow of his bones. When he is starting, the problems are not deep: he is young and strong, can reach full draw, and can hit the target. He practices for a little longer, and the problems get worse: he has not reached old age, yet his ability to reach full draw gradually diminishes. <If he is young and strong but loses the ability to reach full draw, we can safely say he is injured because his strength has not yet declined. If he is old and has lost his strength, then he cannot reach full draw while dry pulling [▶ that is, using 3 or 4 fingers (not the thumb) to draw a bow without an arrow and without shooting], and he also cannot he reach full draw while shooting an arrow at the target either. However, if technical flaws cause his injury, then despite that he can dry pull with no problems, he cannot reach full draw [▶ using the thumb draw] while trying to shoot with an arrow. This is a problem that is extremely difficult to correct, yet this is by far the most common problem people have.> He will not be able to score as many hits as he did before.

The "injury" that Gao Ying refers to is an injury of the draw arm muscles that these days we would call "tennis elbow." The angle of the forearm for a 3-finger draw versus a thumb draw is different. If you fail to use your back muscles to exert most of the effort, or if your draw length is too long or too short, then it is especially easy to injure the draw-side arm muscles.

儻其人無志而退委者 不思改
圖 不必論矣 卽有志之士 欲變其
舊習者 何從而學哉 嘗觀彎弓角射
之人 其間合正法者 百不一覯也

For these people who regress yet lack the determination to correct themselves, we might as well ignore them because no prescription would help. For those people who have the determination to correct their old habits, the only problem is to find the right archery form and to relearn archery from scratch. Among the various archers you will see at a range, very few will have good form.

Most people who know good technique are willing to speak up and teach others. But only a few people are willing to listen and have the willpower to follow the whole learning process. I do not know if I am able to meet the right students. If I meet them, I will definitely teach them everything I know.

Normally, people with bad form will be stubborn and stick to their bad habits. Not a lot are willing to unlearn their old technique. And even though someone might be willing to relearn his technique, the injuries and habits caused by his old form are very difficult to change. His mind knows what the correct technique is, but his hands cannot make that instant correction. His mind knows what habits he needs to change, but his hands cannot follow through. Once he starts shooting, old problems reappear! What can he do? His aspirations turn into immense frustration.

It is a pity he cannot fulfill his aspirations. If he had the right form when he started shooting, he would be entering the correct gate. How can he possibly end up in a pitiful state? A beginner who starts with proper technique, and avoids the problem of failing to reach full draw, cannot fully understand the hardships associated with bad technique. He will not believe the warnings you give him about bad form. Only people who already have technical problems will believe you, but their problems are so embedded that correcting them is out of reach! In either case, the beginner cannot identify bad technique and can be easily led astray. How could he anticipate that things would end up poorly? That is why it is never too early to be able to identify good versus bad form.

When I was young, I loved archery. I was very diligent in my academic studies, and I was eager to serve the country. When I reached out to people, I was very sincere and open-minded. I was a great admirer of Lord Xinling [▶ actual name Wei Wuji, died 247 BCE], especially the stories about his generosity and open-mindedness.

<Now I will tell you the story of how I ran into problems with my shooting, how I painstakingly corrected them, and how I labored to develop better technique.>

合正法之人 肯一見傾倒 欲立
欲達者 又有幾人 安得其人而遇
之 即遇其人矣 肯直言傾倒矣 彼
犯病之人 未必不以先入之言爲
主 孰肯盡棄其學而學乎 即肯盡棄
其學而學矣 奈何病根已深 猝難拔
去 故有心知其法之善 而手不能猝
學 心知已病之當去 而手不能遽
改 纔一動弓 舊病立見 扼腕嘆
息 無可奈何

平生壯志 付之浩嘆而已 向使
初學時 即得正門入之 豈至此哉 <
初學射時 即得正法 不犯不滿之病
者 絕不知犯病之苦 聞言亦不信 惟
犯病之人 聞言始信 然不滿之病已
深 亦不及改矣 惟初不知辨 故爲
邪徑所惑 孰知誤之至於此哉 此辨
惑之不可不早也>

穎少好射 習章句時 便有立功
萬里之志 與人交 便有披肝裂膽之
懷 竊慕相如信陵之風 嘗讀其傳而
悅之 <以下皆述已平生犯病之由 改
病之艱 并求法之勞 與守法之篤>

弱冠时 輒與邑中善射者遊 而
孫履正 孫履和 李茂修 其選也 時
與之講道肆業 而射日益進 然履和
之力居多焉 其人豪爽 慈惠多大 節
朴而能文 仁而能斷 穎深師之 敢
亚及也

In my twenties, I would practice with the best archers in our city. These archery aces included famous people like Sun Lvzheng, Sun Lvhe, Li Maoxiu, among others. We would always talk about archery technique, and I was able to improve very quickly. Especially Sun Lvhe was the biggest influence. He was bold and generous, down-to-earth but also well-educated. He was benevolent but could also kick ass. I learned a lot from all of those guys, and I can say they were true friends.

又有錢三持者 邑中先達賢豪
也 征東大捷歸 辛丑年間 時謁其
門而問業焉 得其射評而讀之 而射
日益進 猶不敢自足也 更與海上諸
營士 及三吳射學者遊 有片長一
善 必虛心訪問焉 數年間 不避寒
暑 廣稽博採 歷試屢更 比十年而
射法成

Then there was Qian Shizhen (錢世楨), the most famous person from our city, and a veteran from the victory in the Imjin War. In 1601, I had a chance to visit him and talk about archery. I obtained a copy of his book *Commentary on Archery* (射評), studied it, and was able to continue to improve quickly. But I still did not feel I could carry out archery training by myself. So I hung out with military officers and other archery aces from the area. If their shooting had good points, I would humbly ask them for advice. Over a number of years, I continued to learn from others and improve my form. Up to this point, I had 10 years of archery experience, and I felt my technique had fully matured.

In 1603, we had the municipal military exam. I would shoot and penetrate the target: almost all of my arrows hit the mark. At that event, I received a lot of praise from my peers from Sanwu, and I was pretty content with the outcome.

But suddenly there came a famous archer from just up the river. He was a very stalwart looking guy. As soon as he opened the bow he would release quickly, and the arrows would hit the target as soon as you heard the string make a sound. I was very impressed and wanted to learn his way of shooting. Although parts of his technique were commendable, who would have known that his form was in fact fraught with problems?

<The first problem was the shoulders hunching up and the joints being misaligned. Under these conditions, you will get injured and eventually lose the ability to reach full draw. The second problem was rushing to full draw and releasing immediately. Although the release is smooth, you will not have a consistent draw length. Third is releasing the arrow too casually without taking the time to aim. As a result, you would have poor control over the distance of your shot.>

At that time I did not know how to differentiate good form from bad form. I learned his technique, as well as the flaws that came with it. After three years the problems seeped into my bones. Day after day my ability to reach full draw diminished. My ability to hit the target was diminishing, too. At that point I realized what I was doing wrong, but it was difficult for me to correct at that time.

After three years, it was 1613. I went to the military exams in Beijing. At that time I was 43 years old. Skilled archers from all the prefectures and townships came. I approached the best of the archers to talk about the details of archery techniques. Rather than just talking about what made a good shot good and what made a bad shot bad, we also talked about potential faults behind an accurate shot, as well as potential merits behind a shot that did not hit the mark. We figured out the causes of, and connections between, all these technical problems. Then it suddenly dawned on me what I had to do to fix my bad habits. For the next five years, I devoted a vast amount of energy to correcting my technique (I had very little sleep and often forgot to eat). I gave myself a very detailed regimen that I followed day and night.

癸卯年 應試鄉舉 開弓破的 幾無虛矢 一時三吳同志者 相推許焉 頗自謂有得

偶遇一名射 江上人也 形貌偉俊 開弓迅發 應弦而中 輒喜而學之 孰知其法固可嘉 其病不能無也 <肩聳而骨節不直 一病也 犯此病者 引弓必漸不滿 引弓一抽即彀 一彀即脫 發矢順利而衡勒不清 二病也 犯此病者 雖滿而難齊 舍矢甚易而神不注 三病也 犯之者 矢大小不準>

當時胸中真贗未明 學其法并學其病 比三年而病入骨 引弓日漸不滿 中的亦稍減 心知其非 未能遽改也

又三年 癸丑 應試京師 時穎年已四十三矣 縱觀九州及九邊列鎮諸材士 挾弓馳射者蝟集 乃遍簡其尤者 與之講究失得 無論射中之善 與射中之弊 無不畢知 并善中之弊 與不善中之美 轉展相因 根連蔓引之病 無不考竟 乃恍然大悟 欲一改舊習 忘寢食者五年 而病不能恃 乃益奮其力于弓矢 多方改圖 日夜不倦

又三年而筋力勞疲 病〈所云不滿之毛病〉根益深 引弓益不能彀 變怪百出 胸中射法了然 奈兩臂之不能爲我用也 時年已四十五矣 知病終不能去 又不忍棄置 於是更爲左射 以精驗之法 訓新習之于 病未生而法備 其比五年而機熟 應弦命中亦幾如意

丙辰年又遊京師 爲時論所推 燕趙齊秦之士雲集而觀 其尤知味者 率其子弟相從不舍也 然旁觀者雖曰善 予心知其非至也 何也 左射者後手弱 不能敵前手之強 強弱不調 發矢終乖 猶作樂者 琴瑟不調 雖強鼓而成音 不知樂者 妄稱其善 終不能入鐘子期之聽

乃又更爲右射 蓋喜右手久不習射 病根消而易改 且不忍右手二十餘年之功 一旦棄擲耳 乃遂大加更改 以弱弓微弦 滌去舊病者五年 射始合法 中微及遠 稍亦如意 然病根之入骨者 猶存十之一二〈不滿之毛病〉 時或間發其端 中數亦不能如癸卯年之多 而筋骸已漸憊矣

After another three years, my muscles were getting weaker, my problems were getting deeper, and I was definitely not able to reach full draw steadily. My form became messed up in so many ways. My brain knew what I had to correct, but my arms were not cooperating. At that point I was 45 years old. I knew the problems but I could not get rid of them. That was when I switched to shooting left-handed: taking all the experience I accumulated to train a new side. No problems emerged, and my technique was solid. After five years, my newly trained form matured. Quite often I could hit whatever I aimed for. [▶ According to our understanding, Gao Ying's previous injury was most likely tennis elbow in his right (draw-side) arm.]

In 1616, I attended the exams in Beijing once again. Due to significant events that happened that year [▶ such as the founding of the Manchu nation, which at the time was called Later Jin], generals from all the provinces (Yan, Zhao, Qi, Qin, etc) gathered together. These generals knew what was going on, and they each brought their own military entourage. Although bystanders said my shooting was good, I knew in my heart that was not the case. Why? When shooting left-handed, my draw hand was weak and could not match the strength of my bow hand. Ultimately, with this difference in strength, the arrow would not behave in flight. The situation was like a musical group with the different instruments out of balance. They might have a strong beat and make loud noises, and people who do not know any better will think it is good music. But people who know music will not appreciate it. [▶ At this point, Gao Ying had only practiced pulling left-handed for a year.]

Later on, I returned to shooting right-handed. Fortunately, it had been so long since I shot right-handed that my injury had mostly gone away and my form was easier to fix. Moreover, I did not want to abandon 20-plus years of practicing right-handed, so I was determined to fix things. I started with a light bow, and for the next five years I worked to get rid of my old problems, focusing on correct technique until I was able to get my form more and more under control. But 10–20% of the problems were still there because of my old injury. The issue of failing to reach full draw steadily would still resurface once in a while, and I was not able to hit the target as much as I did back in 1603. Moreover, my strength was fading.

Alas! I am already 66 years old now. I practiced archery for 40-plus years. As soon as I understood my problems, it was too late to fix them. If I knew correct technique early on, and if I knew how to avoid bad form, then I would not be struggling like I am now.

My body has suffered a lot, yet I now know how to work hard to correct those problems. Although I put in a lot of effort to correct these faults, they were ultimately too deep to eliminate completely. That is why I am writing "Common Mistakes." In this chapter, I discuss ten or so of the most common mistakes in detail. Based on your understanding of these common faults, the other random faults will become easier to diagnose.

2.1 *Pulling the Bow Carelessly*

Beginners will pull the bow clumsily. If they are not paying attention to good technique, they might reach full draw steadily when they start, but will lose the ability to reach full draw steadily later on. The situation only gets worse and they do not know why. If you deviate at all from having good form, it will be very hard to correct later on.

If you over-practice using bad form, within just 3–5 years you will lose the ability to reach full draw steadily. By overexerting yourself with bad form, you can injure your muscles. That is why you lose your full draw so quickly. If you do not practice that often (e.g., if you go days without shooting), your muscles might not get injured right away. Regardless, in practicing bad form the problems will still manifest at a later point in time.

People who develop these problems will eventually listen to technical advice, but by then it is already too late to correct things. Beginners who have not developed these problems will not listen to good technical advice and treat such advice the same as lies and slander. These beginners are sadly mistaken.

I had a friend Tao Chengzhi (陶成之). When he first started developing this problem, he would not listen to anybody. In the end he could not fix his issue and he regrets it to this day. The rest of my shooting buddies who developed the same problem could not correct themselves either. Alas! People who have not injured themselves should pay attention!

嗟嗟 頴今年已六十有六 習射四十餘年 始知受病之根 而悔已無及 使早能辨射法之真贋 不爲江上人所惑 亦奚知流毒至此

予身受其惑之害 且又知去害之苦 雖用苦功以去病 而病根轉深 皆從初之不辨失也 今天下好射者比比 誠不忍其忽于惑 而不知辨也 辨而不及改也 故作 辨惑篇 以覺之 略舉其惑之大者十餘條 詳示其由 其餘俟明者 類推焉

引弓潦草之惑 〈第一〉

初學射之人 妄自引弓 不講正法者 初雖滿 後漸不滿 此必趨之勢 人所不解 入門一差 到老難改 極力用功者 不過三五年 不滿之病即見 以其用功勤 筋力易疲 故不滿速 不用功者 日逐不射 筋不即疲 雖多延幾年 然不滿之病 久後亦見 此病受過者 聞言始信 而已不及改 不曾受過者 聞言不信也 初射者反以爲謗已 誤矣

予友陶成之者 始犯此病 聞言不信 後竟不能改 悔之無及 其他一時同射之友 犯此病而不信者 如衞 如馬 如劉 不能遍舉

嗟嗟 天下之未爲成之諸友者 可以思矣

羿之教人射 必至於彀 今之射
者 亦知爭而言彀矣 然卒莫能彀
者 人但知求彀 而未知所以彀法
也 得其所以彀之法 不求彀而自彀
矣 不得其所以彀之法 雖竭力求彀
能乎哉 或有勇力之人 力能中彀 亦
僅可彀一時 未必能彀久 故有朝彀
而暮未必彀者 有今歲彀 三四年
後 未必彀者 甚者 一廻箭之中 前
四五枝可彀 後七八九枝即不彀
者 此曷故哉 彼恃力而彀 非以法
彀也

恃力而彀者 筋力用事 恃法而
彀者 骨力用事 筋力用事者 前肩
聳而兩臂皆低 骨節不直<此病犯之
者 十人而九> 雖有力之人 引弱弓
而手已顫 射不及久而力已疲 如何
能彀 骨力用事者 骨節相對 前後
肩臂平直如衡 雖無力之人 引勁弓
而久射 悠然不動 此彀之所以易
也 故學射者 可不求所以彀之法 而
徒云彀也乎哉

When Hou Yi was teaching people archery, reaching full draw was a fundamental requirement. These days, archers pay lip service to full draw, saying that it is important. But they cannot reach full draw because they do not know the technique. People who know the right technique can reach full draw without any problems. People who do not know the right technique will exhaust their strength yet still cannot reach full draw. Some people might be really strong and can sort of reach full draw without the right method, but they will not be able to keep that up in the future. These "full draw today, gone tomorrow" people might be able to reach full draw this year, but 3–4 years later they will not be able to reach it. Within a single shooting round, they might be able to reach full draw with the first 4–5 arrows but then fail to reach full draw on the 7th, 8th, and 9th arrows. The reason is that they rely on raw strength to reach full draw. They are not relying on technique.

Hou Yi (后羿) or simply Yi (羿) is the most famous legendary archer in Chinese folklore. He was known for shooting down nine of the ten suns and performing other mythical feats with his cinnabar-red bow.

Archers who rely on raw strength to reach full draw use their arm muscles. Archers who rely on technique use their bones.

When archers use their muscles, the bow shoulder will hunch up and both arms will slope down. The joints will be misaligned <nine out of ten people have this problem>. Although the archer is strong, he will pull a light bow and still tremble. They do not shoot for long before they are tired. How can they reach full draw steadily?

When archers use their bones, the joints coordinate and allow the arms and shoulders to achieve proper alignment. Although these people might not be strong, they are able to pull heavy bows and shoot comfortably for a while without shaking. This is the way to reach full draw with ease.

So when you are learning archery, how can you just talk about wanting to reach full draw without learning the proper technique??

Bottom left: an example of hunching the bow shoulder slightly. Hunching even a tiny amount will disconnect the bow shoulder blade from the rest of the body, and will lead to problems later. Bottom right: hunching both shoulders and scrunching the neck is no good, either. *Courtesy of Chang Pengfei and Mike Loades.*

An example of hunching the bow shoulder dramatically. Gao Ying considered this one of the most fundamental shooting errors. *Courtesy of Glenn Murray, Esq.*

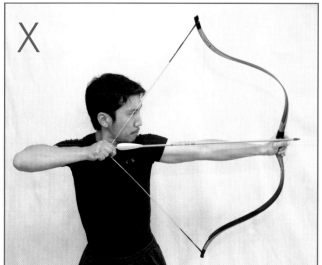

所以彀之法何 學射之初 將欲
引弓 必先數日以左手托在柱上 與
肩齊 以後肩聳起 與前肩齊 令一
人從旁將前肩向前下捲 使前肩低
於後肩 肩臂覺痛乃止 數日內 時
時順前肩下挹 俟其酸痛既定 大約
一月之後 方可以軟竹弓托在柱
上 低手提高 引開 俟前肩下得極
熟 方可搭箭空引

引弓法 前後肩臂 不正平直 旦
使前肩反低 而前掌及後肩臂反
高 方是彀法〈以前肩易聳 而前後
手易低 故初引弓時 必須前肩反
低 方得平直 若前肩不低 僅得平
直 引弓既彀 必然後聳 能平直
乎 故前肩反低者 矯枉太過 方得
合中道耳〉彀法既合 骨節平直 終
日習射 不勞於力 既彀之時 自能
堅持不動 遲速操縱 無不如意 既
到如意地步 則前捷徑工皆從此出

What is the technique for reaching full draw? When you begin to learn archery, even before pulling an actual bow, must spend several days placing your bow hand on top of a post and shrug your draw shoulder. [▶ If you pull the bow right-handed, the bow shoulder is your left shoulder, and the draw shoulder is your right shoulder. If you pull the bow left-handed, the bow shoulder is your right shoulder, and the draw shoulder is your left shoulder.] At the same time, have someone assist you by standing at your side and rotating your bow shoulder forward [▶ when facing the post/target, this is clockwise for a right-handed archer, counter-clockwise for a left-handed archer]. The bow shoulder should be lower than the draw shoulder. If the arms or shoulders start to hurt, then stop.

During these several days, continue this exercise of rotating the bow shoulder forward, and stop whenever you begin to feel sore. About a month later, you can permit yourself to hold a light bamboo bow while your bow hand is still resting on the post, and use your draw hand to pull the bow while continuing the exercise. When the movement of rotating the bow shoulder has become very familiar, then you can nock an arrow and do the pulling without a post.

To draw the bow, the arms and shoulders are actually not in a straight line. The bow shoulder is low, but the bow hand and the draw shoulder are high. That is how you can reach full draw. <There is a tendency for the bow shoulder to hunch up and the bow/draw hands to drop down. To counteract this tendency, make sure your bow shoulder is settled all the way down before you pull the bow. That way everything will be aligned when you reach full draw. If at pre-draw the bow shoulder is not low (but is actually level), then by the time you reach full draw the bow shoulder will hunch up anyway. How can this be well-aligned? That is why you lower the bow shoulder to correct this hunching tendency. Then you will achieve the right outcome.>

When you have reached full draw, the joints are well-aligned. Even after a lot of practice, you will not overexert yourself. When you are at full draw, you can dictate your pace without shaking. You are in full control.

Once you have reached this point of full control, you will be thankful for the previous hard work you spent learning how to reach full draw properly.

Literally keeping the bow arm and the shoulders in a straight line leads to a tense shooting position where the bow and body are crowded together. *Courtesy of Glenn Murray, Esq.*

The key to a "well-aligned" posture is making sure the bow shoulder is settled all the way down and is lower than the bow hand and the draw shoulder. This creates a triangle in the vertical dimension (to complement the triangle in the horizontal dimension described in Book 1, Chapter 1.2). *Courtesy of Chang Pengfei, Mike Loades, and Glenn Murray, Esq.*

若初習射時 即便潦草引弓 前
肩一聳 數日之後 便覺安閑熟習 全
不費力 一月之後 機勢既得 便能
中的 比前下肩法容易百倍 而旁觀
者噴噴稱美 即自己亦以爲射法之
妙 資稟之敏 他人莫及矣

抑孰知 前肩一聳 骨節不直 日
復一日 專用筋力開弓 不三年而筋
疲力億 引弓必漸不滿 中的亦漸
減 又三年而不滿之病益著 始之不
滿者 半寸許 今則二三寸矣 又未
幾而二寸者 將半尺許 此時百病俱
發 終日習射 無中之矢 回視昔
年初射而中的者 已不可得 在明
者 或悔其初引弓之非 而已不及
改 愚者竟托之命蹇 而猶不悟 豈
不悲哉

此皆穎所親試 而親見者 甚
衆 非敢漫言欺世也 嗟夫 潦草引
弓之惑 一至此 初射中第一大惑 故
首舉之以示 智者採焉

郊射太早之惑 〈第二〉

骨節相對 引弓雖合彀法 而射
法尚未演習 手法身法審法茫然 若
遽往郊射 精神外騖 無暇致詳於
手 百病萌生 而不自知矣 故引弓
合彀法之後 必在藁砧上演習

Suppose there is an archer just starting to learn and he haphazardly draws the bow, letting the bow shoulder hunch up. After several days, he becomes familiar with this habit and does not waste much energy pulling the bow. After a month, things just happen to come together and he is able to hit the target. What he is doing is a hundred times easier than learning the proper technique of keeping the bow shoulder low. Bystanders will go "oooh" and "aaah" and think he has beautiful form. He deludes himself into thinking he shoots well and understands the nuances of archery. People like him are not even close to getting it right.

What he does not realize is that as soon as the bow shoulder hunches up, the joints are misaligned. Day after day, he is only using arm muscle strength to pull the bow. In less than three years, his muscles are exhausted and he eventually loses the ability to reach full draw. His accuracy gradually gets worse. After another three years, the inability to reach full draw gets even worse. At first he was short of full draw by a half cun (0.63 in, 1.6 cm), and today he is short by 2–3 cun. Pretty soon he goes from being 2 cun short to being short by about half a chi (6.3 in, 16 cm). At this point a whole slew of problems have emerged. In the end, he has no chance of hitting the target. He cannot reclaim the same success he had hitting the target in his early years. If he is smart, he eventually regrets being careless as a beginner, but it is too late for him to fix things. If he is stupid, he does not realize his mistake and thinks losing his ability is just part of his destiny. How is this not a tragedy?

I am sharing all my experiences and observations in the most candid way possible. I am not trying to deceive you with vague descriptions. Sigh. As for the topic of pulling the bow haphazardly in the beginning, I will wrap up the discussion here. This is the biggest mistake a beginner can make. That is why I wrote about it first. Wise people will heed this advice.

2.2 Shooting Outdoors Too Soon

You are able to coordinate your joints and use the proper technique for reaching full draw steadily. However, your technique is not fully mature, and you are not fully familiar with the details of arm, body, and aiming technique. If you rush to shoot outdoors, you are being too ambitious and will not be able to concentrate. A lot of problems will emerge with your technique, but you will not be aware of them! That is why once you have learned how to reach full draw steadily, you should master your form while shooting indoors at a gaozhen 藁砧 (straw bale).

Your body should be straight, your torso should incline forward, and your two feet should plant solidly. The common saying is that "the front leg should be straight and the back leg should be bent." This is wrong. Why? Releasing the arrow is a function of the arms and is independent of what you do with the legs. Squatting down all the time is unnecessary!

The head should not be vertical/leaning back. Instead, the head should be tilted forward a bit [▶ matching the incline of your torso] so you can look along the body of the arrow shaft towards the target. <I just discussed the overall posture of the body. Next I discuss body posture for drawing and releasing in more detail.>

As for drawing the bow: once you have nocked the arrow, you should point your bow arm towards the ground, your bow shoulder blade should be settled all the way down and rotated, and your bow hand palm should cradle the handle. <You should apply a little tension to the string with your draw hand, then you can cradle the handle with your bow hand palm.> You should incline your torso forward, tuck in your belly, straighten your legs, and stand steadily. At this point your draw arm elbow is pointed up/back and will lift back to draw. As soon as you start drawing, the bow hand lifts up, and the bow arm/shoulder/palm point straight towards the target. How can this not allow you to make the arms and shoulders well-aligned and act as a solid unit? This is the way to reach full draw without even trying!

Drawing of a traditional *gaozhen* (藁砧) or straw bale based on an illustration from the 1638 Ming Dynasty manual *Wu Bei Yao Lue* (武備要略). The straw is aligned longitudinally and bound tightly. When practicing with a traditional gaozhen, you stand in front of the circular face of the gaozhen at a close distance and shoot your arrow so that it lands perfectly straight into the bale (which will allow the arrow to penetrate as deeply as possible). The gaozhen is known in Japanese as a *makiwara*. The Turkish adopt a similar practice known as shooting at the *torba* or *sandik*. *Original illustration by the authors.*

體欲直 胸欲欽 兩足欲站立得穩 俗云「前如折 後如堀者」非也 何也 發矢在手 與足無關也 但不必蹲倒作態耳 頭不欲仰 惟向前側視 以目稍從箭桿審出 以之的可也 <以上言大概體勢 以下細言引弓 發矢時之體勢>

引弓時 先將矢搭在弓上 前臂番直朝地 前肩蓄下捲勢 前掌托實弓心<托實時 先將後手提緊弓弦 而後將前掌托實弓心> 胸欲欽 腹欲挺 足愈直 站愈穩 方將後肘向上 從後一提 前手自肩而臂 而掌 一齊俱直 托出向的 豈非前後肩臂平直如衡乎 故不期彀而自彀矣

發矢時 前肩下捲 已極實 送前
掌注的 後肩從高平瀉 大抵前肩從
下 〈下者 前肩向前下捲〉達上 〈
前拳達上也〉力從前掌而出 後肘
從高瀉下 〈後肘下 後肩切不可
下 若後肩一下 前肩即聳〉力從後
拳而開

此時光景 勢如常山之蛇 盤旋
而引 矢鏃浸進 毫無沮碍 前後手
勻輕兩開 此等工夫 全在藁砧上磨
出 亦必得二三知音士 更相互看迭
爲切磋 乃得入此妙境〈一部射學妙
理在此 不可放過〉若初射時 即往
郊野演習 心動神散 惟務中的 何
暇深求其法 今人不由藁砧演習 遽
往郊射 惑矣

At the moment you are about to release, the bow shoulder is settled all the way down and is extremely solid. The bow palm is extending towards the target. The draw shoulder has moved from a high to a level position [▶ but is still a little higher than the bow shoulder]. The bow shoulder <which is rotated and settled down> sends the bow arm sloping up to the bow fist. Strength comes from the bow hand palm reaching towards the target.

The draw elbow will have the tendency to want to drop down-and-back [▶ because the back and shoulder blades are taking most of the tension and the draw elbow is closed, the release will cause the draw hand to release freely and the draw elbow to naturally drop down-and-back]. <The draw elbow drops, not the draw shoulder. If the draw shoulder drops, then the bow shoulder will hunch up.> Strength comes from the draw hand releasing straight back.

Now your technique looks like a Changshan mountain snake: coiled and ready to strike. The arrowhead draws nearer to the handle without any hint of stopping or stuttering. The bow and draw hands balance the force of the draw and then lightly release.

You can only achieve this kind of technique by diligently practicing your form indoors in front of the gaozhen (straw bale). At the same time, you should practice with one or two knowledgeable friends. That way you can observe and learn from each other. This is really the ideal situation. <You learn a lot about shooting through this kind of practice. You should not give up the opportunity.>

But if you are a beginner and you rush to practice outside, you get too excited and only think about hitting the target. It becomes difficult to develop your form properly under these circumstances. People these days ignore practicing form in front of the gaozhen and rush to practice outside. This is a huge mistake!

Left: during full draw, the draw elbow will be level. Right: as a result of engaging the back muscles and keeping the arms relaxed, the draw elbow will automatically drop slightly down and towards your back during the release. No need to forcefully drop the elbow, and no need to forcefully swing open the draw-side shoulder.
Courtesy of Mike Loades.

Examples of improper draw elbow technique. Left: the error of dropping the draw elbow during full draw before release, which is dropping too early and creates unnecessary tension in the draw arm.
Courtesy of Chang Pengfei.
Right: the error of neglecting to drop the elbow during release (i.e., dropping it too late). The draw hand will have a tendency to kick out sideways.
Courtesy of Glenn Murray, Esq.

前肩自下達上

＜出箭時 前肩必須自下達上 以
前肩之性本易聳 前臂之性本易
垂 只因欲直骨節 故引弓之初 強
將前肩極力下捲 向前番直 前拳亦
極力翰起 引弓既彀時 大難永假 臂
力已盡 前肩必然有復聳之意 前拳
亦復有下垂之勢 安能到底前肩不
聳 前拳起翰者乎 故發矢之際 愈
加注意于前肩 必欲從下者 以殺其
復聳之意 達上者 達其拳向上出
矣 以殺其下垂之勢 則矢發方得超
揚遠到耳 拙射不能用到底之工
夫 初開弓 前肩則下捲 發矢時則
復聳 故矢不及遠＞

Using the Bow Shoulder to Send the Bow Arm Sloping Up to the Bow Hand

<When you are about to release, the bow shoulder must send the bow arm sloping upward to the hand. Otherwise, there is a natural tendency for the bow shoulder to hunch up and the bow arm to drop down. Thus, for the sole purpose of aligning the joints properly, at the start of the draw you must do your utmost to make sure your bow shoulder blade is settling all the way down and your bow hand is lifted higher than your bow shoulder.

At full draw before the release, you do not have arm strength to spare. That tendency, where the bow shoulder hunches up and the bow arm drops down, will return. How do you prevent the bow shoulder from hunching up and keep the bow hand raised?

The answer is that when you are about to release the arrow, you need to pay even more attention to the bow shoulder, making sure that it is settled down to eliminate the shoulder-hunching tendency. For the bow arm sloping up towards the bow hand, the bow hand must extend out and upward. This will eliminate the tendency for the arm to drop down. Only when you release this way will your arrows fly far.

Mediocre archers do not know how to maintain this position throughout the whole process. As they start the draw they are able to lower their bow shoulder, but when they are about to release their bow shoulder hunches up again. That is why they cannot shoot far.>

[▶ Having the arm in this position allows you to keep the bow arm less tense while still being able to support the bow stably.]

An example of settling down the bow shoulder blade and using the bow shoulder to send the bow arm sloping up to the bow hand.
Courtesy of Glenn Murray, Esq.

2.3 *Shooting Carelessly at the Gaozhen (Straw Bale)*

妄射藁砧之惑 〈第三〉

There are people who know they should do form practice while shooting at the gaozhen 藁砧 (straw bale) indoors as they are beginning to learn archery. They practice in front of the gaozhen for a long time, but why do they fail to improve? Although shooting at the gaozhen can be very beneficial for your form, it can also be very detrimental to your form!

If they know the proper technique, then they can improve quickly. But if they do not know technique and shoot carelessly, they can develop problems even more quickly. Why? Because when shooting in front of the gaozhen, they can perform hundreds of shots within a day. If you are in your home shooting at the gaozhen, you could shoot the same number of arrows in one day as you would shooting outdoors for 10 days. If you are learning proper form and practice this way, good technique becomes more and more familiar, and problems occur less and less frequently. Within a month proper technique will become second nature, and you will have reached a milestone in your shooting. If you want to achieve mastery, it is all based on this kind of practice.

人亦有初習射而演藁砧者矣 老而無成 何邪 蓋藁砧雖學法之具 亦入迷塗之具也 故學法而射者 得益甚捷 不知法而妄射者 取害尤速也 何也 射藁砧者 一日可發數百矢 在家射藁砧 一日可當郊射十日之功 是以學法而射藁砧者 合法愈熟 去病愈遠 不一月而法機熟 入門既端 將來漸入巧妙 皆基于此 不學法而妄射者 此非以學法也 學病矣 不一月而病機熟 入病愈深 去病愈遠矣 一日之誤 遂成終身之惑 可忽乎哉

Now for the other case of shooting without knowing proper technique. If you shoot carelessly, you are not learning technique — you are learning mistakes! Within a month the problems become even more ingrained: the faults become deeper, and getting rid of them becomes even harder. A day's worth of mistakes becomes a lifetime of problems. How can you afford to be so negligent?!

There are people who are humble and studious. <The world has people who want to learn but are not humble. They hold fast to their own prejudices. You give them good advice, but they do not bother to think about the reasoning behind it. They think they are hot stuff. People like this have no hope of improving.> Although these humble/studious people are talented, they are not stubborn about their understanding. They will always keep the Five-Step Method in their heart even while they are walking, eating, sitting, and sleeping. Then when they practice in front of the gaozhen indoors, they are able to stand steadily, nock the arrow,

是以虛心好學之人〈世亦有好學而不虛心者 守定一隅之見 一聞善言 不審理之是非 自以爲是者 若人更無上進之機矣〉雖天資敏妙 不敢私心自用 必以審殻勻輕注之法 日嚴諸心 行住坐臥 宛然心目 而後對藁砧 端立搭箭 引定不發 必極於殻 前肩下捲 兩臂平

直　熟視薰砧心一塊　少頃而弛弓　一
日之間　如此數百次　須十餘日

　　前肩下捲熟習　不勞而定　此爲
練肩　審視詳明　舉目便見薰砧中
物　不爲弓弝所障　此爲練目　前拳
握弓　五指安妥　不論滿把與鷹爪　俱
要虎口平仰　殼時　矢鏃引至弓弝中
間　指不碍鏃　掌根手心均貼實安
妥　此爲練掌　前後肩臂平直　一引
便殼　一殼便齊　堅持不動　此爲練
臂　如此又十餘日　此射家築基法
也〈以上只言引弓法　射學根本　全
在引弓滿固　故曰築基　基固而及
遠　命中特易事耳〉

　　築基既定　然後向薰砧發矢　其
法必俟引弓殼時　前肩下捲　得十分
堅實　方能從下達上　送前掌托出　後
肩及臂從高平瀉　向背後而止　是謂
發矢法
　　發矢時　後掌心須向前拳　切勿
用絕法　恐激動機神　矢發不準〈掌
心向前拳發矢時　中指　無名指　小
指須極力緊收　不撒開　只用食指　大
指直開　方捷疾〉

pull the string, and focus on reaching full draw steadily. They settle down their bow shoulder, they make sure their arms are properly aligned, and they focus their vision on a spot at the center of the gaozhen. They do not release hastily. Within a day, they should practice shooting hundreds of arrows in this manner, and repeat this for 10 or so days.

When you become very familiar with settling the bow shoulder blade all the way down, you do not have to labor at it, and the shoulder will be very solid. This is how you practice your shoulder.

Your attention should be focused solely at the point on the gaozhen you want to shoot (you can see through the bow handle to the target). This is how you practice your vision.

When gripping the bow, the five fingers should be holding with the appropriate pressure. Regardless of whether you are using the Full Grip or the Eagle Claw, the web of the hand should be level. When you reach full draw, you pull the arrowhead towards the handle, and the fingers should not obstruct the arrowhead. The root of the palm holds the bow, and the center of the palm holds appropriately. That is how you practice the bow hand. [▶ Please see the discussion in Book 1, Chapter 2.6 for discussion about the "root of the palm" and the bow hand gripping technique.]

Both shoulders and arms should be well-aligned. As soon as you pull you will be able to reach full draw. As soon as you reach full draw the shoulders and arms coordinate as a single unit, all without shaking. This is how you practice the arms.

Practice this way for another 10 or so days. This is the foundation for archery. <Up until now I have been talking about drawing technique. The key to archery is being able to reach full draw steadily. That is why I talk about laying a foundation. Once the foundation is solid, hitting a faraway target becomes especially easy.>

When you have established the basics, then you can face the gaozhen and shoot. As soon as you reach full draw, you must keep the bow shoulder blade settled down and make sure it is 100% solid. Only then can you make the bow shoulder send the bow arm sloping upward to the fist, with the fist reaching out. As a unit, the draw shoulder and arm have settled from a high to a level position, and then the entire unit (draw shoulder/arm closed firmly) will drop down and towards your back and stop. This is the method for releasing.

When releasing the arrow, the heart of the draw hand palm should face towards the bow hand. Do not think about using the "snap back" method of release, or else its abruptness will make your shots unstable. <When the draw hand palm is facing the bow hand, then as you release the middle/ring/pinky fingers should

fold in tightly and not open up. Only the index finger and thumb should open up straight. That will make the release fast. [▶ This is for the case of the double-hook draw hand technique. See discussion in Book 1, Chapter 2.4.]>

When you have committed yourself to the Five-Step Method and become really familiar with it, then the moment you lift your draw hand you have reached full draw. As soon as you reach full draw it will be easier to achieve balance and to make your release light: your arrow will fly efficiently. These steps are so connected that the way you execute them will be like a horse running down a mountain slope: there is no hesitation. If you practice form with the gaozhen for 100 days, your arrows will fly true and go where you intend, and then you will be ready to go outside for military practice.

Although you might practice good technique in front of the gaozhen, when you go outside it is very easy for your technique to change if you are not careful. For military practice, use the same form you practiced in front of the gaozhen! When you are shooting outdoors, your body and arm technique are the same as before. That is the right way to practice. Do not fall into the trap of getting sloppy with your shooting! <Putting in the effort to practice in front of the gaozhen is at least 100 times harder than ad hoc, unregimented practice. But this is one of those times where a moment of toil yields a lifetime of ease: in the end you use your body efficiently, and you are not wasting any energy. That is why I warn you not to fall into the trap of sloppy shooting. People these days are not willing to learn proper technique. As soon as the bow touches their hands, they go outside to shoot. They only think about hitting the target and then hundreds of problems emerge. How can they hope to score? This is what they call "being in a rush to go nowhere.">

If you are outside shooting and your technique lapses, then go back inside to the gaozhen and reexamine your form practice. When you have practiced enough to rid yourself of your faults, go back outside to try again. Repeat this cycle as needed. Do not think of this as a burden: you must hold yourself to a high technical standard. This is the key to becoming accurate.

I always teach archers to focus exclusively on proper form and not worry about accuracy in the beginning. Some people ask me "Mr. Gao, why do you focus on learning form and not on accuracy? We only care about accuracy, so we do not have to stick with form." Alas, how can they be so utterly ignorant?

務使審縠勻輕諸法 熟習巧妙 後手一提便縠 一縠便勻輕而注出 如駿馬下山坡 中間寧有駐足之地乎 如此百日 箭發順利而如意 薰砧之功方足 乃可向郊野演武

凡習射者 仕薰砧上 雖合法 在野外則射法俱變 所云演者 演薰砧上所習之法也 使郊野之射 身法手法與薰砧上一樣 方是習射之正法 不墮世俗妄射之惑矣<如此薰砧上習射工夫 比世人之難 不啻百之 然一勞永佚 終身巧妙 不煩費力 故云 不墮世俗妄射之惑 今人不肯學法 弓一到手 便往郊射 只圖立刻就中 百病交集 如何中的 所謂欲速則不達也> 郊演而或變 則又向薰砧上 溫習射法 溫習而無弊 又復試之郊原 再溫再演 不厭煩瑣 必求合法 而中在其中矣

潁嘗誨人習射 只要合法 不急求中 人輒曰「高先生誨人 只要射一合法 不要中者 何如 我輩只要中的 不必拘於法乎」嗟嗟 何不思之甚也

夫不必法而中者　此偶中不可訓
也　何也　無法而中者　久射機熟故
中　機不可執　無法可守　久不射則
機室　不能中矣　或臨場　得失介懷
則不中　或臨難　喪膽則亦不中矣　故
曰偶中　了所謂不求中而求合法
者　法合而中存　不求中而無不中者
也　此中非偶也　如以予言爲非是　則
孔子祿在其中之意　非與

早射勁弓之惑〈第四〉

今人亦有射藁砧而合正法者
矣　然多歷年所　而引弓時　前後臂
輒動搖　此又何也　射勁弓太早耳　初
習射之人　前肩雖下捲而未熟　骨節
雖平直而猶疎　若遽用勁弓　前後手
爲勁弓所制　竭周身之力　彀弓且不
給　何暇用力復下前肩　何也　初射
之人　骨節俱僵　欲下前肩　已極費
力　若用力彀勁弓　必無力下前肩　前
肩未下　骨節俱虛　引弓安得不搖　發
矢又安能準　故初射藁砧　只用舖筋
軟竹弓　約三十餘斤　百日之後　射
法漸熟　弓漸勁　日增倍之　俟下前
肩熟習之後　骨節自直　直則生力　熟
則生勢　雖無力之人　可彀勁弓　況
強有力者乎　此行遠自邇之理也

The people who do not care about form (and only focus on accuracy) may hit the target accidentally using a method that is unteachable. Why is that? People without form who are accurate only get their accuracy from raw intuition. But their intuition is intangible when there is no form to speak of. If they do not shoot for a while, they lose their intuition and they are not able to hit anymore. Or perhaps when they reach the exam grounds or the battlefield, they become very nervous. They are unable to tame their fear and, of course, they end up missing. This is what I mean by these people "hitting accidentally."

If you focus on form rather than accuracy, then accuracy is reproducible because of your good form. You are not trying to hit, but you hit the target anyway! Your accuracy is not an accident. If you are skeptical of my advice, then you will also be skeptical of Confucius's advice that "the gentleman should strive to understand the underlying process rather than settle for superficial facts."

2.4 Pulling a Heavy Bow Too Early

Suppose you practice in front of the gaozhen (straw bale) and you have good technique. Although you have been doing this for a while, both your arms are shaking as you pull the bow. What is wrong this time? You are shooting too heavy a bow too early!

As a beginner, although you are settling down your bow shoulder blade, it is not yet second nature. Although your joints are roughly aligned, you have not yet mastered the process. Then when you rush to use a heavy bow, the tension of the bow overpowers your arms, you exhaust all your body's strength, and you are not able to reach full draw steadily. It becomes impossible to resettle your bow shoulder blade at full draw. Why does this happen?

Your joints are very rigid as a beginner. Trying to settle down your bow shoulder blade will take most of your energy. At this stage, if you try to divert that energy into pulling a bow that is too heavy for you, then you have no energy for settling your bow shoulder blade, your bow shoulder will not settle down all the way, and your joints will be misaligned. You cannot avoid shaking during the draw, and you cannot attain consistent accuracy.

Thus, when you start practicing form in front of the gaozhen, you should use a sinew-backed bamboo bow with a light draw weight of about 30 jin (39 pounds). Do this for about a hundred days. Afterwards, as you get more familiar with your form, you can gradually increase the draw weight of your bow. After practicing this way for a while, your joints will align themselves automatically, and from that alignment comes strength. Through familiarity, your form takes shape. This is how a weak person can pull a strong bow. Imagine what a strong person with the right technique can achieve! This is a gradual, step-by-step process.

I always teach archers to take things gradually. A lot of people hate taking things slowly, and they do not know how to introduce things gradually. Ultimately, the people who are hasty and want to progress quickly are the ones who make the slowest progress. Some stubborn people will say: "Do not use a light bow. If you begin with a light bow, a lot of problems will develop and you will not be able to use a heavy bow." What a ridiculous thing to say! In response I tell them: "Okay, suppose your reasoning is true. When we teach babies to walk, we always let them lean against a wall. But does that mean they lose the ability to run when they grow up?" People always have a good laugh when they hear this.

Some say: "Of course you should begin with light bows and progress towards using heavy bows. When you start out, your draw hand should use a single-hook thumb draw technique to hold the string, and then you should eventually change to a double-hook thumb draw technique." That saying makes no sense. Single-hook only uses the index finger [▶ covering the thumbnail] to control the string, and it yields less strength. Double-hook uses the index and middle fingers [▶ covering the thumbnail] to control the string, and it yields more strength. More strength is better than less strength. That is pretty obvious!

Most people use single-hook because they believe the release is crisp, whereas the release for double-hook will be sluggish. If you want to use double-hook thumb draw, only use half the tip of the middle finger to cover the thumbnail. You should position the index finger as if you were using single-hook. When you let go of the string, the middle finger should tuck in tightly, whereas the thumb and index finger should open up straight and relaxed. That is the right way to let go of the string. It is as crisp as single-hook technique, but you get added strength for pulling the string. When you release, you avoid the sluggishness of the typical double-hook technique. This is how double-hook technique can be far superior to single-hook technique.

予誨人射 莫不由漸而入 人多嫌其太遲 而不知始之徐徐者 乃其所以速 而世之欲速者 正其所以遲也 彼偏見者 輒曰「弓勿用軟 初射而用弓軟 遂成痼疾 終身不能用勁」此說非也 予聞之曰「信如所言 今人教小兒學步者 循牆而走則終身便不能急趨乎」聞者大笑

或曰「用弓當自軟而勁矣 後手羈弦 亦當自單搭始 而後乃雙搭乎」曰不然 單搭只用食指羈弦 而力小 雙搭用食指中指羈弦 則力大 力大愈於力小 明矣

世多用單搭者 以單搭發矢鬆 而雙搭遲鈍耳 若使雙搭 只用中指第一節之半 搭在大指 而食指仍用單搭法 脫弦時 中指用弦法 極力收緊 而大指食指盡力直開 則得勢而脫弦鬆脆 與單搭無異 且控弦有力 而開時不犯雙搭之遲鈍 則雙搭賢于單搭遠矣

Left: using the double-hook draw hand technique to pull the string. Notice the index and middle fingers covering the thumbnail. Right: Gao Ying's follow through for the double-hook technique, which requires retracting the middle finger back into the draw hand fist during the release. See the box below on Recommended Draw Hand Technique. *Courtesy of Glenn Murray, Esq.*

Recommended Draw Hand Technique

In our experience, executing the double-hook technique successfully highly depends on the dimensions and shape of the ring. The ring has to fit perfectly: it cannot be too thick or have a lip that is too long (lest the middle finger clip the ring while tucking in during the double-hook release). If your thumb becomes sweaty, the ring will also become a little loose, further adding to the difficulties of the double-hook technique. By contrast, single-hook technique is more forgiving overall, and is tolerant of variations in ring size. Please see the following photos for how to execute the single-hook thumb draw.

For single-hook, curl in the three fingers, hook the thumb partially around the string, touch the flat part of the lip of your ring to the side of your middle finger's middle segment, cover the thumbnail with the tip or distal joint of your index finger but do not press too hard (apply just enough pressure to keep the thumb from flipping open accidentally). Ensure that your fingers are not crowding the arrow nock too much. Make sure your hand, wrist, and especially your thumb's base knuckle are relaxed. You will feel as if you have created an imaginary rope between your elbow and the ring as you lead with the elbow behind the arrow to draw the string back.

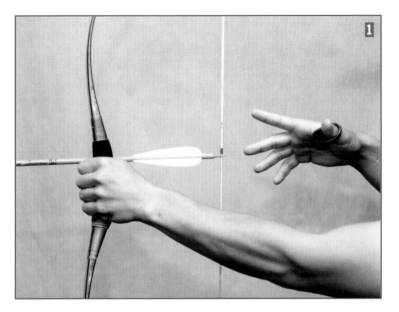
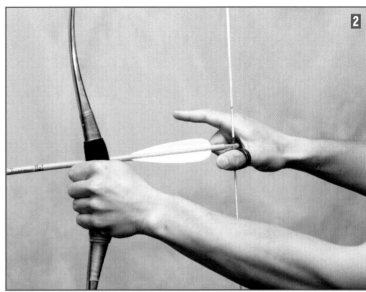
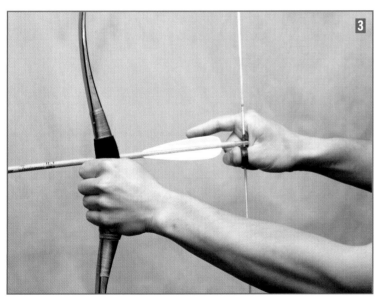
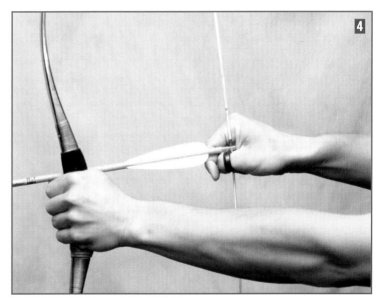

Sequence for single-hook draw hand technique (left-side view of a right-handed archer).
Courtesy of Glenn Murray, Esq.

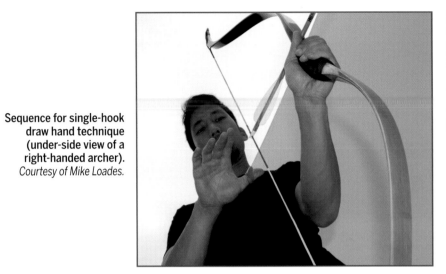
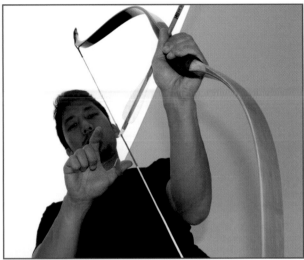

Sequence for single-hook
draw hand technique
(under-side view of a
right-handed archer).
Courtesy of Mike Loades.

The style of practice target that Gao Ying describes is a small flag hanging from a bamboo staff. There would usually be a mound of dirt behind it to stop the arrow. In Book 1, Chapter 3.10, Gao mentions how the front part of a heavy arrow has to be durable because the arrow will penetrate the dirt behind the target flag.

Suppose you have already put in a lot of form practice in front of the gaozhen (straw bale) and your technique is rock solid. Yet when you go outside to shoot at a large target, you cannot attain the same level of proficiency as you did in front of the gaozhen. Your shooting will not become accurate. Why? Because you are using a large target too early!

Beginners hastily choose a large target because they think it is easy to hit, so their mind becomes preoccupied with scoring. They are in a rush to shoot and become greedy about wanting to hit the mark. How can they still focus on the details of the form? Once their form becomes messy, their vision, shoulders, arms, fingers, and palms all become messy. How can they hit the target this way?

Although there are some thoughtful archers who are aware of this problem, they too cannot 100% avoid the greediness that comes with seeing a large target. They will inevitably overlook some element of their form. The moment they get a little greedy, their spirit gets a little sloppy. Once their spirit gets a little sloppy, they pay less attention to their form. How is this not a problem caused by using a large target too early?

If you want to practice outdoors properly, do not use a big target in the beginning. Just use a staff made from the tip of a large bamboo stalk <the base of the bamboo might harm the arrows, so just use the tip>. The staff should be 7-chi long (about 88 in or 2.24 m), and a 1-chi (about 12.6 in or 32 cm) flag should be hanging from it to act as your target. When the target is small, it makes you focus your concentration to the task at hand, with your mind and arms acting in unison. For the Five-Step Method, success depends on whether you are following the method and observing your progress closely. If you are, you will gradually improve your form and gradually rid yourself of faults. When you have done this for a while and your form becomes second-nature, then although you might shoot your arrows relatively quickly, they will all hit the target and your form will be proper. You will be able to hit small targets, so of course big targets will not be a problem!

For this reason, you must recognize the problems associated with shooting at a large target too early. Only after your outdoor shooting technique is mature [▶ from shooting the small flag on a pole] can you graduate to using a standard examination target that is 6-chi (88 in, 192 cm) wide and 8-chi (101 in, 256 cm) tall. The standard practice target should not be too small. If you are always using a small target, but you suddenly see a large target on the archery exam range, you will mistakenly think the target is at close range. It is far away but you think it is near. As a result, your arrow falls short. That is why for your regular practice you should use a standard examination target.

郊射用大的太早之惑 〈第五〉

射藁砧之功既盡 射俱合法矣 而郊射對大的 則不能合法 射輒不中 何也 用大的太早耳 初射之人 遽用大的 見爲易與 好勝之心一生 發矢時 精神俱馳 騖於中的 何暇顧其身法乎 身法一亂 則目審肩臂指掌之法俱亂 安能中的 間有精心謹密之人 亦知簡點 然欲中之心 豈能盡去 一身之間 未免顧此失彼 增一分勝心 精神亦增一分外馳矣 外馳之心增一分 簡點射法之心亦減一分矣 豈非用大的太早乎

是以郊射之法 始初不用大的 只用大竹稍一根 〈竹根恐傷箭 故用竹稍耳〉 長七尺 以尺布爲旗以爲的 的小則求中之心泯 精神常聚于手 所云審彀勻輕注法 合與不合之由 可以潛心簡察矣 察之而法漸合 病漸去 久之而法熟機生 隨手迅發 皆中規矩 小的可中 況大的乎

此用大的太早之惑宜辨也 射法既熟之後 用的只宜合式爲準 〈六尺闊 八尺高 爲準〉 不可過小 若平時常用小的 場上忽見大的 〈考官前爲場上〉 以爲近而忽之 視遠若近 發矢必小 故居常用的 以合式爲準

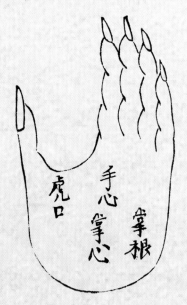

前拳握弓徒緊之惑 〈第六〉

郊射始用小的 演習得法 是宜
中的矣 然發矢忽有左右大小之
偏 此又何也 則前拳握弓徒緊 而
未得其竅也 人恁射學之工夫 只有
三大端 始焉引弓欲彀 中焉浸進欲
勻 終焉發矢欲穩 彀之根蒂 在前
肩之下捲 勻之根蒂 在後肩之旋
運 穩之根蒂 在前拳之把握 前肩
後肩有不合法 其形立見 人易知而
改之 猶人患外傷 藥石可攻 鍼砭
可施也

惟前拳握弓之病 隱在掌心 無
形可見 猶心腹之疾 人不易知 初
學者亦不自覺 何從而改 孰知握弓
不妥 發矢皆偏 〈左右大小之偏〉 縱
使外貌得法 而中的者寡矣 是謂一
惑而喪百善 可無辨與

虎口　手心　掌心　掌根

2.6 *Gripping the Bow Handle Too Tightly*

You are shooting outside using a small target, and you are practicing the right technique. You should be able to hit the target. But when you release the arrow it sometimes veers left, right, up, or down. What is the problem this time? It is because your bow hand is gripping the handle too tightly and lacks finesse!

Overall, archery boils down to three main things: (1) you have to reach full draw, (2) you have to balance the draw weight of the bow, and (3) you have to be stable when you release. The key to reaching full draw is settling down the bow shoulder. The key to balancing the draw weight is getting the draw shoulder involved. The key to stability rests in how the bow hand holds the handle. You can observe if there are problems with the bow-side and draw-side shoulders. It is easy for people see and correct them. As with a man suffering from a disease with external symptoms, you can prescribe the right medicine and apply acupuncture in the right places.

But problems with how the bow hand grips the handle are hidden in the palm. There is nothing concrete to observe: like when someone has heart or digestive diseases, it is hard for others to know. Beginners do not have an intuition for how to diagnose these problems, so how can they correct them? How do you know when it is a problem with the grip? Although the outer appearance looks fine, the arrows will veer all over the place <left, right, up, and down> and hits will be rare. We call it "the one problem that cancels out a hundred other good things." You cannot afford to ignore this issue.

Labels for parts of the bow hand. *Old illustration from the edition of Gao Ying's manual compiled by Jiang Qilong and edited by Ogyuu Sorai (published in Kyoto, Japan, 1780). Live photo courtesy of Glenn Murray, Esq.*

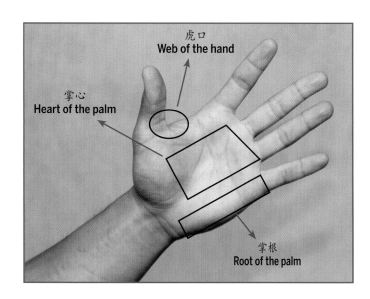

虎口
Web of the hand

掌心
Heart of the palm

掌根
Root of the palm

For gripping the bow, nothing beats the following. At the moment you have you have nocked the arrow (when the bow shoulder is settled down and the bow arm is pointing to the ground, and the draw arm and shoulder are lifting up to apply tension to the bowstring), the root of the palm should solidly support the handle, and the ring and pinky fingers should wrap around the handle. The index and middle fingers are curled but only touch the handle lightly: they should not apply any force. When you are about to release, the thumb is pointing towards the target.

With this grip, although the root of the palm is solid, the arrow will not veer upward because the web of the hand is level. Although the web of the hand is solid, the arrow will not veer downward because the root of the palm also holds solidly. Although the ring and pinky fingers hold the handle tightly, the bow hand will not kick out to the left because the root of the palm is solid. Although the index and middle fingers do not apply any force, the arrow will not veer rightward because the thumb is pointing forward. This is how you get the arrow to release well. It is the best method for gripping the handle. People call it the Big Eagle Claw. <The area between the thumb and index finger is the web of the hand. The part of the palm at the base of the middle and ring fingers is the heart of the palm. The part of the palm at the base of the pinky is the root of the palm. A lot of people mistakenly think the heart of the palm is the same as the root of the palm. If you are holding the handle with the heart of the palm, the web of the hand has to angle upwards, which will cause the arrow to veer upwards. Instead, you should make the root of the palm grip solidly, which will prevent the web of the hand from pointing upwards. This will allow you to point the thumb towards the target, and the arrow will release steadily.>

Suppose you do not grip properly and just do your own ad hoc thing. You might hold the web of the hand tight and let the root of the palm float freely, but this will cause the arrow to veer downward. You might make the heart of the palm grip solidly and the web of the palm point up vertically, but then the arrow will veer upward. If all five fingers grip the handle tightly, then you are using too much force. This will cause the bow hand to kick out sideways, the upper tip of the bow to tip forward intentionally, and the arrow to veer to the left. But then you become afraid of the arrow veering left, so you are reluctant to let the bow move naturally after the shot [▶ that is, you are holding more tightly], which causes the arrow to fly without impetus and veer to the right. You might know the Five-Step Method by heart, but if your arrow flies askew, the rest of your technique is useless. It all stems from a tiny mistake in your grip. You must pay attention to this point.

夫握弓之法 莫善于搭箭時 將
前肩臂向前 番直朝地 後肩臂從高
提緊 就將前掌根托實弓心 次以小
指無名指捲握弓弝 而食指中指屈
曲 附麗于弓 不必用力 發矢時 與
大指一同直叉對的

如此把握 掌根雖寔而虎口不
仰 矢不患大 虎口雖寔而掌根不
虛 矢不患小 小指無名指握弓雖
緊 而不患撇左 以掌根寔也 食指
中指雖不用力 而直叉出 則不患偏
右 以出矢得勢也 如此握弓爲第一
法 人號曰大鷹爪〈大指食指中間
叉口 爲虎口 手掌與中指無名指對
直者 爲掌心 與小指對直者 爲掌
根 世人誤認掌心爲掌根 若握弓時
掌心一實 虎口必仰 矢出插天而大
矣 惟以小指對直處爲掌根 此處一
實 虎口便不能仰 必然直叉而出 矢
出方穩〉

若不講於此 而妄自握弓 虎口
或緊而掌根虛 則矢垂頭而小 掌心
實而虎口仰 則矢插天而大 前拳五
指俱握緊 則用力太過 必撇出而矢
偏左 恐其偏左而不敢撇 則出無勢
而又偏右 縱合審彀勻輕注法 發矢
一偏 百法不驗 皆從握之一字失
也 可不辨與

Big Eagle Claw (Variation 1). The thumb is touching the index and middle fingers in a relaxed manner. Only the ring and pinky fingers hold firmly while the web of the hand acts like a net for the handle. *Courtesy of Glenn Murray, Esq.*

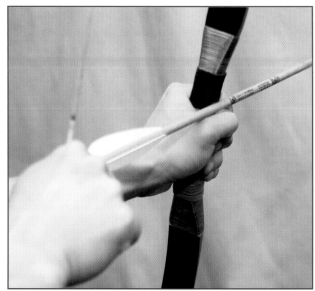

Big Eagle Claw (Variation 2). The thumb is resting above the index finger in a relaxed manner. Only the ring and pinky fingers hold firmly while the web of the hand acts like a net for the handle. *Courtesy of Glenn Murray, Esq.*

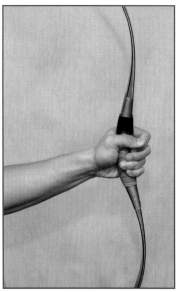

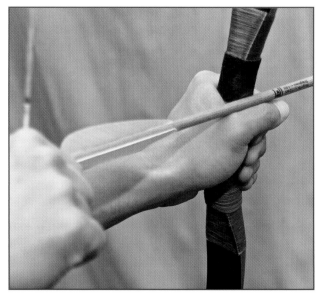

The Full Grip will cause the bow hand to kick sideways most frequently. <The Full Grip is where all five fingers holds the handle tightly.> The Little Eagle Claw ranks next in terms of how frequently the bow hand kicks sideways. <The Little Eagle Claw is where the index finger retracts behind the handle, and only the middle/ring/pinky fingers are holding.> Dull people will not be able to figure out that they have a problem with their grip. Then there are those crude and spiteful individuals who jump to conclusions and do not observe things carefully. When they see the arrow veering many times, they mistakenly think the Five-Step Method is useless, and argue that there is no point to learning proper form for shooting.

Oh man... That is like giving up eating because you saw someone choking.

  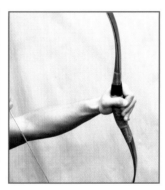

滿把犯撇病者極多 〈五指俱握緊爲滿把〉 小鷹爪次之 〈以食指縮起 只以中指無名指小指握弓 爲小鷹爪〉 犯握弓妄緊之弊 而莫覺 庸愚之人 既不能深求其故 間有粗豪好勝之士 又以欲速而不暇察 見發矢多偏 遂以審彀勻輕注法爲無用 謂射不必學法 嗟夫 是因噎廢食矣

Far left: Little Eagle Claw, where the bottom three fingers hold firmly and the thumb rests over the middle finger. **Middle:** Full Grip, where all five fingers are holding firmly. **Right:** Empty Grip, where the thumb, index, and middle fingers hold firmly, and the fist is slanted so that the ring and pinky fingers are barely touching. (The Empty Grip is not mentioned by Gao Ying but is described in other Ming sources. It is reminiscent of the grip archers use for bows with modern pistol handles.) *Courtesy of Glenn Murray, Esq.*

2.7 *Practicing Too Infrequently*

習射作輟之惑 〈第七〉

Suppose your bow hand holds the bow steadily and you are able to hit the target. You can hit the target as a beginner and you think you are a hot shot. But then a year goes by and your accuracy has not improved one bit. You have not improved this year, and the same thing happens the following year. As time passes, the color of your hair changes but you still shoot poorly. Why is this happening? It is because you are practicing too infrequently!

前拳握弓既穩 自宜舍矢破的 然有始初演射便能中的 人服其敏 乃歷春而夏而秋而冬中數不加 今歲不進 來年復然 時序推遷 顏髮幾改 而射猶夫人者 何也 作輟之過也

If you do not let the water flow, it will get rancid. If you do not use the wood containers for a while, they will get eaten by insects. If you do not give yourself motivation, you will become complacent. If you do not exercise your body, it will become fragile and useless. Especially for archers, having a clean release lies in the fingers and palms, which have the potential to hit a small target one hundred paces

夫水不流則腐 器不用則蠹 人之精神不淬勵則昏 肢體形骸不勤行修煉 則脆弱而無用 況射者 發捷于指掌之間 中微於百步之外 甘苦疾徐之機 得心應手之巧 非精氣

凝注 形神湊泊者不能到 若以作輟
之心乘之 手與弓不相習則法滯 法
滯則機死 機死則巧不著 何以破微
于百步之外哉 故能洞的于百步之
外者 其氣魄光焰 常蓋數百步者
也 精氣能蓋數百少者 必其操持遠
大 旁若無人 能吞吐一世者也 豈
作輟弛廢者所可能哉

故善學之人 攀審彀勻輕注之
法 辨之既拆 行往坐臥宛然心目 郊
射演試 必合竅會 眾人喧嘩 我獨
靜思 舍矢雖多 無不暗記 今日增
何法 去何病 明日更當進何法 去
何法 寸累銖積精進之功 新與日俱
相習滋久 機神自暢 巧妙之來 發
于骨髓 隨其意之所投 無不中矩 而
命中之技在是矣

昔李廣在軍中飲酒遊戲 必以射
爲快心 劉錡握兵暇時 常射矢 室
水桶隙 更拔而更射中之 岳武穆學
射于周同 盡其巧而後已 同死朔望
爲之致祭
古人好學之勤 下人之專 用意
之厚 所以卒成名將 聲施到今 非
偶然也

away. The timing of your movements, the way your instincts guide your hands, the concentration you have obtained, and the synchronicity of your body and mind: all these are crucial for maintaining consistency. If you get lazy about practice, your hands lose familiarity with how to handle the bow, your technique gets stagnant, you lose your sense of timing, and you lose any sense of competence.

So how do you hit a small target a hundred paces away? People who can pierce a target a hundred paces away have an unshakable confidence that can even project several hundred paces away. People with this level of confidence must have all their technique under control. They will not be affected by their surroundings. The world is their apple. But how can you hope to achieve this level of proficiency if you do not practice?

Diligent practitioners pay attention to the Five-Step Method, they can dissect and understand every aspect of it, and they think about it all the time. When they go outside to shoot, they are even more capable of hitting. Although their surroundings are noisy, they are able to ruminate quietly on their technique. Although they might shoot many arrows, they take careful note of what happens with each one. Today, they improve their form a bit and get rid of some faults. Tomorrow, they improve their form even more and get rid of more faults. They work tirelessly to accumulate proficiency day-by-day. Then they are able to shoot fluidly, to understand the nuances, and to have the correct technique ingrained in their bones. They can make the arrow fly wherever they want, and every shot follows perfect form. This is how their shooting becomes accurate!

Back when General Li Guang [▶ of the Western Han Dynasty] was hanging out with his troops, practicing archery was fun for him (as fun as drinking or playing games). General Liu Qi [▶ of the Southern Song Dynasty] would always practice archery in his spare time. If he saw a crack in a bucket, he would shoot at it. The more he shot, the better he could hit. General Yue Fei [▶ of the Southern Song Dynasty] learned archery from Zhou Tong (周同), but practiced so hard that he eventually surpassed his master in skill. Yet Yue would pay bi-weekly tribute to Zhou's tomb after Zhou died. These ancestors enjoyed practicing diligently, putting all their effort in perfecting their skill. They eventually became famous generals whose names we speak up to this day. This is not an accident.

Liu Qi (劉錡) was a general from the Southern Song Dynasty (1127–1279 CE). He was well-known for his battles against the Jurchens/Jin (金) and Tanguts/Xixia (西夏), and he was also a highly-regarded archer. As the story goes, while practicing Liu created a crack by shooting an arrow into a bucket full of water. After removing the arrow, he shot another arrow to seal the crack created by the first one to prevent the bucket from leaking.

Yue Fei (岳飛) was an extremely famous general from the Southern Song Dynasty (1127–1279 CE) and is regarded as a Chinese cultural hero. He gained fame in successful campaigns defending the Song against the Jurchens/Jin, and he was one of the highly-regarded Zhongxing Four Generals (中興四將) of the Southern Song period. His archery and martial arts abilities are legendary, and biographies describe his incredible strength with drawing heavy bows and crossbows even before he reached adulthood. He was also an exemplar of patriotism, and there is a famous story about his mother writing a tattoo on his back saying "serve the country with the utmost loyalty (盡忠報國)."

Nowadays people do not let their form fully mature before they start thinking about hitting the target. They happen to score a few hits, and then they think they do not need technique anymore. In the end, the hands and bow lose coordination and it becomes very difficult to hit the target. They fare more poorly than the people who love archery but do not learn technique (this other group of people can hit the target just by hard training and experience). So the old saying applies here: "talent cannot beat training."

Then some people will say "If you practice enough, you can overcome people with natural talent. Even for people who do not practice proper form, if they shoot enough arrows, they will become accurate! Why bother with technique?"

That is a ridiculous thing to say.

When you ignore technique yet hit the target: that is just intuition. When you learn technique and hit the target: that is discipline. You gain intuition by shooting a lot, so you are just hitting by accident. How ignorant! If you hit, then you do not know why you hit. If you missed, then you do not know why you missed. If you shoot a long time just based on intuition, then when you face a formidable situation you become anxious and nervous. Where is your intuition now? In the end, practicing this way is like shooting blind.

今人學法未就 便思命中 稍能中的 便欲棄置 卒之弓手齟齬 艱于中的 反不若不學法而好射者 機熟而多中也 語云「巧生不如拙熟」此之謂與 或曰「拙而熟 反勝於巧而生 則不習法者 多射亦可中矣 以奚法爲」曰不然 不學法而中者 機熟也 學法而中者 紀律也 機熟之中由於多射 其中時于偶然 不識不知者也 其中也 不知合何法 不中也 不知犯何病 即使久射機熟 一臨利害 中心無主 機不知何處去矣 故終身習射總爲瞎射

學法之人　百法俱備　百病皆
知　胸中利弊了然　其中也　知合何
法　其不中也　知犯何病　即有中的
之矢　亦知其犯何病　以幸合何法而
不害　雖中不爲全美　亦有不中之
矢　如其合何法　以犯何病而不救　雖
不中不爲全非　見一善　知遵而守　見
一病　知戒而改　善日增　病日改　射
之精也　可計日而待　縱久不習射　亦
可計日而溫　或臨利害　中心有主　手
法不亂　其合法者　固已中的　稍不
如意者　亦離的不遠

所謂節制之師　能大勝　不能大
敗者也　不學法之射　猶無紀之兵　不
大勝即大敗者也　此學與不學之辨
也　烏得以不學法之熟　而多中　遂
謂不必學法乎

但學法之人　亦宜多射　不可作
輟　以致生疏　即后羿亦難命中　后
羿之善射　寧獨資性過人哉　要亦好
射中來也　孔子大聖　猶欲假年以卒
學　況其他乎

信道不篤之惑〈第八〉

學射而不作輟　宜巧妙日生　樂
善不倦矣　乃又有躁進之人　嫌法無
速効　好勝之人　訾法爲無奇　忽趨
他途而不肯率由正法者　何也　信道
不篤也　歷變未周之人　邪正未分　識
見未定　與之圖事　必然中變　幸而
有不變者　必其人寡交索居　耳不聞

People who learn form have to understand all the details and recognize all the faults. In their hearts, they know what does and does not work. They know what constitutes good form, and when they miss they know what faults they committed. They can identify mistakes in their successful shots, and they can identify merits in their unsuccessful shots, because they are only interested in improving their form. If they observe something good, they take note and make sure to maintain it. If they observe something bad, they diagnose the fault and avoid it later. Day by day, they improve their form while ridding themselves of problems, eventually becoming excellent shooters. They are able to count the days before they reach this level. If it so happens that they do not practice for a while, they can still recover their technique in a matter of days. They may face formidable situations, but they are not nervous, and their technique will not get sloppy. These people who are serious about technique will definitely hit the target. Occasionally they will not hit what they are aiming for, but then their arrow will not be far off the mark either.

Disciplined soldiers can achieve great victories and avoid crushing defeats. People who do not learn technique are like undisciplined soldiers: they can somehow achieve great victories by luck, but they are at greater risk of having catastrophic defeats. That is the difference between learning and not learning technique. You should not learn proper form halfway, score a bunch of hits, and then come to the conclusion that learning good form is useless.

But people who learn good form should also practice a lot. If Hou Yi were to stop practicing, he would have trouble hitting the target, too. But Hou Yi had archery abilities that far surpassed any mortal man because he loved to practice. The Great Sage Confucius also said that you have to study hard and practice diligently to achieve mastery. If these sages and archery aces need this much practice, what do you think a regular person requires?

2.8 *Being Skeptical of the Method*

If you practice on a regular basis, your mastery will grow day by day as you work tirelessly to get better. But there are impatient people who think learning proper form makes progress too slow. There are also archers who think they are hot stuff, and believe that there is nothing special about learning proper technique (and do not make any attempt to learn it). What is their problem? They do not trust the method!

Inexperienced archers do not know the difference between good and bad technique because they have yet to observe things in a discerning enough way. When they set about their practice in this condition, they are vulnerable to being led astray. Some of these beginners (who live in remote areas with no friends) might be lucky because they can minimize exchanges with those who give them bad advice or display poor form. But once they encounter someone with poor but flashy form, it is tempting to discard proper technique. Why would they maintain proper form, which is so boring?

If beginners happen to run into an experienced archer, they do not know any better and imitate what they see. If they do not understand the benefits of good form, how can they understand the faults of another's bad form?

Learning good form is like going on a smooth and straight highway: you do not have to worry about any weird obstacles. Working towards good form is laborious, and from the beginning you work to improve gradually. This is not a quick process. But if you happen to see a side path that promises good results with less effort, it will seem pretty seductive.

Those who get seduced by side paths will find things easy at first, and the problems that seep into their bones will not show their symptoms right away. How can you prevent beginners from learning this bad form and convince them to learn good form? In less than 3–5 years, the problems become harder to eliminate, and the bad symptoms will inevitably appear. These archers who choose this bad form will no longer be able execute the technique. Even if they want to return to proper form, they cannot. Once the problems seep into their bones, the archers cannot get rid of them instantly <problems such as the joints being misaligned, or failing to reach full draw steadily>. What a pity!

If you are going to teach technique, it is best to choose students who are analytical, disciplined, and cautious. <"Analytical" means being able to identify good and bad techniques. "Disciplined" means never forgetting the basics. "Cautious" means thinking independently and being skeptical of bad advice.> Through your discussions, you can enable them to sharpen their skills gradually, like a whetstone sharpens a knife. The students practice hard, and through helping each other they make a lot of progress. Before long they reach a high level. It is hard to imagine them failing. These kinds of students are your first choice.

As for the others, it is hard to beat students who already have some archery experience. You will want to seek them out because they already have experience with what is good versus bad technique. When you teach them technique, they are receptive to discarding their old form, rectifying their current form, and preserving their newly corrected technique. However, because they have already shot for a while, they may have some lingering bad habits and sports injuries. Although they know

邪說 目不覩匪人耳 儻一遇暗淺執拗之夫 道以可喜可奇之巧 何苦守法而不變乎

初習射之人 偶遇先輩授之法 胸無定見 信而學之 實未嘗見吾法之必善 安能信他法之必不善乎

況正法猶大路然 多坦夷平直 無新奇可喜之說 將來得益雖鉅 其初入門必以序漸升 而無速効 故一見旁門異說 道以省便之功 欹以旦夕之効 用力少而成功多 孰不欣然學之 況旁門異說 能欹動人者 其初亦有小效 但後來之害中入骨者 一時未見 安能禁識見未定之人 不盡棄其學而學乎 不三五年 病根漸深 醜態漸露 新學之捷法 既不獲效 往時之正法 又不可追 而病根之入骨者 卒未能拔〈骨節不直 引弓不滿之毛病〉 豈不深可惜哉

是故欲以法授人者 必擇明通孝謹之士〈明則能辨不爲邪說所惑 孝則不忍忘本 謹則不輕於從人〉 與之講射論德 則砥礪漸磨之 久得力於射者必深 而相資於德業者自遠 立功圖事寧有既乎 此必不可得者也 上也

其外 莫若擇射稍久之人 因而求伸者 與之言射 彼于射中利弊亦已備 嘗授之以法 必覺今是昨非 而守之不失矣 然其人學射既久 病入已深 雖知吾法之善 未必能遽改 第無中變之患耳 次也 又有愚昧之人 以先入之言爲主 而天下無復有

是者 此必不可入堯舜之道也 下也
　嗟夫 上智之士絕少 次者亦不
多見也 得其次者 而可矣 況其上
者哉

私心自是之惑 〈第九〉

　得法而篤信 固可進於道矣 然
或病生於不測 而不自知 只覺控弦
無勢 骨節不妥 審注未明 發矢多
不如意 此又何也 則以私心自是 不
思慮懷訪問 離群索居 而乏箴規之
友也

　夫至勇之人 不能自舉其身 至
明之目 不能自鑑其形 射法胸中雖
已照然 而身之形跡狀貌 手之合法
與否 己不得見也 則習法之久 偶
失簡點 勢不得不趨于弊 控弦決機
之頃 彼雖自以爲法 旁人見之則非
法也 彼雖自以爲非病 旁人視之則
病也 旁人之明 非必過於我也 旁
觀之清 不若當局之迷也

　故得法之射 必賴二三同志之
友 更相鑑戒 見己之所不見 言己
之所不知 乃可去病而守法 己亦須
虛心詢問 時爲體認 然後病根可
去 法爲我有 若少有自足之色 忠
言不聞 馴至病根一深 離法漸遠 始
雖不覺而偶犯 既焉則以爲常 終焉
則以爲故矣 痼疾一深 雖痛加更

what good technique is, it may take more time for them to successfully correct things. It is best if you had the kind of student who did not require major corrections, but being able to work with these experienced students is the next best thing.

Then there are the ignorant students. They believe in the first thing they hear [▶ no matter good or bad], and they think they are so awesome that nobody else in the world can match them. They have no hope of making any progress. They are the worst kind of student.

Oh man... The first type of student is exceedingly rare. The second type of student is not all that common either. You would be lucky to have a student of the second kind, and even luckier to find a student of the first kind.

2.9 *Practicing Alone*

If you sincerely follow proper form, you will definitely make solid progress. Yet somehow another more insidious problem emerges, but you fail to recognize it. All you feel is that you are not able to draw the bow steadily, and your joints are not solid. Your estimation is unclear, and a lot of your arrows do not go where you intend. Now what is the problem? You are practicing alone! You fail to modestly ask others for advice, you work in solitude, and you do not have knowledgeable friends to help you.

People with the best strength still cannot pick themselves up by their feet. People with the best eyesight still cannot look directly at their own face and body. You might feel your shooting technique is fine, but there could be problems with your posture or arm technique that you are unable to see. If you practice alone for too long, you could easily forget some of the fundamentals and have difficulty avoiding problems. As you draw and release you might think you have good form, but bystanders will look at you and see that you have poor form. You will think you have no faults, but bystanders will see the problems. If these bystanders are smart, they can see the whole picture. If these bystanders are observant, you can avoid getting lost on the wrong path.

If you really want to get better, you should practice with 2–3 like-minded friends and supervise each other's practice. It is like observing in yourself would you could not observe before, and giving yourself advice that you did not know before. That is how you can get rid of faults and build up your technique. When you are also modest and open-minded, you will eventually have greater awareness of your body. You will be able address the root of any faults you have, and you will truly attain good form.

On the other hand, if you are arrogant, you will not be able to listen to good advice. Problems will become more entrenched and you will gradually move further away from proper form. At first you will think things are fine and the faults only pop up occasionally. But then the faults will occur more frequently. Later they will be unavoidable. The faults become a chronic illness where the harder you try to expel them, the more futile your efforts seem. <Only people who have gone through the process of correcting deep flaws in their form understand truly how hard it is to change things.> If you practice alone, a lot of problems can emerge. That is why they say: one technical flaw can lead to a hundred problems.

Actually, the same principle applies to anything you do, not just archery. If a military strategist is not completely familiar with his strategy's weaknesses, then he will not be able to maximize his strategy's strengths. If you want to develop accurate shooting, you cannot afford to ignore any faults that can emerge. Instead, you must rid yourself of those faults! Of course it is hard to list every single kind of fault that can happen with your shooting, which is why you should only focus on the basics of good form. Developing good form is like maintaining your health. If your health is poor, many illnesses will emerge. The advice of knowledgeable friends can help you build up good form, much like medicine from a doctor. Once you take the medicine, all the illnesses can be cured and your health can be restored. If you value your health, you have to take that medicine. Likewise, if you value your archery technique, you need to practice with good friends!

Some say that my book only talks about technique and does not talk about problems, so how can friends be able to diagnose those problems? My response is that you can articulate what good technique is. But problems vary from person to person and may manifest themselves differently at different times. How can I write about them ahead of time?

I can diagnose the problems if I can observe them in person. It is very difficult for me to put a diagnosis in writing. That is why I say writing cannot capture everything that I have to say, and what I can say cannot capture everything that I mean. I want to diagnose your problems, but I am not in a proper position to do so. But if your friends are knowledgeable about proper form, you should trust them instead.

2.10 *Ignoring Wind and Weather Conditions*

Suppose you practice earnestly, you are able to rid yourself of any technical problems, and you build up good technique. You should be able to hit, right? But when the wind starts blowing, the arrows veer in all kinds of directions. What is the problem now? You ignored wind and weather conditions! Wind can be heavy or light, and it can come from any direction. Weather can be dry or wet, and it can vary with the seasons.

革 勢必無及〈痼疾受過者 方知改病之苦〉況射中之病 比法百之 故曰 一法立而百弊生

凡事皆然 不獨射也 兵家不能盡知用兵之害者 必不能盡知用兵之利 故欲盡守射中之法 安可不求射中之弊 而盡去之哉 然射中之弊 難以偏舉 只是守法而已 射之正法 猶人身之元氣 元氣不固 百病皆入矣 良朋之言 猶對病之藥石 藥石一入 百弊可消矣 百弊消而元氣固 正法可常守矣 養生者 不可廢藥石 習射者 可去良朋乎哉

或曰 先生之射學 但言其法 未嘗言病 良朋烏得而知之 曰法可言 而病則隨人而變 因時而形者也 安能預擬 若臨事而見之 當自有對病之箴 筆不能盡 故曰 書不盡言 言不盡意 非不欲言也 不能耳 惟能得之言外者 真良朋也

不辨風氣之惑 〈第十〉

虛心詢問 百弊消而法備 是可命中矣 乃一遇風塵四起 矢不免有左右大小之偏 此又何也 則不辨風氣之故也 夫風有大小 又有四方之殊 氣有燥濕 亦有四時之別

夫射而止於數十步之內 弓矢勁
銳 風氣不能奪 即不辨可也 若四
十步之外 射漸遠則矢力漸弱 大小
左右皆爲風氣所使 此而不辨 發矢
皆偏矣

大抵春氣多濕 夏氣多炎 秋氣
多燥 冬氣多冽 氣炎濕則風和 氣
燥冽則風勁 此其大概也 然四時之
中 又有寒暑不常 則就一時之中 亦
有燥濕炎冽之氣 風亦隨之以變
矣 燥冽之風勁 矢遇之而多偏 炎
濕之風和 矢遇之而少偏 且風勁則
弓亦勁 發矢常遠 風和則弓亦弱 發
矢常近 故善射者 將欲發矢 必先
辨風氣 東風則發矢宜頂的之左 西
風則發矢宜頂的之右 對面風則發
矢宜頂的之首 背後風則發矢宜頂
的之足 而頂之多寡 一因弓力之強
弱不齊 與風氣燥濕炎冽大小之不
同 而爲之參酌 變而通之 存于其
人 不可執一 故曰 運用之妙 存乎
一心

識見未充之惑 〈第十一〉

風氣既辨 發矢左右大小宜如意
矣 然或當得失死傷之際 便爾變
色 不能自恃 此又何也 則識之未
充也

If you are shooting within 40 paces (about 70 yards or 64 meters), the bow will shoot the arrow very sharply and wind/weather will have no effect (so you do not have to worry about those factors here). But if you are shooting more than 40 paces, the momentum of the arrow will be more out of your control the further out you shoot. Wind and weather can cause the arrow to veer every which way. If you do not identify these factors, your arrows will go all over the place.

[▶ Gao Ying is accustomed to shooting heavy horn bows with relatively light arrows. Please see our discussion in Book 2, Chapter 2.1.]

Usually spring is more humid, summer is more hot, autumn is more dry, and winter is more cold. The wind is more peaceful when the weather is hot or humid, but is more fierce when the weather is cold or dry. Of course, this is just a rough summary. Within each of the four seasons, you will have variations in climate such that within a short period of time, you could experience dry, humid, hot, and cold weather. The winds will change accordingly. The strong winds of cold/dry weather will cause an arrow to veer strongly, whereas the more peaceful winds of hot/humid weather will cause the arrow to veer less strongly. As it so happens, during the seasons when the wind is strong, the cold and dry climate will increase the poundage of your horn bow, and you will be able to shoot farther. During the seasons when the wind is weak, the hot and humid climate will decrease the poundage of your horn bow, and you will not be able to shoot as far. For these reasons, experienced archers pay attention to the wind and weather before they shoot.

Suppose you are facing south towards the target. If the wind is coming from the east, then you should aim to the left of the target. If the wind is coming from the west, then you should aim to the right of the target. If you encounter a head wind, then aim at the top of the target. If you encounter a tail wind, then aim at the bottom of the target. The amount you have to adjust your aim will depend on the strength of your bow, as well as the strength of the wind.

Considering all these factors, there will not be a single way to deal with the situation. You will have to rely on your experience.

2.11 Failing to See the Big Picture

Now that you have accounted for wind and weather, you have full control of whether your arrow veers left, right, up, or down. But when a critical, life-or-death moment arrives, you panic and cannot shoot reliably. Now what is the problem? You are failing to see the big picture!

Whether you are a candidate on the examination grounds (or a soldier fighting on the battlefield), if you fail to see the big picture then you become too self-conscious about your reputation on the exam grounds (or you become too cowardly to die for the emperor on the battlefield). But if the thought of messing up (or dying) fills your heart and mind with incredible anxiety, how can you expect to concentrate and shoot with good form? When Wang Tanzhi held his writing tablet upside-down while meeting Huan Wen, or when Yin Hao deliberated too much and sent a blank letter to Huan Wen, it was all because they were too nervous.

夫得失之地 莫如應試 死傷之
地 莫如臨敵 人惟識見未充 當功
名之場 便營得失 臨戰鬥之際 便
憂死生 得失死生之念 薰灼于心 不
覺神驚氣奪 何暇持弓審固乎 王坦
之倒執笏板 殷淵源竟達空函 皆此
念也

Wang Tanzhi (王坦之) and Yin Hao (殷浩) were officials in the Eastern Jin Dynasty (317–420 CE). There are famous anecdotes about how each of them reacted in fear to Huan Wen (桓溫), a powerful Eastern Jin general.

People who see the big picture know that fame and fortune are fleeting. When Emperor Yao passed the throne on to Yu Shun [▶ both rulers from the legendary Three Sovereigns and Five Emperors period], they shared a cordial drink of wine. Tang (湯) founded the Shang Dynasty by overthrowing the Xia Dynasty; later on Wu (武) founded the Zhou Dynasty by overthrowing the Shang Dynasty. One major figure gets exchanged for another, just like chess pieces. The trifles of regular people like us are insignificant in comparison. Moreover, a famous high-ranking official could be miserable, whereas a regular person could live a happy life. People worry about getting a high-ranking job in the government, but end up taking orders and becoming somebody's lackey. How is this better than having the freedom to enjoy the world as a normal person? When you look at things from this detached perspective, do you have any reason to be nervous about taking an exam?

Likewise, when you go into battle you do not want to be anxious. The ancients would make careful plans before going to war. Although the actual battle is won on the battlefield, the soldiers know ahead of time that they are certain to win. Hence the expression: "you achieve the victory before you go to war." Under these circumstances, why is there any reason to be anxious? If you encounter a formidable enemy, you fight with no fear. Real men devote their bodies to fighting for the nation. If they should die in battle, they have made a noble sacrifice serving their country. What else do they have to worry about?

Wise men know the conditions in the sky, on the ground, and with the people. When they advance, they devote themselves entirely to the cause and are ready to sacrifice themselves for their country. When they retreat, they do so because it is the prudent thing to do. If they go forward and die, they know their sacrifice is not in vain.

若識見遠到之人 謂功名富貴過
眼浮雲 唐虞揖讓 祈同杯酒 湯武
征誅 猶棋一局 況藐小功名 得之
未必非禍 失之奚必非福 與其位極
人臣而戚戚 何如一丘一壑而肆志
哉 見識及此 又何得失介意乎 至
于臨敵遇變 益不足慮 古人謀定而
戰 決機雖在臨事 勝權握于事先 故
曰 勝兵先勝而後求戰 又何色變
乎 若使果遇大敵 蹈踏不免之禍 丈
夫既以身許國 馬革裹屍 壯志已
畢 又何足患

況大智之人 必能上知天 下知
地 中知人事 事機可為則出身以殉
國 時不可為則明哲以自全 彼其出
身以赴難者 恕其才之足以報稱者
也 決機應變 胸中自有定衡 當其
持弓 自能神閒意定 斟酌而出 動
中機宜者也 又何倉徨失措乎

Although the circumstances around you will change, your heart should always be solid. Then when you hold the bow your spirit will be at ease and your focus will be sharp. You can deliberate carefully before moving to action, and you will execute your movements well. How can you expect to falter under these circumstances?

When Confucius taught archery in Juexiang [▶ part of modern-day Shandong], a large crowd of people would come to watch him. Confucius would say archery is for developing discipline and studiousness. Through archery, people could develop a respect for societal order and also develop skills to bolster military strength. Because Confucius said that archery could help societal order and military strength, the Way of Archery is broad and significant. Only people with wisdom can understand the deep meaning of archery. People who do not grasp this deeper meaning will not be able to reach a high level of shooting skill.

For excellent archers, the possibility of making a mistake or losing their life does not shake them. If you want to reach a high level of archery, you must be disciplined and studious. Nowadays there are people who hold archery in disdain, saying that it is a pointless pursuit. Do not waste your time talking with these people about understanding discipline and studiousness.

2.12 Lack of Inner Peace and Self Discipline

Now suppose that you are able to shoot very accurately in practice, but that once you reach the competition grounds you become stiff and anxious in the public eye. Your shooting suffers as a result. What is the problem now? It is because you have not achieved inner peace.

The key to being a good archer is your understanding. All the movement and timing of archery is a reflection of your spirit, and we use them to judge your courage and temperament. Whether you prosper and whether you can stay alive is a matter of courage. Your career path and prestige are a matter of fate. Likewise, we can observe your cleverness, wisdom, and generosity in your shooting appearance.

People who pull and release too hastily are impatient. People who hold their bows steadily are very calm. People who think about the release before reaching full draw like to leave tasks half done, and they lack perseverance. People who reach full draw and take their time to observe the target have thoughtful temperaments and are very careful about what they do. People who have a crisp release are keen and decisive. The archers who are relaxed have a certain elegance about them. As for the archers who hesitate on their release and are unable to hit the target for several shots: these people are suspicious of others. People whose arrows always seem to be veering in a particular direction (whether it is left,

昔孔子射於矍相之圃 觀者如
堵 語以修身好學之道 且曰 用以
臨民則順治 用以戰陣則無敵

夫射一技也 孔子以臨民戰勝之
略在 是則射之道廣矣 大矣 射之
巧 信非大識之人不能持矣 彼未能
充其識而習射者 必其射之未精者
也 能精於射者 死生利害不能動
也 然欲精于射者 盍于識充之哉 世
有鄙其射爲不足學者 未足與語
識也

涵養未純之惑 〈第十二〉

又有平居習射偏能中的 或當分
曹角射時 榮辱共覩 未免兢持 失
其故步 此又何也 則養之未純也

夫射之一技 根於靈性 其舉止
動盪 張弛發縱之機緘 實一身精神
心術之所著也 膽勇氣魄之所沛
也 貧富壽殀 於此乎膽 事業功
名 於此乎卜 聰明智慧 器識度
量 於此乎顯 故引弓迅者 心必
躁 持弓固者 慮必沈 未彀而先思
發者 殀之徵也 已彀而熟思凝視
者 縝密之士也 發矢剛毅者 果銳
而明敏 雍容和平者 寬柔而雅素 欲
發不發 比發而不中節者 狐疑不斷
者也 忽左忽右 大小無常者 蒙昧
而乖張者也 變性百出 莫知其端

70

right, up, or down) are either ignorant or stubborn. People who make tons of errors but do not stop to consider why have immature and flaky personalities. People who hesitate or are indecisive will achieve nothing in life. People who start by pulling the bow properly but release awkwardly have uptight personalities. People who have no fear and release recklessly after reaching full draw are immature and love to show off. People who reach full draw hastily yet can hit the target are too intense. People who release before they reach full draw yet hit the target out of sheer luck cannot be consistent: the more they practice, the worse they will become. Then there are those who seem to draw stably but cannot hold full draw steadily: although they might shoot alright, they are boring people overall. Then there are people with no technique who shoot sloppily and think they are hot stuff: these people are shallow and have not accomplished anything in their life. Although everyone's personality is different, you can still get a general sense of their personalities by looking at their shooting. Hence the old expression: "Through archery you can observe a person's virtue."

When our ancestors talked about archery, they would say its appearance is like a ritual and its rhythm is like music. Only people with virtue can be proficient in ritual and music. Thus, archery itself is also closely linked with developing virtue. Archers who want to be proficient shooters must develop their virtue.

A key to developing virtue is developing generosity. Generous people are not self-conscious: whether they win or lose, their temperament is pretty steady. Of course they are happy if they win, but even if they lose they are still pleased. When Su Dongpo (蘇東坡) would play games of chess with guests, why would he sacrifice his dignity by worrying too much about the outcome? [▶ Su Dongpo was a famous Song Dynasty official/scholar/gastronome, after whom the famous dish Dongpo Pork was named.]

Another key to developing virtue is developing courage. Whether a person is decisive is a function of his courage. People without courage have a shaky spirit: the moment a situation starts to look bad, they immediately get discouraged. Courageous people are tough and resilient: they are not phased even if they encounter a hundred obstacles in their path, and they do not fear the most dangerous situations. Just like when Bohun Maoren talked about shooting with an empty mind: an empty mind does not become anxious when facing formidable situations. [▶ Bohun Maoren was a famous Daoist monk from the Warring States Period (475–221 BCE).]

The final key to developing virtue is developing qi (氣). Qi is a difficult thing to balance. Too much qi leads to becoming arrogant, overbearing and neglectful. Your shots will sail high and have no direction. Too little qi leads to becoming cowardly and timid. Your shots will fall short and fly askew. People have who have the right amount of qi are at peace with themselves and their emotions do not get ruffled easily. This is just like the story about the fighting chicken with a wooden appearance.

者 浮滑之徒 傴塞滯澁 宜脫不脫
者 困阨之士 始引則是 發矢忽乖
張者 老而貧 蕩蕩無忌 疾滿而速
出者 少而顯 彀弓急促 而發輒中
節者 飽腹而無餘 未彀急發 巧中
而不繼者 始饒而終億 又有彀弓似
穩而不固 矢發順利而無味者 庸常
貧薄無疑 又有滿手皆病 自以爲
妙 而視天下無一是法者 暗淺鄙
陋 沒齒無成可知 夫人品之不齊 雖
不盡然 而其大略已自可見 此射所
以爲觀德之具也

古人論射 以其容貌比於禮 節
奏比於樂 禮也 樂也 非有德者 不
能爲也 而射與之同條共貫 故欲精
於射者 必務養其德也 欲養其德 惟
在於度 度量弘而人己之形忘 勝負
之心泯 分曹角射 勝固欣然 敗亦
可喜 猶東坡之弈也 又何過爲競持
而失其度乎 又在養其膽 膽者勇之
決也 膽不足則神寒 居閑旦餒 當
局必靡 膽旺之人 果而銳 健而能
久 百折不能移 奇險不能慴 是伯
昏氏之射也 曾何利害之足以動
心 又在養其氣 氣者難持之物也 盈
則驕 餒則怯 驕者神奮而疎 怯者
神短而懼 疎者發矢多大而無當 懼
者多小而偏斜 此善養氣者 貴和平
而不撓也 所謂木雞之養者此也

夫度量之弘也 膽勇之壯也 氣
局之和平也 皆射之所托 以行其巧
妙者也 舍此三者而徒言法者 法豈
爲其所用哉 彼射而不知法者 固不
足道 知法而不托根於三者 法固不
靈也 此射之大惑也 不可不辨也

辨惑 總結

夫射之惑 非止一端 而僅舉其
十二條者 此皆相承相倚 射中必趨
之弊 惑之大者也 有一於此 必且
以誤成誤 弊端互起而射法紊 猶植
嘉穀者 惡草不除 勢必蔓延而嘉
穀廢 故善植嘉穀者 必先盡去害苗
之草 而嘉穀自茂 工於射者 必先
盡去迷心之惑 而射法始純 況射之
巧 至微而至精 發於心而應於手 胸
中少有所惑 則心無主而神搖 神搖
則氣餒而機沮 機神搖沮 發矢皆
偏 雖有巧法 無所復施 此惑之不
可不辨 而辨之不可不早也 辨之早
而去之盡 滿腔之中 無之非道 日
習巧妙 勿助勿忘 手舞足蹈 皆中
繩墨而機巧自生矣 故曰樹德莫如
滋 去害莫如盡 知此者可與進道 可
與語射矣

Generosity, courage, and calmness: these are the hallmarks of a good archer. If you practice proper form but lack these personality traits, then you will not be able to make use of your form. (We will not even talk about people who ignore proper form in the first place.) Although your technique is solid, you will not be able to reach a higher level of archery. This is a very major problem! You cannot afford to ignore it!

2.13 Conclusion

When it comes to common problems in archery, it does not stop with these discussions. However, these twelve most commonly-encountered problems are interrelated. Once you develop one of these problems, the others are likely to spring up because they are linked. Like when growing crops: if you do not get rid of the weeds, they will spread like mad and render the field useless. That is why successful farmers get rid of all of the weeds: only then will the field be suitable for growing crops. When you practice archery, you must first rid yourself of technical faults: only then will your technique begin to be solid. Especially with archery, the details are very fine-grain. The release starts with your heart and manifests itself in the hands. If you have even a tiny bit of confusion in your heart and mind, you will lose your stability and rhythm. Like this, your arrows will all fly askew. Although you have the technique in your mind, you cannot apply it. Thus, you must identify these technical faults, and it is never too early to do so. If you identify faults early and completely eliminate them, then your mind and body will definitely be on the right path. As you strive to improve in your daily practice, you have to follow the correct form by eliminating these faults, eventually making the form second nature. That is why they say "nourish your virtue entirely, and eliminate your vices completely." People who know this are on the right Way and can truly talk about archery.

3.0 *Introduction*

If you want to be a good craftsman, you must first sharpen your tools. If your tools are not up to the task, then you cannot effectively apply your skills. If you cannot effectively apply your skills, then you will surely make mistakes. Especially in archery, there are many tricks and nuances, and there are many possible ways to make mistakes. If your equipment does not suit you, then you might have the skill to hit an eagle in the sky, but your equipment will prevent you from reaching that potential. I do not want to talk about the people who do not know how to fix common technical faults in their practice. However, even if you are able fix those faults (and rid yourself of every little technical error), shooting with the wrong equipment will create discord between you and the bow. The hand is fighting with the bow and the bow is fighting with the arrow. Before you even reach full draw, you are guaranteed to have a bad result. If the bow's brace height does not match the guidelines, and if the height and thickness of your thumb ring is unsuitable, then how can you hope for the arrow to reach the target and hit? This is not a problem with technique or even a problem with the equipment itself: the problem is that you are choosing the equipment incorrectly. This chapter is on Choosing Equipment, and it is a continuation of the previous chapter on Common Mistakes.

3.1 *Choosing the Strength of the Bow*

Select the arrow based on the strength of the bow, and select the bow based on the strength of the archer. This is common sense. Over-ambitious people like to choose heavy bows without considering whether the draw weight of the bow is suitable. Timid people like to use light bows and do not care whether the arrow can reach far. Both of these mindsets are wrong!

To choose the draw weight of a bow, you need to first measure your own strength. However, there are different kinds of strength: arm strength, hip strength, and leg strength. Each has their purpose. Leg strength lets you hike long distances. Hip strength lets you carry heavy things. Neither of these will help with archery. If you have good arm strength, then you can draw a heavy bow, which for our purposes is about 100 jin (130 pounds). If you can dry-pull a 100 jin (130 pound) bow to full draw, then you should be shooting a 50 jin (65 pound) bow. [▶ Dry-pulling means drawing the bow without nocking an arrow. Remember, do not let go and dry loose.] In general, the

武經射學入門正宗 （卷下） 擇物門

擇物門 序

夫工欲善其事 必先利其器 器械不利 良工無所施其巧 寧猶無所施其巧 抑亦不能不生其弊矣 況射者眾巧之門 百弊之府也 使弓矢不調 縱有落鵰貫蝨之技 豈施其巧乎 彼習射而不知辨惑者 固不足道 即使惑辨矣 百病皆消矣 設以不調之弓矢畀之 則弓手不習 強弱不和 手之性既與弓抗 弓之性又與矢仇 當控弦彀弓時 已齟齬而不相合 況弦之長短大小恣其制 指機之高下厚薄失其宜 又安望矢道同的 應弦命中乎 此非射之過也 亦非弓矢機弦之過也 不擇之過也 此擇物之章 所以繼辨惑而作也

弓力強弱宜擇 〈第一〉

因弓制矢 量力調弓 此不刊之典 今好勝之人 喜用勁弓 而不顧力之不稱 退怯之人 過用弱弓 而不顧矢之不能及遠 皆非也
夫弓之強弱 必須量我力之大小 然力有不同 有臂力 有腰力 有足力 各有所用 足力能致遠 腰力能負重 與射無益也 惟臂力多者 能引勁弓 大率以百斤為準 空引弓能彀百斤者 射時只用五十斤 大約用力之十分之五 不可過竭其力 寧過於軟 過勁則非矣 蓋用弓過勁 則筋力為弓所束縛 操縱緩急不得如

意 安能盡射法之巧 此弓力之強弱
所當擇也 稱弓法 以弓置地上 以
足踏定弓弝于地 以稱鉤弦稱起 將
箭鏃頂在弓弝上 稱起弦至箭根
齊 方可言彀 而知弓之重輕 用矢
輕重法 在後第八章

弓套長短宜擇 〈第二〉

弓之長短不齊 則力量亦因之而
異 長弓之力量長 故能彀長箭 短
弓之力量短 只能彀短箭 不可紊
亂 如使長弓而用短箭 箭已彀而弓
力量未彀 如此而遽發矢 則不能及
遠 且弦口鬆 箭發亦不準 短弓而
用長箭 則箭未彀 弓之力量先彀 若
復過引 不惟弓之筋角易斷 且肩臂
骨節爲弓所局 不得展舒其巧 發矢
烏能如意 是以人長則臂長 而弓矢
之長亦稱之 人短則臂短 而弓矢之
短亦稱之 此爲定論

或曰 有短人喜用長弓 長人喜
用短弓 奈何 曰短人臂短 而用長
弓者 必須勁弓 勁則弦口急 雖未
能彀弓之力量 只以臂骨盡處爲
彀 發矢亦準 故短人欲用長弓者 勁
則無妨矣 若長人而用短弓 弓力量
已彀 強欲過引 須用軟弓 然弓軟
發矢不遠 何取於短 但人長而無
力 若用長弓而勁 則不能彀 用長
弓而軟 恐弦口鬆 發矢不遠 故不
得不用小套弓耳

bow you shoot with should weigh 50% of your dry-pull strength. You should not exhaust your strength by choosing a bow that is heavier than this guideline. It is okay to err on the lighter side. Again, you should not use a bow that is too heavy. If you do, then your muscle strength will be at the mercy of the bow, you will lose control of your timing, and you will not be able to properly develop your technique.

This is how you should choose the strength of your bow. To measure the strength of the bow itself, first place the bow on the ground. Secure your feet on the handle while letting the feet face towards the ground. Then place the arrow on the handle with the arrowhead at the handle, and pull the string until it reaches the other end of the arrow [▶ do not nock the arrow on the string]. At that point the bow is at full draw, and you will be able to measure its draw weight. The method for selecting the weight of the arrow comes later in Book 1, Chapter 3.8.

3.2 *Choosing the Size of the Bow*

Bows come in different lengths, which in turn affect their draw strengths. Long bows reach their full strength at a long draw length, so they are suitable for long arrows. Short bows reach their full strength at a short draw length, so they are suitable for short arrows. Do not mix these up. If you use a long bow to shoot short arrows, then full draw for the arrow is still not full draw for the bow. In this situation, the arrow will not travel far when you release. Moreover, the brace tension will be soft, so you will not be able to release the arrows consistently. If you use a short bow with a long arrow, then before you reach full draw with your arrow, the bow is already at its maximum draw length. If you continue to pull, you risk breaking the bow. Moreover, your arms, shoulders, and joints will be cramped by the bow, so you will not be able to extend yourself. You will not be able to control where your arrows go. Tall people have long arms, so the bow and arrows must be long to match. Short people have short arms, so the bow and arrows should be short to match. These guidelines are firm.

Some people will point out that there are short people who like to use long bows, as well as tall people who like to use short bows. What do you do in each case? Because short people have short arms, the bow must be strong if they want to use a long bow. A long bow that is strong will have a higher brace tension. Although the short archer will not be able to pull the bow to its max draw length, at least his arms and joints will be able to reach full draw, which in turn will let him release the arrow cleanly. Thus, there is no harm in a short person using a long bow if the bow is strong.

Now if a tall person wants to use a short bow, he will already reach the bow's max draw length even though he would prefer to draw further. In that case he has to use a short but light bow, but then such a bow will not shoot far. There is no reason for a tall person to choose a short bow. However, if a tall person does not have strength and he chooses a long bow that is strong, he will not be able to reach full draw. If he chooses a long bow that is light, then the brace tension will be soft and he will not be able to shoot the arrow far. In this case, a long, strong bow with a lower brace height (小套弓) is the better choice.

The acceptable alternative is to choose a "small loop" bow (小圈套弓, which is a bow with a lower brace height). The string would be about 2–3 fen (0.25–0.38 in) to a half cun (0.63 in) longer than the original string. This will make the bow usable. When you choose a low brace height bow, then if it is too heavy you will not be able to reach full draw, and if it is too light you will not be able to shoot far. Neither of these extremes is a good idea.

3.3 *Choosing Horn Bow Materials*

Long ago, the Tang Dynasty's Taizong emperor (Li Shimin) took dozens of his best bows to show to a bowyer. But the bowyer said the bows were no good! The wooden cores were not straight because the grains were running in a diagonal direction. This would cause the arrows to fly off course. You can select great materials to make a bow, but if the construction is incorrect, then you cannot call it a good bow. The materials that go into making a bow are a composite of sinew, horn, bamboo, and wood. You can put the four materials together, but if any one of them has problems then it makes the whole bow unsuitable. You should not choose a bow in this condition! When people these days choose bows, they pay attention to whether the outside of the bow is shiny and pretty. They do not realize the most critical element of the bow is the core, followed by the tips, then the horn, the sinew, and lastly the glue.

The core of the bow must use old and dry bamboo. You can use local bamboo or bamboo from within your province. You should not use fresh bamboo. Why? When old bamboo has dried for a while, it is strong and is not crooked. When you use it to make a core, it maintains elasticity [▶ and does not take a permanent set]. New bamboo is soft, and if you use it to construct a core it will not make a crisp sound [▶ i.e., it will have poor elasticity]. Bows made in Zhenjiang (鎮江) [▶ a city that is part of modern-day Jiangsu province] make a crisp sound when they are at brace [▶ you can pluck the string lightly and listen to the sound]. And it is not just because of their excellent craftsmanship. The bamboo that goes into Zhenjiang bow cores comes from Jiangxi (江西), where it is dried for two years before being brought to Zhenjiang by merchant boat. If you are not able to obtain

酌權宜之術　可取小圈套弓式　略
故長二三分或半寸許　方可適用　若
竟用小套弓　勁則難彀　軟則發矢無
威　不能及遠　斷不可也

弓之材料宜擇〈第三〉

昔唐太宗取良弓數十　示弓工　工
曰非良弓也　木心不正　脈理皆斜　發
矢多偏　夫以良材爲弓　而心不正　猶
不得爲良弓　況弓之材料　筋角竹木
連合四者而後成　有一不善　必不相
調　可不擇乎　今人擇弓　只取外面
色澤光美　而不知弓之大病在胎　弓
稍次之　角次之　筋膠又次之　弓胎
竹須乾透者　可用本地竹　行中竹　新
嫩者　不可用　何也　竹乾久者　性堅
剛不屈　作弓胎　多有還性　新嫩
竹　性柔　作弓胎則弓聲不清　鎮江
弓　弦口聲清者　非獨做法佳　以鎮
江一路弓胎竹　皆江西糧船帶來隔
年乾透之物　絕無近地竹　行中竹之
故也　若江西竹不可得　不得已而用
竹　行中竹者　須去頭段三尺許　以
其節多　故不用　只用中間五六段　其
餘竹稍　不可用　又須陰乾五六個月
後　方能剛性不屈　燒去竹油　多去
黃　而少去青　胎欲極薄如錢　取兩
頭竹節相對　則上下均調　此擇胎
法也

弓稍須用杜桑　勿用沙桑　以杜
桑木紋細而堅　沙桑木紋粗而鬆故
也　兩稍俱要一色相配　木心與木心
相配　皮與皮相配　則性和同而發矢
平直矣　弓稍體式須細小　不必粗
大　小則脆而捷　粗則壅而緩　弓腦
須堅勁穩實　不取薄而狹　薄則發矢
無力　狹則活而易滾　但不可太厚而
過闊耳　又不可太鉤〈鉤　彎曲也
〉而致滾　署圓而不必太直　方爲定
準　若大稍弓下插袋者　專取穩實爲
主　稍不妨于大　腦不妨于厚　但不
宜太過　大約稍與腦　或軟或勁　俱
要與弓弰心相配　此擇稍腦法也

　　角面須出廣中者佳　然不可必
得　只取老而黑　勿取嫩而黑也　綜
紋者爲老　細紋者爲嫩　白色而老者
次之　黑色而老者爲上　凡弓之最劣
者　兩頭角面一老一嫩　始雖上下相
勻　後必相欹　打滾歪斜之患生矣　角
面又不取太長　太長則腦活　活則發
矢無勢且不準　而腦上角面又易起
綻　今人見角面長大　便以爲材料富
而愛之　誤矣　此擇角面法也

　　筋不必過多　多則易滾　且射時
烘弓或火力不透　筋亦易鬆　若筋過
少　弓力又易疲　矢發不遠　故筋角
必相對配者佳　大約弓六十斤者　筋
用二兩五錢　軟弓三四十斤者　筋用
二兩　筋骨細而白者爲可　粗而紅者
爲下〈細白粗紅俱指絲筋時言〉鋪
筋法　須刷得筋平安紋直者佳　膠須
用麻布絞得細膩白淨為美　黃魚膠
可用　米魚膠不可用　薄而白者爲黃
魚膠　粗而白者為米魚膠　不粘〈薄
白粗白　俱指未煮時言之　非既煮時
有薄白粗白之分〉此擇筋膠法也

Jiangxi bamboo, then bamboo from within your province will do. But in this case, you should cut off about the top 3 chi (38 in, 96 cm) of the bamboo: there are too many segments up there, so you do not want to use that portion. You only want to use the middle 5–6 segments and discard the remainder. Then you should dry the piece in the shade for 5–6 months, after which it will become strong and will not be crooked. Then, you should heat treat the bamboo to evaporate the oils. The more you heat treat, the more yellow the bamboo comes. The less you heat treat, the more green it remains. You want the core lamination to be as thin as a coin. Select two laminations (one for each bow limb) and join them at the handle, making sure they are symmetric and properly aligned. That will make the top and bottom limbs balanced. This is how you choose the core!

For the bow tips, you should use Du (杜) mulberry. Do not use Sha (沙) mulberry. The grain on Du mulberry is very fine and the wood is very firm, whereas the grain on Sha mulberry is very coarse and the wood is more brittle. The construction of the top and bottom tips have to match perfectly in every respect. The grain of the two tips should match, from the heartwood through to the sapwood. When the tips are constructed to match each other perfectly, then the arrow will fly straight!

The shape of the tips should be thin and small. They should not be bulky. If they are small, they will make the arrow fly fast and sharp. If they are bulky, they will make the arrow fly sluggishly. The "brain" of the bow [▶ the joint between the working limb and the tip of the bow, also called *kasan* in Turkish] has to be absolutely tough and stable. Do not make it too thin or narrow. If the brain is too thin, the arrow will fly without impetus. If the brain is too narrow, the bow is unstable and liable to twist. Of course you cannot make the brain too thick or too wide. Moreover, you should not make the brain hook forward sharply (or else the bow limbs will have a tendency to twist). The brain should be a gentle curve; it should not be too straight. This is the proper shape. If you are selecting a Dashao (big-tip) bow, you should focus more on choosing a stable bow. In this case, it is okay for the tip to be longer and the brain to be thicker, but these properties should not be too exaggerated. Regardless whether the tips and brains belong to a light or heavy bow, they have to match bow handle [▶ aligning with the bow handle in a straight line]. That is how you select the tips and brains of the bow!

As for the horn that goes on the belly of the bow, the best horn is from Guangzhong (廣中) [▶ an area in Guangdong province]. If you are not able to obtain that, then select black horn from an old animal. Do not select black horn from a young animal. Old horn will have thick grain lines, whereas young horn will have thin grain lines. White horn from an old animal is okay, but black horn from an old animal is the best choice. The worst bows will have two kinds of horn:

old horn on one limb and young horn on the other limb. Although the bow will begin with the top and bottom limbs in balance, eventually the limbs will lose their balance and all sorts of twisting and crookedness will emerge. The horn layer should not be too long or else the brain of the limb will become unstable, which in turn causes the arrow to fly wobbly. Moreover, the horn risks cracking [▶ likely due to linear cracking, or perhaps the horn layer delaminating from the brain]. Today, people see a bow with an overly-long horn section and think the materials are great, and they fall in love with the bow. What a mistake. Anyway, I have explained how to properly select the horn of the bow.

There should not be too much sinew or else the bow is liable to twist. Moreover, when you warm up the bow limbs over a fire prior to shooting, the heat will have no effect, and the sinew layer will be too soggy and become loose. But if there is too little sinew, the bow will develop a set [▶ "set" means the limbs will become more deflexed over time as they lose their elasticity], and it will not be able to shoot arrows as far as before. That is why it is best to have the right proportion of sinew. Roughly speaking, a 60 jin (78 pound) bow should have a layer using about 2 liang and 5 qian worth of sinew. [▶ 1 jin = 16 liang, and 1 liang = 10 qian. So 2 liang and 5 qian is 2.5 × (1.3 pounds / 16 liang) = 92 grams of sinew.] Light bows weighing 30–40 jin (39–52 pounds) should have 2 liang (74 grams) of sinew. It is good if the lines of sinew are fine and white. If the sinew lines are thick and red, that is bad. <Whether the sinew is fine/white or thick/red is a matter of how finely the sinew is separated during processing.> As for how to lay the sinew onto the bow, ideally you should use a comb to brush the sinew so that the layer has a uniform thickness and the lines are straight and parallel with the bow limb. Use a hemp cloth to strain the glue so that it has a fine and clear consistency before using. Glue from the Yellow Croaker is good. Do not use glue from the Miiuy Croaker. If the glue is thin and white, it is Yellow Croaker glue. If the glue is thick and white, it is Miiuy Croaker glue, whose adhesion properties are inferior. <When I refer to thin/white and thick/white, I am referring to the color before the glue is cooked. I am not referring to the thin/white and thick/white consistencies you see after the glue is cooked.> This is how you select the sinew and glue for the bow.

Xiaoshaogong (小稍弓) Structural Diagram

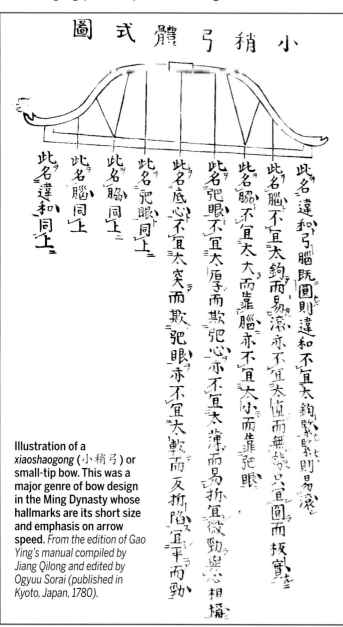

Illustration of a *xiaoshaogong* (小稍弓) or small-tip bow. This was a major genre of bow design in the Ming Dynasty whose hallmarks are its short size and emphasis on arrow speed. *From the edition of Gao Ying's manual compiled by Jiang Qilong and edited by Ogyuu Sorai (published in Kyoto, Japan, 1780).*

此名違和　弓腦既圓則違和不宜
太鉤緊　緊則易滾
　　此名腦　不宜太鉤　而易滾　亦不
宜太直而無勢　只宜圓而板實
　　此名脇　不宜太大而靠腦　亦不
宜太小而靠弛眼
　　此名弛眼　不宜太厚而欺弛心　亦
不宜太薄而易折　宜微勁　與心相稱
　　此名底心　不宜太突　而欺弛
眼　亦不宜太軟而反折陷　宜平而勁
　　此名弛眼　同上
　　此名脇　同上
　　此名腦　同上
　　此名違和　同上

This is called the *weihe* (違和). The brain of the bow is already round, so the *weihe* does not have to hook too tightly. If it is too hooked, it can twist easily.

This is the brain or *nao* (腦). It should not be too hooked or it is liable to twist, and it should not be too straight or else it will lack energy. Making it round will make it strong enough.

This is the working limb or *xie* (脇). It should not be too big or else the bending will occur too close to the brain. It should not be too small or else the bending will occur too close to the handle eye.

This is the handle eye or *bayan* (弛眼). It should not be too thick or else it will overpower the handle base. But it should not be too thin or else it will fold easily. It should be just thick enough to match with the handle base.

This is the handle base or *dixin* (底心). It should not be too bulging or else it will overpower the handle eye. But it should not be too thin or it will fold. It should just be straight and tight.

This is the handle eye, same as above.

This is the working limb, same as above.

This is the brain, same as above.

This is the *weihe*, same as above.

Dashaogong (大稍弓) Structural Diagram

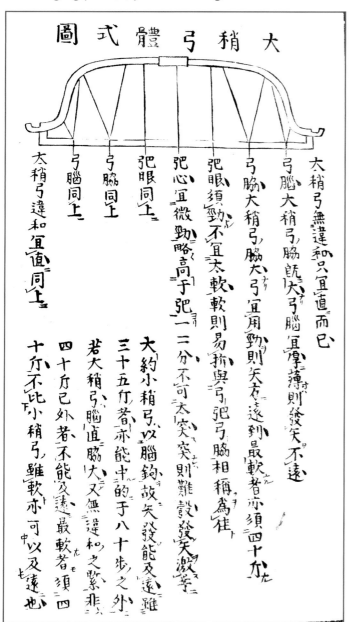

圖式體弓稍大

太稍弓無違和只宜直而已
弓腦大稍弓脇既大弓腦宜厚薄
則發矢不遠
弓脇大稍弓脇大弓宜用勁則
矢方遠到最軟者亦須四十斤
弛眼須勁不宜太軟軟則易折與
弓弛弓脇相稱為佳
弛心宜微勁略高于弛一二分不
可太突突則難彀發矢激手
弛眼同上
弓脇同上
弓腦同上
大稍弓違和宜直同上

Illustration of a *dashaogong* (大稍弓) or big-tip bow. This was another major genre of Ming Dynasty bow design which is characterized by a longer-length bow with larger tips and an emphasis on stability.
From the edition of Gao Ying's manual compiled by Jiang Qilong and edited by Ogyuu Sorai (published in Kyoto, Japan, 1780).

Big-tip bows or *dashaogong* (大稍弓) do not have *weihe*. The tips only have to be straight.

Brain of the bow or *gongnao* (弓腦). In a big-tip bow, the working limb is already big, so the brain has to be thick. If the brain is thin, the arrow will not travel far.

Working limb or *gongxie* (弓脇). The working limb is big on a big-tip bow. The bow has to be strong, only then will the arrow fly far. The lightest bow of this genre must be at least 40 jin (52 pounds).

The handle eye or *bayan* (弛眼) must be strong. It cannot be too soft or else it will fold easily. Matching it with the handle and the working limb is best.

Handle base or *baxin* (弛心). The handle base should be relatively strong. It should be thicker than the rest of the handle by about 1–2 fen (0.13–0.26 in, 3.2–6.4 mm). But it should not be too bulging, or else it will be hard to reach full draw and it will cause strong vibration in the hand after release.

Handle eye, same as above.

Working limb, same as above.

Big-tip bow *weihe* must be straight, same as above.

大約小稍弓以腦鉤 故矢發能及
遠 雖三十五斤者 亦能中的于八十
步之外 若大稍弓腦直脅大 又無達
和之緊 非四十斤以外者 不能及
遠 最軟者須四十斤 不比小稍弓 雖
軟亦可以及遠也

挑盤體式宜擇〈第四〉

弓材料雖擇 而挑盤不勻 亦不
適於用 然挑盤之法 妙在一心 良
工祕而不傳 雖忌心使然 亦不學無
文 未能筆之書也 能學而善書者 又
未必工於挑盤 此法所以不傳於
世 邊疆重鎮造弓者 不一其家 工
於挑盤者不過幾人 而最精者未
聞也

穎少好射 因好弓矢 見工人所
造 多不如意 乃講求其故 良工祕
而不言 拙工雖欲言之 而不詳也 於
此訪工之最良者 與之言 雖得其
概 而未敢盡信也 又約同志者 出
資買材料 同工人親造而試之 乃得
其詳 又恐其未盡善也 遍訪良工而
察其利弊 考其規制 必極其變而
後已

予少時 以好學之心好射 中年
推學射之心學弓 滋久乃得其巧 大
抵射之巧在手 而心爲主 挑盤之巧
在目 而手爲主 心爲主者以神運
也 射之所以難也 手為主者 以形
用也 挑盤之所以易於射也〈新弓
上弦時 以膝揉其上下之勁處 使之
勻 謂之盤弓 看弓之上下硬處 銼
而去之 謂之挑弓〉然其巧妙 筆不
能盡 大要惟在目力審視之無偏〈
弓之上下軟勁勻調 謂之無偏〉右

Overall, because the brain on a small-tip bow is hooked, the arrow will fly far. Even with a 35 jin (45.5 pound) draw weight you can still hit the target at 80 paces (140 yards or 128 meters) and beyond. With the big-tip bow, the brain is straight and the working limb is big. Moreover, there is no additional power since it lacks a *weihe*. Unless the bow is at least 40 jin (52 pounds) in draw weight, it will not shoot far. The lightest of this genre you can use is 40 jin. Still, a big-tip bow cannot compare to a small-tip bow: although the small-tip bow is light, it can shoot far.

3.4 *Making a Balanced Horn Bow*

A bow might have good materials, but if its construction is imbalanced then it is still useless. Getting the construction right takes a tremendous amount of skill. Good bowyers are very secretive and often refuse to pass on their methods to others. In addition to being paranoid, they are uneducated and illiterate. There is no way they could record the details of what they do in a book. By contrast, there are bowyers who are educated and can read and write, but they are not necessarily skilled in constructing balanced bows. That is why it is difficult to pass on these skills to the next generation. There are a lot bowyers in the frontier towns, but only a handful of them can make a balanced bow. I have yet to hear of anyone from those regions who is an extremely outstanding bowyer.

When I was young I really liked archery, so I took an interest how to make the bows and arrows themselves. However, most of my meetings with bowyers were unproductive. I would go around to different bowyers asking for advice. The good ones were secretive and would not say a word. The mediocre ones were willing to talk, but what they said was not detailed. A while later, I finally had a chance to talk with one of the most famous bowyers. Although most of what he said was correct at a high level, I did not entirely believe all of the details he conveyed. Later, I got together with some archery friends to buy materials for that bowyer to use. That way I able to observe how he constructed a bow and I finally got to understand some of the details. However, I was not entirely confident in my understanding, so I visited various other bowyers to observe their strengths and weaknesses, and to critically analyze their theories. I continuously improved my understanding because I got to see things from these multiple perspectives.

So when I was young, I put a lot of effort into studying archery. But when I was middle age, I applied that same dedication to learn bowmaking. After studying for many years, I became a pretty good bowyer. Overall, the nuances of shooting rest in the hands, but the foundation of shooting is in the heart. The nuances of balancing a bow rest in the eyes, but the foundation of balancing a bow is in the hands. Shooting is hard because a skill rooted "in the heart" is rather intangible. By contrast, balancing a bow is more concrete because its foundation is in the hands. Thus, I find balancing a bow easier than shooting. <When you brace a bow for the first time, you use your knees to knead the belly of the bow, which will flex the parts of the top or bottom limbs that are too stiff. This phase of balancing out the bow is called the "uncoiling" (盤) phase of balancing a bow. Check the top and bottom limbs to see if there are overly stiff areas, and use a file to adjust them. This is called the "tillering" (挑) phase of balancing a bow.> The nuances of balancing a bow are hard to completely articulate in writing. You use your eyes to observe the bow closely and make sure every part is correctly proportioned <in particular, whether the relative strength of the top and bottom limbs are appropriate>. At the same time, the right hand performs the shaping to bring the bow into balance. <Below, I talk more about the guidelines for balancing a bow.>

The body of a bow is like the body of a person. If you can understand anatomy, then you can definitely understand bow balancing! A bow has the following parts: handle base, handle eyes, working limbs, brains, and tips. The handle base is like a person's heart. The handle eyes are like his back and waist. The working limbs are like his arms. And the brains and *weihe* (達和) are like his fists. [▶ The "tip 稍子" of the bow consists of both the brain, the *weihe* (the segment between the brain and string notch), and everything else above of the string notch.]

A man's character is in his heart. If he is noble, his heart has fortitude and temperance. Likewise, the handle base must be balanced. It should not be too thin or concave, or else the character of the bow is too soft. <A "thin" handle base will be soft and concave. It is what people call a "hollow" handle. When the bow has this kind of design flaw, you will not be able to shoot far.> Of course it should not be too thick or bulbous, or else the character of the bow is too hard. <When the handle base is too thick and sticks out too much, it is what people call a "bulging" handle. When this problem emerges, not only is it hard to reach full draw, but upon release there will be a lot of hand shock.> Only a straight and solid handle base will do.

A man's entire strength comes from his back and waist. That is why the handle eye should not be weak at all. If it is weak, then the handle eye will have a tendency to fold. Of course, the handle eye should not be too strong, or else its stiffness will overpower the handle base. The handle eye must be strong, but you must account for the strength of the handle base to calibrate things appropriately.

A man has two arms, which allow him to transfer his strength to his fists. They must be quick and sharp. Thus, the working limbs should not be "too big," or else the bow will lack strength. <When the working limb is "too big," that means the limb bends too close to the brain. When this happens, the arrow will release with low energy.> The working limbs should not be "too small" either, or else the handle eye

手運斤之勻調而已 <以下皆言挑盤法>

夫弓之體勢　猶人一身　然明於身之理　而挑盤之理在是矣　故弓有底　有弝眼　有脇　有腦　有達和　弓底者　猶人之心也　弝眼者　猶人之腰脊也　脇者　猶人之兩臂　腦與達和者　猶人之兩拳也

心者　性之所發也　人之性　貴於剛中　故弓底須中和　不宜太薄而下墮　以失之柔 <薄則底軟而下墮　俗呼曰鍋底弝　犯此病者　發矢不遠> 亦不宜太厚而反突　以偏於剛 <太厚反突者　俗號突底弝　犯此病者　不惟彀弓難　發矢時弓激手> 惟平直微勁者佳也　腰脊者　周身之力之所發也　故弝眼不宜微弱　弱則弓腰傾折而無力　不宜太強　強則弓腰板勁而欺底　須壯勢活潑　與弓底強弱相稱者佳　人之兩臂　所以達其力於拳者也　欲捷而銳　故脇不宜太大　大則無力 <太大者　俗號靠腦脇者此也　犯此者　發矢無力> 不宜太小　小則弝眼易傾 <小者　俗號靠弝脇者此也　犯此者　弝眼易折> 必須脇在弝眼外半寸許者佳　既不靠腦　又不靠弝　脇道勻調　與弝腦相配　發矢方銳　人之兩拳者　所以致其力於搏擊者也　欲其猛而剛　故腦不宜太直　直則無勢　不欲太鉤　鉤則易滾　而但期於圓　圓則外向捷　而達和自緊 <弓稍內寸許名達和> 弦口急　而發矢遠到　此挑盤之大概也

是以良弓體式　必期弝底平勁 <弓心爲弝底　平勁者　不太突　不傾折也> 弝眼與脇道勻調 <弓弝外四寸許爲脇道> 弓心與兩腦相應 <弓面上角木相接處爲弓腦> 弓雖弱而弦和鳴 <弦聲響亮緊急爲和鳴> 性

雖勁而底掌不悖＜弓性雖緊急勁
銳 然挑盤勻調弓之底 與人之手掌
相和而不悖戾＞ 巧妙之要是在良工
之一心

弓弣大小宜擇 ＜第五＞

弓弣不宜太大 恐握之易緊 發
矢時 常犯撇病 撇則矢易偏於左 弣
亦不宜太小 小則難握 彀弓發矢
時 常犯括臂之患 與其過大 寧過
小 須得中為妙 蓋握弓之法 掌根
得力而實 無稽于指之力 自然不用
大弣 惟握弓不得法 掌根不實 必
須指上用力 若弓弣小 指握不能
緊 撇出無勢 必然括臂 故不得不

will buckle under pressure. <When the working limb is "too small," that means the limb bends too close to the handle. When this happens, the handle eye could break easily.> The working limb should start about a half cun (0.63 in, 1.6 cm) beyond the handle eye. It should not bend too close to the brain, it should not bend too close to the handle. The taper of the handle/limb transition should be balanced and should match well with the handle and brain. Only then will the arrow release sharply.

A man's two fists take his strength and use it strike. They should be fierce and solid. Thus, the brain should not be too straight, or else it will lack energy. But it should not be too hooked, or else it will twist easily. The brain only has to be round, which will allow the arrow to fly quickly and allow the *weihe* to be tight automatically. <The *weihe* is the roughly 1 cun (1.3 in, 3.2 cm) segment on the tip that is closest to the brain.> This configuration gives the bow higher brace tension, which will allow you to shoot far.

These are the overall guidelines for a balanced bow.

The shape of a good bow will have the following properties. The handle base should be flat and solid. <The center of the handle is the base, which should be straight and solid. The handle base should not be too bulbous, and it should not be too concave.> The taper of the handle/limb transition should be balanced <the 4 cun (5.0 in, 12.8 cm) portion outside the handle is the taper of the handle/limb transition>. The handle base should coordinate with the two brains <the joint between the limb's horn and the tip's wood is called the "brain">. Even if the bow has a light draw weight, the string will make a pleasant ring <a "pleasant ring" means the braced string makes a bright, high-pitched sound>. Even if the bow has a high draw weight, it does no violence to the hand. <That is, although the bow is strong and sharp, the handle base of a well-balanced bow will not shake or cause discomfort for the bow hand.> Understanding these subtleties comes with experience.

3.5 Choosing the Appropriate Handle Size

The bow handle should not be too large, or else you are liable to grip the handle too tightly. When you release the arrow, you will have a tendency to "thrust forward" the bow arm [▶ i.e., you will let the bow hand kick out to the left during release], which in turn will cause the arrow to veer to the left. The handle should not be too small either, or else it becomes difficult to grip. When you reach full draw and release, the string will often slap your arm. Given these two extremes, you should prefer the handle that is too small instead of the handle that is too big. Of course, it is best if you have a handle of just the right size. As discussed in the method for gripping the bow, the root of the palm [▶ which is aligned with the pinky finger] should hold firmly. Do not rely exclusively on the fingers to grip forcefully. Therefore, you should not use a large handle because it encourages you to use improper gripping technique: the root of the palm will not hold firmly, which causes you to use your fingers to exert force. Now when the handle is too small, the fingers will not hold tightly, which will cause the bow to move unpredictably after the release, in turn causing the string to slap your arm. Then you might want to switch to a large handle again and perform the thrust forward movement. However, although you might be able to avoid exposing your bow arm to slapping, remember that a large handle will cause your hand to kick left and the arrow to veer left! All in all, using a large handle is still a bad idea.

Good archers favor small handles and eschew large handles. However, the reason is not because of handle size. People who can hold the bow properly make sure the root of their palm is firm, so they do not require a large handle. Only people who do not know how to hold the bow are oblivious to proper palm placement, so they should use a large handle. When the root of the palm is firm, the arrow will exit straight and level. When it is not firm, the arrow will skew to one side. The key is whether the root of the palm is firm, and has less to do with the size of the handle. Mediocre archers do not know what to do with the root of their bow palm, yet they covet small handles. This is wrong.

There are some archers whose bow elbow is double-jointed (when they lock their bow arm, their elbow is actually sticking out in front). If they want a small handle, the string will definitely slap their arm. Thus, they should be using a large handle as a temporary workaround. If they are willing to put in the extra effort, they should practice rotating both the bow shoulder and the bow arm clockwise [▶ for a right-handed archer] so that the cup of the elbow is facing towards the ground [▶ normally a person who is not double-jointed only has to focus on rotating the bow shoulder, not the bow arm]. There will be a space between the string and the inside of the bow arm [▶ because the arm is rotated clockwise], thereby allowing these people to avoid getting slapped by the string. At that point, they do not require a large handle.

Then there are the archers who are extremely double-jointed. Their elbow angles in front of their body about half a chi (6.3 in, 16 cm) when they lock their bow elbow. These people are exceedingly rare, about one in a thousand. If they do what I described in the previous paragraph, they will have a tough time avoiding string slap. Instead they should rotate the arm counterclockwise so that the cup of the elbow is facing upwards. When they are about to release, there will be a space between the string and the outside of the bow arm [▶ because the arm is rotated counterclockwise]. This will allow them to avoid string slap, and they do not require a large handle. There are many variations in arm shape, so you have to adjust your technique accordingly to find something that feels natural and comfortable. The super double-jointed people who need to revolve their arm counterclockwise are very rare. Among the Taicang guards, I only saw one guy named Sun who was like this. That is why I noted this for your reference.

用大弝撇出 雖免括臂之患 孰知矢易偏于左乎 此用大弝者非也

善射者貴用小弝 而不貴大弝者 非弝大小有貴賤 以善握弓者手掌實 故不必用大弝 惟不善握弓者 手掌不知實法 故必用大弝 掌根實者 發矢平直 掌根不實者 發矢多偏 貴賤在掌根之實與不實 不在弝之大小也 拙射不知求實掌根之法 但慕弓弝小之可貴 則誤矣

人有一種臂曲前突者 弓弝若小 必然括臂 則宜稍用大弝 亦救弊之法耳 若能用苦功者 將前肩及臂 極力向前 番下朝地 弓弦從臂上邊出 自可免括臂之病 亦奚必用大弝為

又有一種臂向前曲出半尺許者 此等異相 千人中間亦有之 若番下向地 亦不免括臂者 則將臂番轉朝天 使發矢時 弦從臂下邊出 亦可免括臂之患 而無稽於大弝 臂形異 則法因之以異 亦自然之理也 臂曲極而番轉朝天者 世不多見 予於太倉衛 曾見一孫姓者爲然 故記之 以備參考廣見聞云

Left: normal bow elbow in natural canted position. Middle: archers who are slightly double-jointed should rotate their bow elbow so that the cup of the elbow faces down. Right: archers who are extremely double-jointed should rotate their bow elbow so that the cup of the elbow faces up. *Courtesy of Mike Loades and Glenn Murray, Esq.*

弓弦長短宜擇〈第六〉

弦之長短 隨弓體式 弓長則弦宜離弓弛七寸許 弓短則弦宜離弓弛六寸五分 今人以拳按弓弛 以大指頂著弦爲準者 則弦太長 非也 何也 弦長則口鬆 弦口鬆 則發矢時振蕩不定 矢發不準

大抵 江北人多用短弦 離弓弛八寸許 則嫌于太短 故江北人多用短箭 以官制爲準 恐長人用短箭 骨節俱縮 力亦易疲 不能久射 久後 必有不穀之病 且弦太短 弓亦易傷 穀弓亦不能盡一 矢亦隨之以大小矣 此北方之病 而人不察也〈邊制箭 小尺算 二尺七寸五分 官制箭 小尺 二尺六寸五分〉

3.6 *Choosing String Length (Brace Height)*

The length of string will correspond with the length of the bow. For a long bow, the string should be about 7 cun (8.8 in, 22.4 cm) away from the handle. For a short bow, the string should be about 6 cun and 5 fen (8.2 in, 20.8 cm) away from the handle. People these days place their fist on the belly of the handle and stick their thumb up: if the thumb touches the string, then they think that is a good brace height. But the string will be too long with this method [▶ i.e., brace height too low], which is not what you want. Why? When the string is too long, the brace tension is loose, thereby making the string oscillation inconsistent at release time. You will not be able to shoot accurately.

Overall, Northerners (people who live North of the Yangtze River) like to use short strings, which are about 8 cun (10.0 in, 25.6 cm) away from the handle. Because the string is short, Northerners like to use short arrows. They find the Official Standard arrows most suitable. But you do not want tall people using short arrows, or else their joints become cramped and their strength becomes exhausted easily. They should not shoot this way for long. If they persist, they will develop the habit of failing to reach full draw. Moreover, too short a string will overstress the bow limbs. It will be harder to reach a consistent draw length [▶ because of the limitation of the maximum draw length], thereby making it difficult to control the elevation of the arrow. This is the problem that Northerners experience, yet no one seems to notice. <Using the "small chi" standard, Frontier Standard arrows measure 2 chi, 7 cun, 5 fen (2.75 small chi, 34.6 in, 88 cm), and Official Standard arrows measuring 2 chi, 6 cun, 5 fen (2.65 small chi, 33.4 in, 84.8 cm).>

Southerners like to use long strings because it is easier to reach full draw without harming the bow. When I started shooting, I liked using long strings. But there was a Northerner named Zhang who told me about the disadvantages of using a string that is too long. At that point I was convinced that I should try shortening my bow string. As a result, I found that I had a more consistent release, and the bow had less tendency to twist. I could also hear the bow make a crisp, clear sound at brace. Overall, it was much better. Of course, the string should not be too short: it should be somewhere in the middle. Roughly speaking, if you want a bow with a lower brace height (小套弓), then extend your thumb and index finger straight to measure from the belly of the handle to the string. If the distance matches the span of your thumb and index finger, then that is a good brace height. If you want a higher brace height (大套弓), then use the span of your thumb and middle fingers (extended straight) to measure that distance. Tall people have long fingers, so the brace height will be higher. Short people have short fingers, so the brace height will be lower. People have different heights, so you choose the length of the bow accordingly. And because people have different finger lengths, you use this to determine the length of the string [▶ i.e., the brace height]. These are the guidelines.

We actually recommend asking the bow maker for the recommended brace height, rather than using your own fingers (whose lengths will vary from archer to archer) to dictate the brace height for the bow.

3.7 *Choosing Arrow Length*

The length of the arrow should correspond with the length of your arms. These days, over-ambitious people who have short arms like to use arrows that are too long. They like to boast about how far back they can draw the bow. Timid people who have long arms like to use short arrows because they think it is easier to reach full draw. Both of these ideas are wrong.

南人多用長弦 取其易彀 而弓
不傷也 穎初亦好用長弦 因北人張
姓者 言長弦之害甚悉 乃悅而從
之 稍稍用短弦 殊覺發矢準 弓亦
不滾 且弓聲清響 得益多矣 但弦
不宜太短 以得中爲貴 大約小套
弓 以大指食指托直 從弓弝上量至
弦口 一托爲準 大套弓 以大指中
指 托直量之 亦一托爲準 若人長
指亦長 弓套亦隨之而長 人短指亦
短 弓套亦隨之而短 各以其人形之
長短 以定弓 因人指之長短 以定
弦 是爲定論

箭式長短宜擇 〈第七〉

箭之長短宜隨臂之骨節 今好勝
之人 臂短而過用長箭 以誇其能 退
怯之人 臂長而喜用短箭 以圖易
彀 皆非也

長人用短箭 骨節俱縮 百病易

生 固不足道 短人用長箭 是專以
力彀 非以骨節彀也 力彀者 力衰
則不彀矣 彀安能齊 骨節彀者 不
勞力而彀自齊 至老不衰者也 故臂
長矢亦長 臂短矢亦短 以骨節爲
度 此不易之理 引弓必令前後肩臂
平直如衡 後肘平屈向後垂下 大約
後手指機 與後耳齊 如向南射之
人 彀弓時 體勢反覺向西北 則彀
法方爲極致 骨節既定 則箭之長
短 亦因之以定 安可妄用

　　量箭法 自有定理 將左臂及左
手中指 俱向左伸直 須以箭鏃頂在
左肩下脇骨上 量至左手中指頂
止 指頂外又加二寸五分 〈小尺算
〉 是爲箭之定式 長短之人 各隨其
臂指爲量準 此天定之理 穎嘗考訂
多方始得 〈其法 識者遵之 庶無差
錯 若力小之人 自脇骨上 量至中
指頂 外加二寸亦足矣〉

　　　　箭體式輕重宜擇 〈第八〉

　　力大之人 弓用勁 力小之人 弓
用弱 弓勁則箭重 弓弱則箭輕 此
自然之理 今有貪平之人 弓本勁而
好用輕箭 以示發矢得平狠之法 抑
孰知箭輕則體桿柔弱 不能勝弓猛
力之發遣 矢縱脫弦 箭桿即鈎 發
矢無定準 寧特不能平直 矢且不知
偏於何所矣 又有好名之人 弓本

When tall people use short arrows, their joints are cramped and many problems will emerge with their shooting. This is not a good path to follow. When short people use long arrows and overdraw, they only use muscle power to reach full draw, and they fail to use their joints to reach full draw. When you use muscle power to reach full draw, you will get tired even before you reach full draw. How can you maintain a consistent draw length? When you use your joints, you can reach full draw effortlessly. Even as you become older, you will not get tired! That is why tall people should use long arrows, and short people should use short arrows.

Measure the arrow according to your joints. This is an unchanging principle. When you draw, you want the bow-side and draw-side shoulders/arms to be aligned, and the draw elbow to be level (with a tendency to want to drop down-and-back during release). Your thumb ring should be next to your ear, approximately. If you are shooting towards the South, then at full draw your stance should have a Northwest orientation [▶ when projecting a ray from the left foot to the right foot, the ray will face Northwest for a right-handed archer]. This is how you reach the full extent of your draw. When your joints are set, then you use this position as a basis for choosing the length of your arrows. You should not deviate from this.

There is a set method for measuring the length of your arrow. Extend your bow arm and middle finger straight out to your left. Place the tip of the arrowhead at the first rib just below your armpit [▶ Translators' warning: do not use sharp points for this], measure directly towards the tip of your middle finger, and then add 2 cun, 5 fen (which is 3.1 in or 8 cm using the "small chi" standard). This method of choosing arrow length works regardless of the individual's height or finger span. It is quite universal, as I have gleaned from my experience in experimenting with many different variations. <This method is usually pretty error free. But for people who have less strength, they should instead measure from the armpit to the tip of the middle finger and add 2 cun (2.5 in, 6.4 cm).>

3.8 Choosing the Weight of the Arrow

Strong people use strong bows, and weak people use light bows. A strong bow requires a heavy arrow, and a light bow requires a light arrow. This is the natural principle. These days there are archers who become too greedy and like to use a heavy bow with light arrows. They think that doing so will let the arrow fly ruthlessly with a flat trajectory. What they do not realize is that the shaft is weak in a light arrow, and it will not be able to effectively receive the full might of the bow's energy. Before the arrow leaves the string, the shaft immediately bends, and the arrow flight will be inconsistent. The arrow always flies crooked, and these people have no idea what direction it has veered off to! There are also people who want to show off and like to use light bows with heavy arrows. They think that doing so will give them stable arrow flight. They do not realize that a heavy arrow flies more slowly. The bow exhausts most of its energy trying to move the heavy arrow, and there is little energy left to give the arrow any extra cast. The arrows will not fly accurately. These people occupy two extremes.

Getting the bow and arrow to match is a delicate balance. You cannot have the slightest deviation. In particular, for every 10 jin (13 pounds) of draw weight, you want to add 1 qian, 2 fen (4.4 grams, or 68.25 grains). For a 100 jin (130 pound) bow, you should use a 1 liang, 2 qian (44.3 grams, or 682.5 grains) arrow. For heavy bows approaching 100 jin (130 pounds), it is okay to have an arrow that is a little heavier than 1 liang, 2 qian. For weak bows approaching 30 jin (39 pounds), the arrow mass will approach 3 qian, 6 fen (13.3 grams, or 204.8 grains). This is extremely weak! You should not use a bow that is any lighter, and you should not use an arrow that is any lighter! Why? If the bow is any weaker, the arrow will not be able to reach the target. If the arrow is any lighter, you will not be able to have a consistent release. When the arrow is light, the shaft is soft: the arrow will wobble on the way out and will not be able to effectively receive the bow's energy.

[▶ You can read our recommendations for a safe arrow mass ratio in the "Choosing Arrows" section in the Appendix.]

3.9 *Choosing the Age of the Bamboo Shafts*

You have matched the weight of the bow and arrow, yet for some odd reason the arrow will still veer too left, too right, too high, or too low, sometimes as much as one zhang (3.5 yd, 3.2 m) off course. The reason is because the arrow is made of soft, young bamboo. It cannot effectively receive the force from a heavy bow. The arrow bamboo from Guangzhong has the best quality, and Jiangxi bamboo is the next best. However, getting Guangzhong bamboo in large quantities is very difficult, so it is okay to settle for Jiangxi bamboo: but you have to know how to choose it! Old arrow bamboo is the best [▶ that is, the bamboo is grown for a longer period of time before being cut], whereas young/tender arrow bamboo is the worst.

There are different kinds of old bamboo shafts. There are wide diameter and narrow diameter shafts. Moreover, among the wide and narrow shafts, the walls of the shafts can be thick or thin. Thin-walled shafts are good for making light arrows, and thick-walled shafts are good for making heavy arrows.

If your supply of suitable bamboo runs low, your remaining choices are suboptimal. If you only have thick-walled bamboo shafts for making light arrows, you have to

弱 而顧用重箭 以示發箭得疾遣之
法 豈知 箭重則行遲 竭力遣之 力
必不齊 矢亦不準 是二人者之所爲
皆過也

夫弓矢相配 如權衡然 不可分
毫過差 大約弓力量十斤者 用箭一
錢二分 百斤之弓 箭可重一兩二
錢 弓勁至百斤 箭重至一兩二錢
者 猶可復重 弓弱至三十斤 箭至
三錢六分者 弱亦甚矣 弓弱至此 不
可復減 箭至此 不可復輕矣 何
也 弓過弱 矢不能及的 箭過輕 發
必不準 以箭輕桿軟 發出必搖 矢
不能勝弓力之遣耳 此弓箭輕重定
法也

箭竹老嫩宜擇 〈第九〉

弓矢相配 重輕合宜矣 乃發矢
時 忽有左右大小之偏 至甚丈者 以
箭竹柔嫩 不能當勁弓之發遣耳 箭
竹性出廣中者最佳 江西次之 然廣
竹不可多得 即江西竹中亦有可
用 在人知所擇耳 箭竹以老者爲
佳 嫩者爲劣 老有不同 有桿粗大
而老者 有細小而老者 而粗細中 又
有厚薄之殊 以薄者作輕箭 厚者作
重箭 方適于用 若偶值箭竹缺少
時 不及揀選 或以竹厚者作輕箭 勢
必多去竹青 而矢易曲 或以薄者作
重箭 必桿大而矢行遲 不可不辨也

竹嫩者 無論粗細 俱不可用 今
人看老嫩者 俱以色辨 以黑者焦黃

者爲老 以白者淡黃者爲嫩 皆非
也 何也 已成之箭 皆從沙泥火中
燒出 其色非本色也 如使嫩竹而多
燒 色亦可黑而可黃 老竹而火力未
透 色亦可淡而可白 故色不足辨其
老嫩 惟于竹成紋之 紋粗者爲老 紋
細者爲嫩 又須揉其體桿 硬者爲
老 軟者爲嫩 指甲上撚之 聽其
聲 清響者爲老 木樸者爲嫩 乃爲
定論 又有箭桿上多大白痕者 此必
以粗竹作細箭 多去竹青故也 此箭
之最劣者也 發矢必不準 且嫩極不
耐久用

箭體式宜擇〈第十〉

用輕箭者 須牛奶頭 以其輕而
小也 約重不過二三分 用重箭者 須
蝴蜂翅頭 以其重而大也 約重六七
分 蓋箭體重 頭亦重 箭體輕 頭亦
輕 欲其稱也 稱則不惟能及遠 矢
發亦有定準 今人用箭鏃 輒以己意
爲好 尚非也

重箭 肚宜在前段 輕箭 肚宜在
後段〈箭體中間大處爲肚〉 何也 箭
重體必粗 後半不患其軟〈箭體以根
爲後 鏃爲前段〉 只患弓力猛遣 箭
頭入土深 故前半體易曲 亦易折 必
須肚在前段 以壯其體 且弓力勁
者 矢發至的 猶不肯垂頭 須肚在

shave away the green parts of the shaft wall. However, the arrow could easily become crooked. If you only have thin-walled bamboo shafts for making heavy arrows, then you have to pick a wide-diameter shaft. However, the arrow will fly slowly. You cannot afford to ignore these details!

When bamboo is young, it does not matter whether it is thick or thin: you should avoid it at all costs. Nowadays when people judge the age of the shaft, they think that blackened or dark yellow shafts are old and that white and light yellow shafts are young. That is wrong! Why? Finished arrows all undergo heat treatment over a fire pit. The resulting color has nothing to do with its original color. Over-heating a young shaft for a long time can make it black or dark yellow. Under-heating an old shaft can make it light yellow or white. That is why you cannot judge the age of the shaft by its color. Instead, you should judge by the grain of the shaft.

When the grain lines are thick, the shaft is old. When the grain lines are thin, the shaft is young. You should also flex test the shaft: old bamboo will be stiff, whereas young bamboo will be more flexible. You can also roll the shaft lightly atop your fingernails and listen to the sound it makes. If the sound is light and crisp, it is old bamboo. If the sound is dull, then it is young bamboo. These are the guidelines.

You might encounter arrow shafts with a lot of white marks. In fact, these shafts are thick bamboo that have had the green parts shaved down to make thin arrows. These kinds of arrows are the worst! You will not be able to have a clean release with them, and they will be just as fragile as shafts made with young bamboo.

3.10 *Choosing the Proportions of the Arrow*

With a light arrow, you should use a cow nipple arrowhead because it is small and light. The weight of the head should not be heavier than 2–3 fen (0.74–1.11 grams, or 11–17 grains). With a heavy arrow, you should use a butterfly wing arrowhead because it is large and heavy, weighing roughly 6–7 fen (2.2–2.6 grams, or 34–40 grains). If the arrow shaft is heavy, then the arrowhead should be heavy; if the arrow shaft is light, then the arrowhead should be light. When these proportions are suitable, not only will the arrow fly far but the arrow flight will be very consistent. Nowadays people choose arrowheads on a whim. This is wrong!

In heavy arrows, the belly should be towards the front of the shaft. In light arrows, the belly should be towards the back. <The thickest section of the shaft is the belly.> Why?

With heavy arrows the shaft will be wide/thick. Thus you do not have to worry that the back half of the arrow would be too soft. <Regarding the body of an arrow, the part with the nock is the back, and the part with the arrowhead is the front.>

However, such a heavy arrow will receive the full force of a heavy bow, so its arrowhead will deeply penetrate the dirt behind the target. Thus, the front half of the shaft risks becoming crooked or broken. That is why the belly of the arrow should be in the front half to strengthen the arrow body. Moreover, if the bow is heavy then the arrow will have a tendency to veer upwards. Placing the belly in the front half of the arrow will mitigate this tendency.

With light arrows the shaft should have a narrow diameter, but this makes the back half of the arrow liable to fishtail. For this reason, the belly should be in the back half to reduce the fishtailing tendency. Moreover, when the bow is light, the arrow will not penetrate deeply. As a result, the front half of the arrow will not become crooked or broken on impact, so you should not bother putting the belly in the front half. Moreover, with a light bow, the arrowhead will have a tendency to sink downwards when the arrow is halfway towards the target. You must make the front half of the arrow narrow and light to help flatten its trajectory.

Heavy arrows should use horseshoe arrowhead sockets. Light arrows should use beansprout arrowhead sockets. Horseshoe sockets are thick and solid, so they match well with heavy arrowheads. Beansprout sockets are thin and light, so they match well with light arrowheads.

Big fletchings will slow down the arrow, so you should not make the fletching too large. But with a heavy arrow and a heavy bow, the fletchings should be a little bigger. If the fletching is too short, the arrow will not fly straight. But with a light arrow and a light bow, fletching should be a bit smaller. If you wanted a light arrow with large fletchings, it is pretty obvious the arrow will not fly very far.

Do not use the small vane of a goose feather as fletching. A goose feather has a stem in the middle, a large vane on one side, and a small vane on the other. The dimensions of small vanes are inconsistent, so if you use them as fletching you will get poor aerodynamics and erratic arrow flight. I have experimented with this already, so do not take my advice lightly. These days way too many people use small vanes. But these kinds of people do not understand proper archery technique either. If they are not able to hit, they cannot figure out whether their technique is to blame or whether their use of small vane fletchings is to blame. That is all I have to say about vane selection.

You should not use black feathers. If you shoot them into the grass, black feathers are difficult to find. It is better to use white feathers. These days, people want to mimic the style of Beijing arrows, which use black feathers. Being superficially fashionable cannot be practical.

前半 以殺其勢 輕箭體必細 後半
常軟而易鈎 故肚須在後半 則體不
鈎 且弓力弱 發矢入土淺 前半不
患其鈎而折 又何藉於肚在前乎 弓
力弱者 矢至半路而頭已垂 須前半
細小輕利 以無沮其進步

重箭宜用馬蹄口 輕箭宜用荳板
口 以馬蹄口粗壯而牢固 故與重箭
鏃相配 荳板口尖小而輕捷 與輕箭
鏃相配

翎大箭行遲 翎不宜太大 但箭
重弓必勁 翎宜稍大 以稱其勢 儻
翎過小 矢發亦不準 箭輕弓弱 翎
宜稍小 以稱之 若箭輕翎大 矢亦
不前 此易曉也 但不可用鵝毛小邊
翎耳 鵝毛中有一梗 一邊翎大 一
邊翎小 小邊翎 大小不關風 矢發
不準 此已試之功 非虛語也 今人
用小邊翎者 甚眾 但不知射法之
人 中則不知合何法 不中亦不知犯
何病 故中則以爲手之能 不中則以
爲手之病 小邊翎之病 人不知察
也 故特表而出之 以示君子 黑翎
切不可用 以射入草中 色黑難覓 不
如白翎之爲愈也 今人欲學京箭樣
式 故用黑翎 是備虛名而受實禍矣

指機之名 古未嘗有也 古號爲
決 決者 取其決機捷而無凝滯也 今
人所用指機 名一盞燈者 四圍口太
廠 中間四邊 又薄而無內 控弦
時 大指必極力扣緊 開時 已不脫
灑 一不便也 射時用皮襯 二不便
也 指機口太廠 彀時機礙箭開 指
機底離箭根半寸許 矢亦難彀 三
不便也 指機底薄 彀時傷弦 四不
便也

又有荷新樣者 前口獨廠 後邊
及兩邊口 稍斂而薄 此式稍善 而
未盡美 何也 前口廠雖善 而嫌中
間無肉 則控引時 大指亦須扣緊 又
用皮襯 且兩邊既薄 指機底如刀
口 則控弦時 亦傷弦 其三不便 與
一盞燈同 惟兩邊薄 控弦彀時 則
矢根離指機底 不過一二分 則控弦
易彀 故云稍善而未盡美也

穎嘗創一指機 式與荷新樣相
似 前口廠 而中多分肉 控弦時 大
指不必極力扣緊 則彀時脫弦鬆
快 一便捷也 後面稍厚 兩邊極薄
如錢 引弓彀時 指機底離箭根 不
過一線許 則箭易彀 二便捷也 然
兩邊既薄 指機底如刀口 恐彀時傷
弦 故於指機底前 用兩足砥住弓
弦 不使控在兩邊薄處 只以指機前
邊平底 控弦則弦不傷 一弦可當五
弦之用 三便捷也 且前兩足 砥住
弦 則弦不礙指 而不必用皮襯 四
便捷也 邑中諸友 愛之者 號曰高
公四捷機云 三吳好射者 倣其式而
爲之 不約而同也

3.11 *Choosing a Thumb Ring*

The name "*zhiji* 指機" (thumb ring) was not a common term in the old days. Back then they called it "*jue* 決." They called it "*jue*" because the word meant "decisive and without hesitation." Among the rings used nowadays, one is "The Lantern 一盞燈." The four outer walls of the ring are rather wide and flat, and the portion surrounding the thumb is very thin. When you use The Lantern to hold the string, you are forced to hook your thumb very tightly. As a result, the release will not be crisp. That is problem number one. When you shoot with it, you have to use a leather lining [▶ this is the same idea as the Turkish *kulak*, a leather lining placed between the front of the thumb and the ring to protect the thumb skin from being pinched by the string]. That is problem number two. Because the ring is too flat and wide, at full draw it will interfere with the arrow. The base of the ring [▶ the bottom opening of the ring immediately surrounding the thumb] is about a half cun (0.63 in, 1.6 cm) away from the arrow nock. It will be hard to pull the arrow to full draw. That is problem number three. Moreover, because the base of the ring is thin, it will cut into the string at full draw. That is problem number four.

There is also "The Lotus Petal 荷新樣" design. Only the lip of the ring (the front of the ring) is flat and broad. The sides and back walls are narrow and thin. This design is better but still not ideal. Why? Having a broad lip is good, but because the parts surrounding your thumb are thin, you will find yourself hooking your thumb tightly during the draw and you will be forced to use a leather lining. Because the side walls of the ring are thin, the floor of the ring is like a blade that will cut into the string during the draw. The Lotus Petal shares these three faults with The Lantern. However, because the side walls of The Lotus Petal are thin, the base of the ring is at most 1–2 fen (0.13–0.25 in, 3.2–6.4 mm) away from the arrow nock at any time during the draw. Thus it is easier to reach full draw. That is why I say this design is better but not completely ideal.

I created my own ring design similar to The Lotus Petal. The lip is flat and broad but is also thicker. Thus, when you are about to draw you do not have to hook the thumb tightly around the string. This will make the release very crisp. This is the first advantage. The back wall is a little thicker, but the side walls of the ring are as thin as a coin. At full draw, the base of the ring will be no more than the width of a thread away from the arrow nock. It becomes easy to reach full draw, which is the second advantage. Because the thin side walls could act like knives cutting into the string, I put a two-pronged guard at the front base of the ring to protect the string. The string does not touch the thin side walls: it only touches the lip. This will prolong the lifespan of the string, letting it last five times longer than with any other ring. This is the third advantage. Moreover, because the two-pronged guard blocks the string, it protects the thumb from getting pinched by the string and there is no need for a leather lining. This is the fourth advantage. All my friends in the city love this design. They call it "Gao's Four Victory Ring." All the archers in the Sanwu (三吳) region imitated this design and came to the same conclusion.

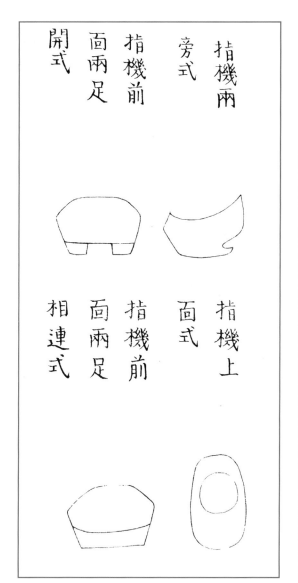

Illustrations of thumb rings from Gao's manual. The original Chinese captions are as follows. Top row (right to left): "Ring side view. Ring frontal view with two-pronged guard." Bottom row (right to left): "Ring top view. Ring frontal view with linked guard." *From the edition of Gao Ying's manual compiled by Jiang Qilong and edited by Ogyuu Sorai (published in Kyoto, Japan, 1780).*

More illustrations of thumb rings from Gao's manual. The original Chinese captions are as follows. Top: "Ring back view, tall style." Bottom: "Ring back view, short style." *From the edition of Gao Ying's manual compiled by Jiang Qilong and edited by Ogyuu Sorai (published in Kyoto, Japan, 1780).*

做指機法

指機之適用 全在中間之眼與大
指形相肖 然大指形合有不同 有
圓 有扁 又有指後突起高骨者 故
指圓 眼亦宜圓 指扁 眼亦宜扁 指
機前面宜高 而中間稍宜留肉 此大
指形圓與扁者 指機眼宜然也 若大
指後面突起高骨者 則不然 指機之
眼 後面亦宜挖作一凹 與大指突骨
形相肖 指機前面又不宜高 只宜平
塌 中間又不宜多留肉 方爲貼妥 在
于通變 不可執一

指機前兩足間 可連 亦可斷 隨
其人之所欲爲之 不必拘也 又須一
人用大小二指機 以備相代 久不射
則指小 久射則指漸大故也 故欲令
人做指機者 必須先以指形示人 使
做指機之眼與大指形相肖 方不必
皮襯而安貼 若不以指形示人 妄取
人指機 帶而不妥 不得不用皮襯爲
穩矣 此特論平時習射則然 若臨戰
陣 手執枹鼓 安用此有足指機爲 莫
若用平底銅圈 方爲寔用 花羊角圈
亦可用 外此 牛角竹木圈 皆不堅
固 不適於用者也

How to Make a Thumb Ring

Making a comfortable ring is all about making sure the eye of the ring [▶ the opening of the ring] matches the shape of the thumb joint. Thumbs joints come in different shapes: round, flat, and protruding (where the bone at the back of the thumb joint sticks up). For round thumbs, the eye of the ring should be round. For flat thumbs, the eye of the ring should be elliptical. For round and flat thumbs, the lip of the ring should be high, and the middle of the lip should be just a little thicker. For protruding thumbs, you need a different shape: the back-inside wall of the ring should be more concave to comfortably accommodate the protruding bone at the back of the thumb joint. The lip of the ring should not be high, only flat. The lip of the ring should be less thick. Only then will the ring be suitable. You have to account for these variations. This is not one size fits all.

The guard at the base of the ring can be linked or two-pronged. The choice between one or the other is just a personal preference. Moreover, a person should own two rings for different situations. When you do not shoot for a long time, your thumb is small. When you shoot for a long time your thumb gradually becomes bigger. If you want someone to make a ring for you, you should show the ring maker your thumb in-person. That way he can make the eye of the ring match your thumb shape and size, and you will not need to glue in a leather lining. If you do not show the ring maker your thumb, he will have to make guesses and the resulting ring will not fit properly. You might be forced to use a leather lining to have a stable fit.

The preceding discussion about rings with guards pertains to peacetime practice. When you are fighting a war, you are wearing armor and carrying all sorts of equipment, which makes using a ring with a guard impractical. In this case, nothing beats a bronze disc with a flat bottom if you want a practical ring for battle. A disc made of ram's horn is also practical. Otherwise, discs made of water buffalo horn, bamboo, and wood are not durable enough to be useful.

An example of a lipped ring with a two-pronged guard made from wood modeled after Gao's Four Victory Ring.

3.12 *Choosing Bamboo vs. Wooden Arrows*

Northerners mostly use wooden arrows, and Southerners mostly use bamboo arrows. This is not because Northerners like wood and Southerners like bamboo. Wood grows in the North, and bamboo grows in the South. It is simply the case that people use whatever resources are available locally! There are three kinds of arrow wood: shafts made from birch are the best, followed by catalpa, followed by willow. Birch shafts are very strong and do not become crooked easily. Willow shafts are soft and become crooked easily. That is why I rank them this way. Of course if the shaft is firm, it could be very heavy. That is why you should use birch shafts with heavy bows and use willow shafts with light bows. Some people say that because wood is heavier than bamboo, then bamboo arrows do not have as much penetration power as wooden arrows. But hearsay is not the same as empirical observation. One time Qian Shizhen, the famous general from my hometown, performed an armor piercing experiment. He used the same archer and the same bow to shoot one bamboo arrow and one wooden arrow at the bow's maximum strength. The wooden arrow barely made a dent in the armor, whereas the bamboo arrow penetrated 3 cun (3.8 in, 9.6 cm). Thus, wood is inferior to bamboo in terms of penetration power. If you are shooting a long distance, bamboo is better than wood. If you are shooting a closer distance, then wood and bamboo are both fine.

3.13 *Conclusion*

When you are shooting with friends in good scenery, drinking wine makes the experience more enjoyable. A strong wind and a good sail make it possible to travel long distances. I have just finished writing about choosing equipment in great detail. When you choose the right archery equipment, you are not just putting yourself in a position to perform heroic feats: you are putting yourself in a position to develop your virtue. When you are just about to start learning archery, you should modestly seek out proper instruction. When you have already started learning, you need to make sure your tools are in good order. Choosing good equipment is of the utmost importance. Some students get very cocky and ignore proper technique. They shoot poorly because of their bad form yet blame their equipment for their poor performance. Then there are stingy folks who, despite learning proper technique, stick with using shabby bows and shabby arrows. They cannot hit the target, and this is the equipment's fault. These people do not blame their equipment, and instead think the technique they learned is useless. Both of these mindsets are flawed!

竹木箭宜擇 〈第十二〉

北人多用木箭 南人多用竹箭 非北人好木而南人好竹也 木產於北邊 竹產於江南 各因其土之所產而用之耳 木箭有三 樺桿爲上 楸桿次之 柳桿又次之 樺桿堅而難曲 柳桿鬆而易折 亦易曲 故有上中下之分 然堅者恐傷於重 故勁弓宜用樺桿 弱弓宜用柳桿爲稱 人又有謂木重竹輕 竹不如木箭之能洞堅也 抑孰知 臆逆何如目睹而親試之爲真 吾邑參戎公錢三持 曾蹲甲試之 只用一弓而竹木箭各一 令一人恣力射之 木箭洞甲不過一粟許 而竹箭則貫甲三寸 是木不如竹之勁利可知 若射遠則木益不如竹 射近則不甚相遠也

擇物門 總結

良朋美景 豪飲之助也 風帆迅利 長驅之資也 筆墨俱妙 淨几明窗 揮灑之具也 弓矢既調 機引善制 豈非豪士逞懷之助 修人輝德之資乎 習射者 當未入門時 宜虛心博採求益爲先 既入門之後 又當利器以善用 擇物爲急 世乃有好勝之徒 茫不知法 射不佳 手之過也 乃不罪手而罪弓 以掩其拙 又有鄙吝之夫 學法已成 輒以敝弓劣矢 而不中的 弓之過也 乃不罪弓而罪法之不驗 皆非也 甚者 手之過而罪弓 必欲更其弓 弓之過而罪法 又欲易其法 妄更其弓 害猶可言 妄

易其法 展轉乖誤 害不可言矣 惟
明智之士 利弊昭然 功過莫掩 弊
在弓則更弓 弊在法則易法 弓無留
弊 手無微疵 人弓相親 心手相
悅 機神和暢 而射之道盡矣
　　嗟嗟 以此道推之 天下亡事可
幾而理矣 非明智之士 安能見之哉

武經射學入門正宗　後序

　　夫射之法 深且繁矣 然以道通
之 則又至簡而至易 何以明其然
也 習射之初 以法求射 則見其
繁 習之滋久 法熟而理暢 理暢而
機洽 機洽而道通 則千條萬緒皆可
一貫 安見射法之繁乎

　　穎弱冠時 以好功名之心好射 遂
忘寒暑 晚年頗得力於射 而通其
道 遂以好道之心好射 并忘功名 行
住坐臥 非射不思 居閒燕處 非射
不樂 憂患非射不息 怨仇非射不
解 疾痛疴癢 非射不忘 推之九地
九天 觸目驚心之事 無之非射者也

If the problem is in their technique but they blame the bow, they will change the bow. If the problem is with the bow and they blame their technique, they will alter their technique. If you are carelessly changing your equipment, you at least have a chance of knowing the reason. If you are carelessly changing your technique, a lot of problems will emerge and you will have no chance of knowing the reason why. Only smart people are able to analyze things objectively and eliminate unknown variables. If the problem is with the bow, they will change the bow. If the problem is with their technique, they will change their technique. Only when the bow is free of problems and the technique is free of faults will the man and his equipment match well. This way, his heart and hands will act as one, everything will go smoothly, and he can fully realize the true Way of Archery.

Alas! If you can master the Way of Archery, then any other challenge you undertake in this world is within reach. Ignorant people are not able to see this connection!

Conclusion to Book 1

Archery has a lot of depth and complexity. But if you approach it with the right methods, things that seemed deep and complex at first will become simple and easy. How so? In the beginning, learning with proper technique seems complex. But after practicing for a while, your familiarity with the technique helps you understand the principles. When you understand the principles, your timing becomes intuitive. When your timing becomes intuitive, you are on the Way and have reached the pinnacle where thousands upon thousands of threads work together as a single unit. At this point, how can shooting seem complex?

When I was about 20-plus years old, I practiced really, really hard because I wanted to be famous. In my later years, I had become quite a skilled archer, but at that point I enjoyed archery because I enjoyed the challenge, not because I wanted to be famous. Throughout my life, there was never a moment when I was not thinking about archery. Most of the time, shooting was a joy for me. When I was anxious, shooting became my relaxation. When I would puzzle over something, shooting would give the moment of clarity I needed to solve the problem. Even when I was sick or injured, archery would help me forget my pain. Through all the triumphs and tribulations, there was not a moment that did not involve archery.

Although this year I am quite old, my love for archery has not diminished. People who do not know me think that practicing archery is a painful and laborious waste of time. But I find it extremely enjoyable. People who know me think that practicing archery is just a silly obsession that is all fun and games. They do not realize that the source of my joy comes from the bitter hard work that I put into practicing.

As for the Way of Archery, the outside is coarse but the inside is refined. The body moves while the spirit is tranquil. Achieving a high level of skill is not impossible, but it does take a lot of work. You have to be modest and open-minded in adopting good suggestions. Your willpower should be vigorous, your strength should be solid, your gaze should be penetrating, and your breathing should be peaceful. This way you will be able to improve without being too stubborn or self-conscious. You will be able to take all the work you have invested and apply it to real situations. Understanding the nuances of the art and having discipline undoubtedly lead you to the best Way. When you have reached the true Way, you understand its many facets. Archery is not a one-dimensional art!

I have studied archery for over forty years, but I feel like I have only just started understanding the high-level principles. When times get difficult, I have the willpower to carry on. And as I get older, I still have strength. I am still able-bodied and able-minded because of archery, even though my time is running short. I want to be able to take my experience and pass it on to my children. Although my oldest son Wumeng and my grandson Nianzu are very studious, their left arms are crippled. I have tried hard to teach them, but it was hard for them to learn because of their physical impairment. I have also tried to teach my second son Xiumeng and my youngest son Shengmeng. But these two are not studious. They are the kind of people who do not care for learning or developing their talents. Teaching them would be a waste of time, because they would not apply what they learned to anything useful. It is better to let them stay at home as farmers.

Nevertheless, I cannot afford to miss the opportunity to pass on what I have learned! When I see someone shooting carelessly, I get really offended. I do not care what their social status is: when I see problems with their technique, I start correcting them. Even if I encounter overbearing and self-righteous people, I will work extra hard to try to enlighten them with the hope that they will come to a realization. I do not do this because I enjoy lecturing people. The reason is because when I was younger and started archery, I did not have anyone to teach me. I ended up trying a lot of different things, changing my technique many times. I did not realize that changing things left-and-right would take a toll on my muscles and bones. Sometimes I would

今年齒雖漸加 長而好樂不倦 不
知予者 以為勞且苦 而予則彌覺其
樂也 知予者 以為樂且癡 而不知
予之樂 皆從苦中來也

夫射之道 外粗而內精 形動而
神靜 功非驟得 養非襲取 其存心
欲虛 取益欲廣 志欲猛 力欲實 瞻
欲旺 氣欲和平 精進欲無已 然後
可以收其功 而推其用 其精神心術
之微 涵養持循之功 無非至道 通
其道而遊之 與之上下 非可一藝
目矣

予講求四十餘年 而始得其略 貧
而益堅 老而益壯 頗得力於此 而
精神已憊矣 欲以授之子若孫 而長
子武孟 孫念祖 雖喜讀書 左臂俱
折 不能學也 強授之 而亦不能
精 是天限之也 欲授之次子修孟 幼
子聲孟 又不喜讀書 則不學無術之
人 授之技而不善用 不若農焉而已

又不忍此術之無傳也 每見彎弓
角射之人 不覺欣喜神動 無論賢愚
貴賤 見其射中之弊 必徐為指引 即
有強項自是者 亦必多方開導 冀其
一悟 非好為人師也 深恨少年初射
時 以無人指示之故 廣求博採 淘
洗更革 不知幾番變易 徒罷筋骸 或
以片時可得之法 而流汗數年 或以
不費絲力之法 而深求玄算 形神俱

稿 此何異欲尋友於咫尺之地 不知
其家處所 乃周行千里 轍迹幾遍天
下 復還故處 而遇之者乎 回視四
十餘年 艱辛之苦 今幸得之 雖可
喜也 亦可悲矣 是以一見持弓妄遫
之人 何惜一開口之勞 不以貽人終
身之惑 無奈 知音者絶少 徘徊四
顧 無與為偶

甲子春 有毛連生 名廣者 婁陰
人也 好學樂善 予愛而授之 幾盡
其法 而又性懶 恐其不能記臆也 因
作射略以遺之 予友嚴求思名衍
者 樂道不仕 博洽君子也 聞射略
成 索而觀之 嫌其略而不詳 雜出
而無序也 丁卯春 遂作射法三十餘
條 分之為三門 則各自為始終 而
為一小成 合之為一門 則共為始終
而為一大成 自表及裏 由粗入細 肢
節相承 各有其序 如四時之代謝 不
可紊也 如臟腑之相因 不可缺也 使
學者得望道而趨 歷階而進 故總名
之為射學入門 噫 高山流水 可以
入琴神相契也 公孫舞劍書法斯
成 道相通也 予所言者 射也 意之
所指不止於射也 後有得予法者 實
有望於斯人

—崇禎丁丑仲春
既望 高穎 識

stumble across the correct technique, but only after years of sweat and labor. Sometimes I would waste a lot of effort trying to figure out very simple details. In the end, I was mentally and physically exhausted. It was like traveling thousands of miles around the world just to search for my friend's house, and then returning home by chance just to realize that my friend is actually my neighbor! I look back on those forty years and think about all the hardships I suffered. Although I have been very lucky and learned a lot, I still cannot help feeling that the whole journey was a bit tragic. Thus, when I see someone picking up a bow and shooting recklessly, I do not regret opening my mouth to lecture them if it saves them a lifetime of misery. Alas! I have very few good friends who can fully understand me.

In Spring 1624, a met a man from Louyin named Mao Liansheng. I liked the guy because was very studious and strived to improve himself. I decided to teach him everything I knew about archery technique. I was afraid that he would not be able to remember all the details, so I wrote a little summary to give to him. My friend Yan Qiusi was a very well-read gentleman. When he heard that I wrote a summary on archery, he asked for a copy and read through it. He felt that the summary lacked detail and was disorganized. Then in Spring 1627, I wrote more than thirty sections on archery technique and split them into three chapters. They started out as multiple small standalone sections. But when I joined them together as chapters, the whole work started to become more substantive. The work started as a laundry list of topics, but it eventually became a coherent piece. It contained coarse-grained descriptions at first, but eventually it would describe things in great detail. There were logical transitions between the different sections, and everything was finally coming together.

Like the four seasons, no discussion is out of sequence. Or like a person's internal organs: no topics should be left uncovered. Students who read the book will make measurable progress if they follow the book step by step. That is why this work is called *An Orthodox Introduction to Martial Archery*. Alas! "High Mountain 高山" and "Flowing Water 流水" are canonical music pieces that embody the spirit of the qin (琴). When Zhang Xu witnessed Gong Sun's sword dance, he saw in her the spirit of a master calligrapher. Although I write about the subject of archery, the deeper meaning behind my work is about more than just archery. I hope that later generations who learn from my book can realize this point.

— Chongzhen Era, Ding Chou Year, Second Month, Sixteenth Day
(1637 CE, March 12th): Gao Ying

Book 2

An Orthodox Guide
to Martial Archery

射為六藝之文　與禮樂詩書並
陳　古者天下選諸侯卿大夫士　亦必
以射為殿最　且取師於是　觀德於
是　則射之義　不為不深且遠矣　故
古者男子生　懸桑弧蓬矢　以射天地
四方有以也　然考之三代而下　凡好
為論議　負一長一技者　多創為一家
之言以垂不朽　自古迄今以善射名
者　后羿　由基　而後如樂伯　非衛賈
堅之流　穿石洞鐵　志目夾胭之才　代
不乏人　卒無一書垂訓於後　即有宣
洩其祕者　亦不過一二言而止　辭不
盡乎其意　不盡乎其言　此又何也　穎
嘗反覆推之意者　古人得力於射者
深　故其發之言也訒　夫是以言簡意
精　誠不欲以射中隱如躍如之機
趣　滯之於言語文辭之粗　而存其甘
苦疾徐之妙　於微辭婉轉之間　以俟
人之自悟未可知也　無奈　後人不能
深惟其奧　往往以文害辭　以辭害
意　失之毫厘　謬之千里　而射法之
不明於世所從來矣　且又有好事
者　創為偏執迂疏之說以惑世　而愚
者爭趨之　則愈趨愈遠　而射法益不
可明矣

Introduction to Book 2

Archery is one of the Six Noble Arts, along with ritual, music, poetry, literature, and charioteering. [▶ Here, Gao Ying seems to have mixed the Six Noble Arts with the Six Confucian Classics. The Six Noble Arts come from the Rites of Zhou 周禮 standard, which includes ritual (禮), music (樂), archery (射), charioteering (樂), literature (書), mathematics (數). The Six Confucian Classics include Book of Changes (易經), Book of Documents (書經), Book of Poetry (詩經), Book of Rites (禮經), Book of Music (樂經), Spring and Autumn Annals (春秋).] Among the selection criteria for rulers and officials in the old days, archery skill was of the utmost importance. It was a way to select officials and a way to demonstrate virtue. As a result, archery was a very serious pursuit. Back then, when a boy was born, there was the custom of hanging a mulberry longbow (桑弧) and reed (蓬) arrows, as well as shooting arrows in six directions (towards the sky, towards the ground, and in the four cardinal directions). During the Three Dynasties of Antiquity [▶ Xia, Shang, Zhou from 21st–3rd centuries BCE] and after, there were great thinkers and talents, and they were each able to establish their own schools of thought and secure their place in history. From that time to today, there were famous archers like Hou Yi, Yang Youji, Lebo, Fei Wei, Jiajian. People do not tire of hearing stories about amazing feats such as piercing stone, penetrating iron, and using willpower to robin-hood arrows. However, all these famous archers never left any books for future generations to study. Once in a while, they might begrudgingly divulge a few of their secrets, but what they reveal will be rather superficial and uninformative. What is going on here?

I pondered this point for a long time, and I came to the conclusion that the ancients were cautious. They chose to use simple descriptions because it was difficult to use the written word to describe the nuances of archery in great detail. Unfortunately, future generations are left speculating about the true meaning of their ancestors' terse writing. Their speculation manifests itself as bad oral advice, which in turns messes up their understanding. It is the fraction-of-a-mile deviation that ends up taking you a thousand miles off course. In the end, they have a cloudy understanding of technique and their form is ruined.

Still worse: there are those self-styled "masters" who make up cockamamie theories about archery that end up misleading many a new student. These students will never be able to learn good form: the more they shoot, the worse they will become.

For Zhu Yuanzhang, as the founding emperor of a dynasty the world was his apple. But even during peacetime, he placed great emphasis on military training. As a result, the archery ritual was written into law as part of the Code of the Great Ming (大明會典) [▶ a compendium of laws, as well as regulations concerning the structure and offices of the Ming government]. There are a lot of military training schools in the former capital of Nanjing, and other local governments all around the country have established archery ranges in the regular schools. Unfortunately, a long period of peace makes people focus their attention on literature and painting, and they look down upon archery as a brutish activity for military people. And even for military personnel, they are more concerned about getting promoted: they superficially go through the motions of practicing archery, so they do not have a deep understanding of archery's nuances. That is why both civilian and military officials seem to ignore archery. But the literature these days has become wishy-washy, and military training has become laxed.

Today's emperor [▶ Chongzhen] decreed that all the scholars must study military texts, as well as practice horsemanship and archery, in order to bolster the strength of the military. Local governments were also ordered to establish new military schools, with the purpose of attracting military talent who would work with scholars to practice military skills and discuss military theory. The emperor hoped that all the country's citizens would renew their motivation to revitalize the country with him. At the time, the scholars answered the call and trained like soldiers.

In the military, practicing archery caused a lot of headaches because they had ignored it for a long time, and there was a lack of qualified instructors. As a result, everybody had to rely on ancient anecdotes and old military books as a last resort. Unfortunately, all these materials are very problematic: you do not know the true source (as modern people will write books that pretend to be ancient texts), and they also contain a lot of errors. For this reason, I meticulously quote relevant passages from all of these books and (a) point out the reasonable parts so people can follow them, (b) modify uncertain parts so people will not misunderstand them, and (c) identify the bad parts so that people can avoid them. Meanwhile, I also added my own commentary so that I can organize the material and make it more accessible to a future audience.

馴至我太祖高皇帝 爲萬世計深遠 天下雖定 武備之嚴 歲時加㦸 射儀之制 載在會典 不啻詳矣 神京留都 俱有武學之設 列省郡縣復設射圃於學宮 址可按而數也 奈承平之久 舉天下聰明絕異之資 醉酣墨瀋 既以射爲鄙事 即業於武事 率皆以急功苟且之意 習爲蹴張之儀容 未暇研窮其精義 故語射於今日 無論文士武弁 皆不得而知矣 今皇上赫然振勵 悼文詞日益浮 武備日益弛 勅天下文學士 誦韜鈐 習騎射 使有文事者 盡有武備 而又郡縣設爲武學 羅天下奇才 劍戟之士 工騎射而精武略者 進之泮宮 咸與儒生等 是慨然欲與天下相更始也 故一時章縫之彥 跗注之儔 非不奮焉 戎務 以射爲馳神 當此射學久湮之後 莫適所從 不過因古人之遺言及昭代紀效武略諸書所載者習之耳 抑孰知 諸書所載 未必盡出古人 足爲後學之模範 其爲好事者之勦說 所謂偏執迂疏之弊 以誤成誤者不少也 愚故遍錄其文辭 以列之篇 取其論議無偏 足爲後世法者 明著其美 使之知所趨其有 膠固失宜 足爲後世蔽者 詳指其瑕 使之知所避 又有意甚美而辭未達者 明於此 而暗於彼者 舉其端而未竟其全者 則補綴其缺略 以暢其所欲言 使人得以因顯察微 由粗入奧

夫射之正法 前射學入門已詳具
之矣 此又錄諸說之利弊 而條著
之 庶幾天下後世 不為邪說所惑 而
直趨正道 故名其集為射學正宗指
迷云 雖然迷一途指矣 知而行之其
在人與 知而弗明 猶弗知也 行而
弗致 猶弗行也 知明而行致 文弱
者懦而不前 凡庸者淺而不入 勇悍
剛銳者 又粗浮而不精 一切勤始惰
終 欲速苟簡者 皆不足以語此也 精
深獨到者 惟明智沈雄之士稱焉 天
子之所向 天下精神才力之所向
也 今明天子以武備 望諸有文事
者 則天下明智沈雄之士 投袂而起
者 霧集矣 知而行之 其在斯人
與 其在斯人與

—— 崇禎丁丑仲春既望

武經射學正宗指迷集 卷一

錄 古人射法遺言 共七條

『孔子射於矍相之圃 觀者如
堵 曉以孝悌忠信之道 播以修身好
學之義 而他日又曰 用之以戰陣則
無敵 用之於臨民則順治』〈第一條
〉

The previous book, *An Orthodox Introduction to Martial Archery*, already discusses proper archery form in great detail. This current book quotes and discusses the good and bad parts of popular archery texts. I hope this text will help future readers to correct their form and avoid being misled by bad advice. That is why this volume is called *An Orthodox Guide to Martial Archery*. Although this book can point out the various kinds of confusion and errors that occur in practice, true understanding roots with the way you practice as an individual. During practice, if you only understand half of the technique, that is just as bad as having no understanding. If you practice half-heartedly, that is just as bad as not practicing at all. You need both a clear understanding of technique and the discipline to practice diligently.

Overall, knowledgeable but weak/cowardly people do not understand how to act upon what they have learned. Common people have a superficial understanding of technique. Courageous people who are rash always miss the fine details. We do not even need to mention the people who are in a rush to make progress: they start strong but eventually become lazy. Only people who are patient and wise can reach a high level.

The entire country should follow the emperor's will. The current emperor is requiring scholars to train their fighting skills to bolster the strength of the military. But all the country's talented people should join the effort as well. Ultimately, the strength of our country rests with the contributions of each individual.

— Chongzhen Era, Ding Chou Year, Second Month, Sixteenth Day (1637 CE, March 12th)

Book 2, **Chapter 1:** Last Words on the Archery Technique of the Ancients

1.1 *Purpose of Archery (Confucius)*

For the first four chapters of Book 2, Gao Ying quotes old sayings and contemporary writings about archery, and then provides his own commentary.

『 Confucius would glare at his students during their archery practice, observing whether people would flinch from protocol. He hoped that this sort of practice would make clear to people the meaning behind devotion (to the parents), respect (to older brothers), loyalty (to the rulers), and honor (among friends). At the same time, archery cultivated the mindset of discipline and studiousness. Later, Confucius also said: "The public must practice archery to improve the strength of the country's military and to establish social order and harmony." 』

Archery is a martial skill, but why did Confucius talk about "devotion, respect, loyalty, honor" as well as "discipline and studiousness"? The reason is because the Way of Archery has a rough outside and a detailed inside, as it requires the coordination of your physical strength and mental spirit. Although it looks tough and powerful, the whole process requires patience and discipline. How is this not "devotion, respect, loyalty, and honor"?

If you lose during an archery competition, you cannot blame your opponents: you must examine yourself and figure out a way to improve. The so-called "discipline and studiousness" mentality is just the same. Given the above discussion, if all the people who met these standards joined the army, you would have a strong and capable military with moral fortitude (fighting for a good cause). The country would be truly invincible. If you used archery to help govern the country, then it would cultivate peace and humility in the people so they can follow the rituals. This would establish order in the whole country. This is what Confucius meant.

Alas! If today's archers could commit themselves to the way of harmony, then they would be walking the path of "devotion" and "respect." If they could commit themselves to the way of patience and discipline, then they would be walking the path of "loyalty" and "honor." If you constantly reexamine yourself, then you will be on the path to "discipline and studiousness." If you promote the ritual standards and train the soldiers, then the country will achieve prosperity. Meanwhile, if you train yourself with all of these standards, how can people look down upon you as a simple military ruffian? They cannot!

1.2 *Virtue and the Bow Shoulder (Book of Rites)*

『The Book of Rites says you need to follow the ritual standard when you are shooting. When your inner spirit is true and your outer body is straight, then you can hold the bow and arrow with concentration and solidity. When you hold the bow and arrow with concentration and solidity, then you are truly able to hit. This is the path to virtue.』

Accuracy is important in archery, but you need to know the ritual inside and out. That way, you are able to connect your spirit with your movements. That is why during ritual archery, shooters are grouped into pairs, shoot side-by-side, and later drink the ritual wine. The reason we have all of these ritual requirements is because we want to standardize the archery process. This will allow archers to reach an optimal mental and physical state so they can focus on the target and hit it. This is why you must follow the ritual part.

射一技也 孔子以孝悌忠信 修身好學之道 悉具於 是 何也 射之道 外粗而內精 形動而神注 以剛猛勁銳之事 而雍容和平 沈毅而出之 非孝悌忠信之道乎 分曹耦射 不怨勝己 反身克治 殫慮以求之 修身好學之道 不是過也 故用此以戰陣 剛柔竝施 仁者之兵也 其誰與敵 用此以臨民 和易嚴明禮義之教也 何難順治 此孔子之意有如斯也

嗟嗟 今之工於射者 果能體雍和之道 以存心 則孝悌之行也 體沈毅之道 以踐言 則忠信之友也 推反身之道 以改過 則好修之士也 推禮義之教 以治兵臨民 則遠近悅懷 頑梗歸化矣 國家得若人焉 尚可徒以蹶張之夫目之 否

『禮記曰 射者 進退周還 必中禮 內志正外體直 然後持弓矢審固 持弓矢審固 然後可以言中 此可以觀德行矣』〈第二條〉

射期於中的而已 然必於進退周還 中禮者 以射發於心而應於手 故射必先比耦 設爲升階降階揖讓 左右周還 飲觶之體 以肅其形容 然後凝神定志 乃可言射耳 故射必先周還中禮也

射必內志正 而後持弓矢審 外

體直 而後持弓矢固 此二句射中妙
法 萬世不能易也 然觀今人 志正
而能審者有矣 體直而持弓固者絕
少 何也 以直之一字經文發之未
明 故後世知之未析 即古之以善射
名者亦未有极言所以直之道 以示
人 故後世言體直者 或以站立正直
爲直者 或以前臂番直爲直者 此皆
體直中之一事 而直之本不專在此
也 何也 站立直者 身形直耳 於持
弓矢何益 而能固乎 前臂番直者 引
弓將滿 臂力已竭 必然顫動 如何
能持弓矢牢固乎 抑孰知 直之標在
直身與番臂 直之本在前肩 不直前
肩 徒直前臂 是爲無本之直 引弓
將彀 前肩即聳 骨節不對 如何能
直 故直肩之法 後弓工妻章內 及
前捷徑門 辨惑門郊射章內言之已
詳 引弓如是 則前後肩臂并力 凝
結一片 平直如衡 方可云外體直 體
直而彀弓者 箭鏃引至弓弝中間 而
肩臂之力交至 前肩從下達上 送前
掌托出 後臂從高瀉下 徐徐發矢 目
力審定可高可下 方可云持弓矢審
固 可以言中矣 涵養若此 其人必
禪心好學 樂於禮義 和平恭敬 用
志不分者能之 故曰此可以觀德行
矣

〈此段又當與後雜錄四卷 或問
第八章同看 方得體直之全法〉

While shooting, you must make your inner spirit true (that is, it should be steady and patient) so you can concentrate on the target. You must make your body straight, and then you must hold the bow steadily. These two sentences describe the immovable pillars of archery. When you look at people today, there are people who can focus their inner spirit to attain concentration. But when it comes to keeping your outer body "straight" to achieve a solid stance, such people are few in number. Why is that? The problem: "straight" is vague description, so later generations have a hard time interpreting what it really means. The archery aces of the old days did not clearly explain the meaning of "straightness." That is why in later generations, some people think that standing with a vertical, upright posture constitutes "straightness." Some think that straightening the bow arm constitutes "straightness." These are two ways to look at it, but these do not reflect the real meaning of being "straight." Why?

People who stand upright and vertical are only making their body straight. How can this possibly benefit solid shooting? If it is the bow arm that should be straight and level from the beginning, you are only using your arm strength to draw and hold. By the time you reach full draw, your strength is exhausted and you will shake. How can shooting this way possibly be steady? Those who have a superficial understanding of "straightness" think it is in the body or arms.

In fact, the basis for "straightness" is in the bow shoulder. If your bow arm is straight but your bow shoulder is hunched up, you have achieved straightness without a foundation. Just as you reach full draw, your bow shoulder will be hunched and your joints will be misaligned. How can this be straight? With respect to the method for straightening the shoulder, "The Tale of the Bowyer's Wife" (later in this current chapter), "The Shortcut" (Book 1, Chapter 1), and "Common Mistakes" (Book 1, Chapter 2) all explain this in detail. When you pull the bow this way, the both shoulders and arms will coordinate their strength [▶ using back tension and squeezing the shoulder blades together], as if they were fused into a single unit. Only then can you say that the body is "straight." When you reach full draw (the end of the arrowhead reaching the handle is full draw), the strength of the shoulders and arms coordinate, with the bow shoulder settled low and sending the bow arm sloping up towards the bow-hand palm (which reaches out), and with the draw shoulder starting high and settling down, both gradually leading to the release. You can concentrate your vision on whatever you want to hit. This is truly a "concentrated" and "solid" way to shooting. At this point you can talk about hitting the target! If you can reach all these requirements, you will develop into a humble, studious person who can follow all the rituals with proper etiquette. People with determination can accomplish this. Hence the old saying: "through archery, you can observe a man's virtue!"

<I will repeat these points again in "Miscellaneous Questions and Answers" Question 8 (Book 2, Chapter 4.7.8). There you will see the whole discussion about the body being straight.>

『 The Book of Rites says that in the old days, the emperor used archery skill as a means for selecting rulers and officials. Archery was a manly pursuit. As such, proper etiquette and music always accompanied these archery rituals. Because of the addition of etiquette and music, these archery rituals became the premier stage for assessing a man's virtue (whether he can follow the ritual completely while practicing archery). That is why emperors and kings focused so much on archery. Talented candidates from the various fiefdoms would convene at the Imperial Court. The emperor would personally examine each candidate as they were practicing. Only those who shot according to proper etiquette, who were in sync with the music, and who were very accurate, were qualified to attend the Grand Ceremony. The archers who shot in the Grand Ceremony would receive commendations from the monarch, and in turn receive larger fiefdoms. The candidates who did not qualify for the Grand Ceremony would receive the monarch's scorn, while their fiefdoms would be reduced. That is why people say archery played a critical role in selecting rulers. As a result, rulers and officials paid a lot of attention to archery, through which they could demonstrate their obedience to the system of etiquette. Candidates who succeeded in the ritual would always go on to rule their fiefdoms successfully (none of them would be banished). 』

According to the Book of Rites: "Archery was a manly pursuit. As such, proper etiquette and music always accompanied these archery rituals. Because of the addition of etiquette and music, these archery rituals became the premier stage for assessing a man's virtue. That is why emperors and kings focused so much on archery." The ancient emperors had foresight: they intentionally mixed ritual and music with archery. This way, people who loved ritual and music could practice archery, and people who loved archery could understand ritual and music. But they might not realize that archery already has "ritual" and "music" ingrained in it. Why?

Although archery is a physical activity, the inner essence of archery is spiritual. Thus, if you shoot under extreme physical or mental duress (e.g., being too full or too hungry, too happy or too angry, too sick, too depressed, or too bored), then you will not be able to find your balance and you will not be able to shoot well. When you practice archery, you need to maintain a sense of balance and tranquility. Any unbalanced conditions will affect your form and performance. That is why in archery (as with ritual and music) you have to follow the proper procedures.

When good archers shoot, they can keep calm and control their pace. They are able to make their form steady and solid without being affected by their surroundings. They pull to full draw briskly and decisively, and they incline their torso forward so

『禮記曰 古者天子以射選諸侯
卿大夫士 射者男子之事也 因而飾
之以禮樂也 故事之盡禮樂 而可數
爲以立德行者 莫若射 故聖王務
焉 是故古者天子之制 諸侯歲獻貢
士於天子 天子試之于射宮 其容體
比於禮 其節比於樂 而中多者得與
於祭 其容體不比於禮 其節不比於
樂而中少者 不得與於祭 數與於祭
而君有慶 數不與於祭而君有讓 數
有慶而益地 數有讓而削地 故曰 射
者 射爲諸侯也 是以諸侯君臣盡志
於射 以習禮樂 夫君臣習禮樂而以
流亡者未之有也』〈第三條〉

按禮記以射爲男子之事 故飾之
以禮樂 使後世知事之盡禮樂 可以
數爲以立德行者 莫如射 故聖王務
焉 嗚呼 是先王以射教天下 爲後
世計深遠也 但以飾之一字繹之 得
無以射中本無禮樂 特以禮樂飾
之 使後之好禮樂者 不得不因禮樂
而習射 使習射者 不得不因射而知
禮樂矣 抑孰知 射中原自有禮樂 何
待飾之始有禮樂乎 何以明其然
也 射雖以形用 其實以神運也 故
飢飽失中者不能射 喜怒失中者不
能射 凡疾痛疴癢抑鬱無聊之事 感
于外而動于心者 亦不能射 何也 射
固有中和之道也 心神一動 形體乖
違 中正和平之度失耳 由此觀之 射
之中果原有禮樂乎 果無禮樂乎 抑
待飾之而禮樂始見乎 其故可思矣

they can hold full draw steadily and carefully. From a relaxed state, they release crisply, clearly, and decisively. There is an underlying sequence and rhythm to this kind of shooting, much like ritual and music have a sequence and rhythm.

Later generations have a crude understanding of "ritual" and "music." That is why they cannot reach this kind of level. The ancient sages compared archery to ritual and music because they saw archery's deeper meaning. When all the rulers and officials follow the ritual and music while they are shooting, not only can they understand the deeper meaning of the ritual and music, but they can also understand the deeper meaning of archery. You can see the underlying "ritual and music" in archers who can reach a high level. Those who treat archery as a rote exercise will never be able to figure it out.

> The archery ritual (射禮) has a very long history in China dating back to the Zhou Dynasty (1046–256 BCE). This was a ritual where archers would pair off and compete, while shooting according to the prescribed etiquette and music. The customs of the ritual would have a strong influence on East Asian archery.

1.4 Draw Sequence (Tale of the Bowyer's Wife)

『 The bowyer's wife told the King of Chu: when shooting, the bow hand is like repelling a person [▶ when pushing the handle], and the draw hand is like handling a twig [▶ holding the string in a relaxed manner]. The draw hand releases and the bow hand does not react. 』

"The bow hand is like repelling a person, the draw hand is like handling a twig" is talking about the method for drawing the bow. "Handling a twig" means the holding the string in a relaxed manner, so that the draw hand does not push too hard against the arrow, or push too hard against the string. When your bow hand is pushing the bow handle and your draw hand is holding the string in a relaxed way, you will reach full draw.

"The draw hand releases and the bow hand does not react" is referring to the method for releasing. When you release after full draw, the draw hand will move backwards lightly, clearly, and without hesitation. The draw hand releases lightly, and the bow hand holds the handle steadily without intentionally forcing the post-release bow movement. That is what they mean by "the bow hand does not react."

When you draw and release the bow this way, it looks appropriate. But if you practice that way for a long time, you will develop the issue of failing to reach full

是以精于射者 彎弓對的必先并
氣以固形 安心以全神 得失不棲于
情 喧雜不留于意 其引弓也 捷疾
果銳以彀之 欽躬敬慎以持之 雍容
和平婉以出也 而又輕鬆脆裂 迅以
節之 其此芑庇佮 心宜中節之巧 何
者非禮樂之精意 豈若後世之禮
樂 僅僅飾之聲容末節之粗哉 古聖
王以之比禮比樂 良有深意 而諸候
君臣盡志于射 以習禮樂者 是不特
得禮樂之精意 抑亦得到射中之精
意者矣 故得射中之精意者 手舞足
蹈 無之非禮 無之非樂矣 彼以射
求射者 烏足以語也

『弓工妻之對楚王有言 前手如
拒 後手如附枝 後手發之 前手不
知』〈第四條〉

前手如拒 後手如附枝 此言引
弓法 附枝者 輕鬆依附之謂 言後
手引弓不逼弦 不逼矢 前手推定弓
弝 後手輕引而彀也 後手發之 前
手不知 此言發矢法 後手引弓既
彀 輕輕瀉脫 不可一毫凝滯 發矢
既輕 前手托定全然不動 故曰前手
不知
如此引弓發矢 雖見安安 然恐
坐不彀之病 何也 大抵引弓之力在
臂 彀弓之力在肩 分開之力在拳 善
射者 將欲引弓 必先以前臂番直向
地 前肩向前下捲〈捲即番也〉 極其

draw. Why? Overall, the key to drawing the bow is in the arm muscles, and the key to holding full draw is in the shoulder muscles [▶ using both shoulder blade and back strength]. The key to opening the bow from two sides [▶ one being the handle, the other being the string's point of contact with the thumb ring] is making sure the two fists coordinate.

At pre-draw, if you are a good archer you know how to extend the bow arm downward, and how to get the bow shoulder to rotate and settle down <please see previous chapters>. Your draw shoulder hunches and coordinates with the settled bow shoulder to act as one unit.

At this moment, the draw hand nocks the arrow and holds the string. Then, the draw elbow lifts backwards to initiate the draw. The bow shoulder is locked down and does not move, and only the bow fist lifts up to the level of the eyebrow. At the same time, the draw hand pulls the string back until the hand is near the ear. The tendency is for the bow shoulder to be lower than the draw shoulder, and the two arms are level. Use your shoulders to drive the arms, and use your arms to drive the fists. When you hold full draw this way, the strength originates from your shoulders, and you are able to divide the force between the two fists and arms. That is why you are able to lift the draw hand backwards to reach full draw.

In the end, when you divide the force evenly and release lightly, then you will achieve the so called "draw hand releases and the bow hand does not react."

Suppose you only use the strength of your two arms to open the bow and you fail to use the strength from your shoulder blades. Although you want to have your draw hand pull the string in a relaxed manner, your draw hand will be unsteady because you are using arm strength and you will be limited by the strength of the bow. How can you pull to full draw in a relaxed manner? If you fail to reach full draw yet still want to release "lightly," then even if you force yourself to achieve "the bow hand does not react," then the arrow will not fly efficiently. How can you shoot far? Thus, only when you combine my method of settling down the bow shoulder and the bowyer's wife's light release method are you practicing the ancient method in the correct way.

<Please see The Shortcut (Book 1, Chapter 1) for the method on reaching full draw. You should also compare this section with Book 2, Chapter 4.7, "Miscellaneous Questions and Answers" so that you can fully understand how to reach full draw.>

堅實 後肩聳起 與前肩迫力 凝結
一片 後手搭箭掛弦 後肘向上提緊
開弓 前肩向下捲實不動 只將前拳
殽<音窵>起與眉齊 後拳平引與耳
齊 前肩之勢反低 後肩之勢反高 兩
臂平直如衡 以肩使臂 以臂使拳 如
此引弓則周身之力盡爲兩肩 分達
于拳臂之間 後手一提便殽<前臂番
直向地 後手搭箭扣弦 後肘向天一
提 前掌托實弓心 兩臂一齊迫力撐
開 豈非一提便殽乎> 前後拳臂分
勻輕脫 方可謂後手發之前手不知

不然只用兩臂之力開弓 不知用
肩 縱然後手如附枝之易輕 恐後手
之力有限 輕輕引來如何能殽 後手
既不能殽 而又輕鬆發矢 欲使前手
不知 矢發必無氣 如何能及遠 故
弓工妻之言 當善用之 用其輕鬆之
法以發矢 用予實肩之法以殽弓 則
古法誠爲我用

<殽弓法詳于捷徑門 此段又當
與四卷或人問合看 方得殽弓法>

『烈女傳曰 怒氣開弓 息氣放
箭 蓋怒氣開弓 則力雄而引滿 息
氣放箭 則心定而慮周』〈第五條〉

怒氣開弓者 則力雄而引弓易
滿 息氣放箭者 則心定慮周 發易
中的 此法極是 然今人多不能 怒
氣開弓者 一彀隨脫 不能少留而息
氣凝定者何 其病皆在用臂而不能
用肩耳 夫臂之力小而肩之力厚 只
用臂力開弓者 怒氣引弓一滿 臂力
骨節已盡 必然急脫 又焉能息氣放
箭 凝定周詳於怒氣振蕩之後哉

故善射之法 將欲引弓 必先將
前肩下捲 前後肩臂骨節 凝結一
片 而後怒氣開弓 將彀之時 臂力
已竭 肩力繼之 力量有餘 自能息
氣放箭而收心定慮周之功 中的始
穩

〈用肩法 詳于四卷內或問十發
中 宜合看〉

『紀昌師非衛 先學不瞬 次學
視 視小如大 視微如著 以髮懸虱
於牖 三年如車輪 射以朔蓬之幹 貫
虱之心』〈第六條〉

1.5 *Timing of the Draw* (Biographies of Eminent Women)

『*Biographies of Eminent Women* (烈女傳) says that while shooting, you should draw the bow briskly with anger, and you should release the string with tranquility. When you draw the bow with anger, you muster all your strength to reach full draw quickly. When you release the string with tranquility, your heart is settled and you can think [▶ and aim] carefully. 』

Drawing the bow in a state of anger [▶ i.e., reaching full draw briskly] allows you to use full power and reach full draw without hesitation. Releasing with tranquility allows you to be calm and settled, and your accuracy will be stable. This is the right way. But a lot of people these days are unable to grasp the concept.

A lot of people can pull the bow with anger, but they are unable to release the arrow with tranquility. After reaching full draw, they are unable to hold and aim. Why? Because they do not know how to use their shoulder and back muscles to support the full draw. Arm strength is weak. Shoulder and back strength is very strong. If you only use your arms, then if you pull to full draw with anger your arm strength will already be exhausted, and your release will be very hurried. How can you "release with tranquility" after "drawing the bow with anger" this way?

Here is the right method. Before drawing the bow, first settle down the bow shoulder. Make sure the bones and joints of the bow-side/draw-side shoulders and arms become a single unit, then you can start to draw with anger. By the time you reach full draw, your arm strength is already exhausted and your back and shoulders take over to hold full draw. This way you will have enough strength in reserve to hold full draw steadily, and naturally you will be able to "release the arrow with tranquility" and your accuracy will be consistent. <Detailed discussion about the method for using the shoulders is in Book 2, Chapter 4.7, "Miscellaneous Questions and Answers.">

1.6 *Training Vision (Ji Chang Piercing the Heart of a Louse)*

『Ji Chang learned archery from Fei Wei. Fei Wei told him to first learn not to blink, and then learn how to focus his vision on small objects. Fei Wei tied a louse to a hair, hung it on the window, and asked Ji Chang to focus on it for three years. After three years, the louse looked as big as a wheel. Then Ji Chang shot an arrow and penetrated the heart of the louse. 』

To "first learn not to blink" is talking about how to train your vision. A human's spirit is concentrated in the eyes, and the whole body's strength and willpower will direct themselves to where the eyes are focusing. That is why training your vision is the first step. If you can estimate and see the target clearly, then you can achieve accuracy. If you can achieve a high level of concentration, then you can "penetrate the heart of the louse." Actually, this story is a tall tale, but the lesson it conveys is correct.

Nowadays, the moment a beginner grabs a bow he wants to shoot outdoors, only using brute force to pull the bow and not using his joints [▶ and shoulder/back strength] to hold full draw. Like this, the chest will stick out and the head will be vertical. His bow fist will block his vision. He will practice for many years without actually seeing the target. For people who keep their head vertical, the arrow is to the right of the bow [▶ for a right-handed archer], but they are looking past the left side of the bow. They cannot really see the arrowhead. In the end, they are just shooting blind.

[▶ In this section, Gao Ying is talking about shooting long distances. When shooting far away, looking over the left edge of the bow does not allow you to look along the arrow shaft, to the arrowhead, through to the target. It will be hard to estimate distance.]

Here is the proper method for training your vision as a beginner. The torso should be inclined forward, your belly should tuck in, your two legs should be straight, and your head should be tilted sideways [▶ keeping your neck relaxed to naturally match the incline of your torso], and the top tip of the bow should be slightly canted [▶ rotated clockwise for a right-handed archer]. When you are about to reach full draw, your joints are already aligned [▶ the back and shoulder muscles get involved], and the arrowhead has already reached the outside of the handle. Use your peripheral vision to look along the arrow shaft, to the arrowhead, through to the target. Aiming like this will give you a visceral sense of where the arrow will go, so your accuracy will be consistent. Your arrows will go wherever your eyes are looking, and this is the right way to train your vision.

These days, people learning archery know they need to work on their vision, but their accuracy is not very good. Why is that? Although most people can estimate the target carefully before full draw, they will be in a hurry to release once they reach full draw. Thus, training your vision requires you to focus on the target from before you draw until after you reach full draw. Only then can your arrow follow your vision.

<Please read this section in conjunction with "The Shortcut: Focus" (Book 1, Chapter 1.1).>

先學不瞬　此練目之法也　人之精神皆萃於目　目之所注　一身之筋力精氣俱赴矣　故射以練目爲先焉　審視既明　發矢自準　神馳意到　虱心可貫　不必有其事　而有其理也　今初習射者　弓一接見　便往郊射　不藉力於骨節　惟憑筋力引弓　胸突頭仰　目光爲前拳所障　習射數年　兩目未曾見的　即欲審視　頭仰之人　箭在弓右　視在弓左　目終不能見鏃　故曰　終身習射只爲瞎射　烏何中的

練目之法　在初學時　胸欲欽　腹欲脡　足欲直　頭欲向前側視　弓稍欲斜　引弓將彀　骨節已平直　鏃至弓弝中間　以目稍自箭桿至鏃　以達於的　視之了然　發矢可準　東西遠近毫髮不爽　目注于此　矢亦至於此　方爲練目之法

今人習射　亦知練目矣　然卒不能中微破的者　只因初引弓時　目雖能審　既彀將發　心手俱忙　倉皇撒放　何以中微　故練目之道　自初引弓時　目固審視　發矢時尤宜加審　目到意到手到　發矢如意　方可收練目之功

〈此段當與前捷徑門注字篇合看〉

1.7 *Training Courage (Bohun Maoren on the Edge of a Cliff)*

『伯昏瞀人立於巉巖峭壁 萬仞
之巔 背不測之淵 足垂二分 射百
發而百中』〈第七條〉

此練膽之法也 今人習射 平時
或可中的 一當角射分曹 則得失介
懷而不中 或臨戰鬥 死傷在前 則
目眩心駭而益不中 此無他 不練之
故也 人之智慮以練而深 筋骸以練
而固 況射之功力 中微於百步之外
者 而可不練乎 練目 練掌 練臂 練
肩 練身 練足 一身之中 無所不
練 而膽為先 何也 膽者心之衛
也 膽不足則心懾 一臨利害 則耳
目手足俱非我有 尚可挽強命中
乎 此習射者 學法既成之後 必須
練膽 練膽之道莫如臨敵 然戰不可
得而試 於何而練之 北方之人 地
勢高阜 無川澤溝池之限 山陵糾
紛 草木翳薈之所 練之以射獵 騰
山超谷 搏兔伐狐 擊猛獸如田兔 何
有于即戎乎 南方之人 見丘陵城
塹 則登高履深 練而習之 熟習之
久 高下在心 發矢如意 臨變倉
猝 自有定衡 而命中可機矣
〈練掌練臂諸法 詳于辨惑門妄
射藁砧章第三 宜合看〉

『Bohun Maoren [▶ a famous Daoist teacher] stood near the edge of a cliff to shoot, with his back facing towards the canyon below. Each time he shot, he took a step closer to the cliff until part of his feet were hanging over the edge. He could still hit every time.』

This is a method for training your courage. Nowadays, people might be able to have accuracy during normal practice. But when they reach the examination field or the battlefield, they might miss the target because they are thinking about winning and losing, or life and death. This happens because they lack practice. You can train your thoughts and wisdom to be deep, and you can train your body and muscles to be solid and powerful. Furthermore, archery requires you to penetrate a small target from 100 paces away, so you need even more training to achieve this. You need to practice your vision, your hand techniques, your shoulders and arms, and your body posture. You need to practice every detail of your body.

And training your courage is the most important of all. Why? Because courage helps gives you stability when you face critical situations. How can an archer without courage achieve accuracy in a crucial moment? Thus, archers who finish learning proper form must then spend a lot of effort training their courage.

By far the best way to train your courage is in the battlefield. But wars do not occur that frequently, so you need to find another way. In the North, there is high-altitude terrain with thick forests and a few rivers and lakes. Here, you can use hunting to train your courage. Stalking in the forests and mountains to hunt large beasts without hesitation will definitely help you increase your courage. In the South, there is hilly terrain. Here, you can practice shooting uphill and downhill so that you can familiarize yourself with how to adjust your aim. Then, when you face these situations in the battlefield, you can easily handle them.

<A detailed discussion of the method for training your hands, arms, and so on is in "Common Mistakes: Shooting Carelessly at the Gaozhen (Straw Bale)" (Book 1, Chapter 2.3).>

2.1 *Choosing Draw Weight and Arrow Mass*

『Choose the bow according to your strength, choose the arrow according to the bow.』

Build the bow with a draw weight according to the archer's strength, and build the arrow with a mass according to the draw weight of the bow. This point is pretty obvious and difficult to dispute. However, to choose a bow to fit the archer, and to choose an arrow to fit the bow, there is a prescribed method for choosing how heavy or light they should be. For those who want to find a good draw weight for the bow, they have to determine the strength of their arms. If you can stick your arm straight and level while holding a stone weighing 10 jin (13 pounds), then you can use a bow with a draw weight of 20 jin (26 pounds). If you can hold a 20-jin (26 pound) stone, then you can use a bow with a draw weight of 40 jin (52 pounds). The more you can lift, the heavier the bow you can use. To determine the mass of the arrow, you have to know the draw weight of the bow. For every 10 jin of draw weight, the arrow should weigh 1 qian and 2 fen. As the draw weight of the bow increases, you can use this ratio to calculate the mass of the appropriate arrow. Therefore, when you match the bow with the archer and match the arrow with the bow, you will have full control of how far you shoot the arrow.

<Book 1, Chapter 3.1 is a section called "Choosing the Strength of the Bow" (part of "Choosing Equipment"), which also talks about the method for finding a suitable bow. You should take a close look.>

In the Ming dynasty, 1 jin (catty) = 16 liang, 1 liang (tael) = 10 qian, 1 qian (mace) = 10 fen (candareens). Thus, 1 qian and 2 fen = 0.12 liang = (0.12 / 16) jin = (0.12/16) × 1.3 pounds = (0.12/16) × 1.3 × 7,000 grains = 68.25 grains. Since 10 jin is 13 pounds, then when you convert the suggested ratio to the modern standard of grains-per-pound (gpp), you get a recommended arrow mass to bow weight ratio of 5.25 gpp. You should check with your bow maker to see if it is safe to use such a light arrow with your bow.

武經射學正宗指迷集 卷二

錄《紀效新書》射法 共十九段

『量力調弓 因弓制矢』〈第一段〉

因人力之強弱以制弓 因弓力之軟勁以制矢 此法極當 無容議矣 但以弓稱人 以矢稱弓 其輕重俱有定法 大抵欲定弓之軟勁者 須量臂力 直臂能平舉石十斤者 弓宜用勁二十斤 舉石二十斤者 弓宜用勁四十斤 以外舉石多者 弓依例加之 欲定矢之重輕者 須量弓力 每勁十斤者 用矢一錢二分 自此以上 弓力勁者 每以例加之 則人弓相配 弓矢相調 發矢大小有定衡矣

〈稱弓法詳于擇物門弓力強弱篇 宜合看〉

『凡打袖皆因把持不定』〈第二段〉

打袖之弊 非止一端 而紀效書
云把持不定 非也 打袖者或縶袖未
妥而然 或因前掌突出弓弣之右而
然 或因前掌不實 發矢時撐開無勢
〈前掌指掌根而言 非掌心也 對小
指之掌爲掌根 對中指之掌爲掌
心 掌心實則虎口太仰 矢出插天而
大 矢不能平疾 惟掌根實 則虎口
不甚緊 亦不太仰 故發矢平疾而遠
到矣〉弦隨臂括出亦然 又或引弓
時 前肩太突 前拳未能觥（音窹）
出亦打袖 弓弣太小 手汗多而滑 持
弓發矢無勢 亦不免于打袖 打袖之
病無常 而大略總不出此 欲免是病
者 發矢須帶撇勢 前臂觥起 掌勁
硬直推出 而後以肩力從下達上送
前掌 直叉而出 決無括臂打袖之
因 若概以把持不定論之 何以曉後
學乎

『 The bow string hits the sleeve of your bow arm because you are not holding the bow steadily. 』

There are many reasons why the bow string would slap your bow arm. The *New Book on Discipline and Effectiveness* excerpt blames it on failing to hold the bow handle steadily. But this is not the only explanation. One reason is that the front sleeve is loose because the archer fails to bind it properly. Another reason is that the bow hand's palm rests past the right edge of the bow handle [▶ which happens because handle is settled deeply in the left side of the web of the bow hand, causing the forearm to rest in the way of the string]. Another reason is that the bow-hand palm is not gripping appropriately [▶ see Gao's footnote below], so the release will lack a foundation, and the string will move erratically towards the arm. Yet another reason is that the bow shoulder is sticking up, so the bow hand does not have clearance, which exposes your bow arm to being slapped by the string. Other (more rare) causes: the bow handle being too small, a sweaty hand causing the handle to slip, and anything else that causes the release to be unsteady. If you want to remedy these problems, first you have to allow the bow to move naturally after the release [▶ due to having a sufficiently relaxed grip, so as not to interfere with the action of the bow/arrow]. The bow arm should rise with the bow-hand palm pushing out firmly. The shoulder is settled down and will send the arm sloping upwards to the bow-hand palm, which is reaching towards the target. This avoids the problem exposing your bow arm to slapping. Putting the blame squarely on "holding the handle unsteadily" is misleading because there are multiple causes involving various aspects of your technique that you have to examine carefully.

Gao's footnote: I want to provide a quick word about bow hand technique, which involves using the fingers and root of the palm, rather than the heart of the palm. The part of the palm underneath the pinky is the root, and the part of the palm underneath the middle finger is the heart. If the heart of the palm is gripping, then the web of the hand is tilted too vertically [▶ in modern terms, this is a low-wrist grip], so the arrow cannot fly level because it veers upwards as it exits the bow. Now if the root of the palm is solid, then the web of the palm will not be too tight and will not be too vertical [▶ this describes a straight-wrist or medium grip]. For this reason, the arrow will fly level and far.

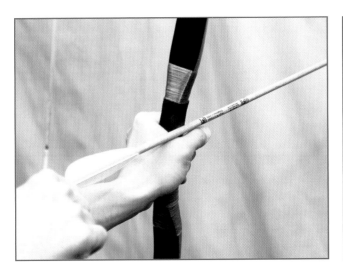

Left: the error of letting the bow hand palm rest too much past the right edge of the handle (for a right-handed archer). Notice the angle of the wrist is far to the left. **Right:** proper angle of the bow hand wrist.
Courtesy of Glenn Murray, Esq.

2.3 *Posture and Draw Sequence*

『Holding the bow and arrow should emphasize concentration/estimation and solidity. "Concentration/estimation" means devoting your fullest attention to estimate the target. "Solidity" means holding the bow firmly.』

What *New Book on Discipline and Effectiveness* means by "concentration/estimation" is to focus intensely on the target: that is, having archer's vision. In "The Shortcut" (Book 1, Chapter 1.1), I already discussed "estimation" in detail, so I will not repeat it here. What *New Book* means by "solidity" is to hold the bow firmly. But a firm grip on the bow does not fully explain what "solidity" means. Basically, "solidity" refers to the body's position. While drawing the bow and releasing the arrow, the hands, arms, shoulders, legs, chest, belly, waist, and back have to be settled. This way, the body and arms will be aligned properly, again using the right form. Only then can you say things are "solid."

Regarding the body, the head should be tilted sideways, the chest should inclined forward, the belly should tuck in, the legs should be straight, and the feet should be in an open stance (不丁不八). This posture is solid as an anvil. Why is that? When you tilt the head sideways [▶ to match the incline of your torso], you avoid the fault where the head is floating and could drop unexpectedly. When you incline the chest, you avoid the fault where the back is vertical and the front of the chest is sticking out [▶ this is the fault where the shoulders overextend themselves, and your center of gravity causes you to lean backwards]. When you tuck in the belly, you avoid the fault where the butt sticks

『持弓矢審固　審者詳審　固者把持堅固也』〈第三段〉

按紀效書講審字義　曰詳審　是專用目力也　前捷徑門審法已詳具之　此不復論　講固字義曰　把持堅固　殊欠明暢　愚謂固者　指全體而言　凡引弓發矢　須全體之間　拳臂肩足胸腹腰背　無不安妥　則身法手法皆中乎節　方可言固

以身法言之　頭欲斜側向的　胸欲欽　腹欲脡　足欲直　步欲不丁不八　立站穩便　此身法也　所以然者何也　頭側則無卻垂之病　胸欽則無背仰前突之病　腹脡則無露臀之病　足直則無蹲倒之病　站立穩便則無竝足體浮之病　諸病俱消而身法始固

以手法言之　前拳掌根欲托實　前

臂肘節欲番直〈番直向地為直〉前
肩下捲 後肩反聳 兩拳欲平對 引
弓彀時 前後肩臂須平直如衡 此手
法也〈平直如衡詳俱見五卷體式圖
〉所以然者何也 前掌根實則虎口
下緊 前臂伸則臂直 前肩下則肩
實 後肩聳則前後高而中低 前肩愈
實 兩拳相對 則出矢平 彀極時 前
後肩臂平而肘垂則後拳脫弦得勢 諸
法畢集則手法始固 身法手法俱
固 彀時方能堅持不動 以目審定
的 必發矢始準 若只以把持堅固四
字 講固字之義 後學如何能解 然
此特論持弓之大略耳 若對的發矢
時 忽偏左 忽偏右 忽大 忽小 隨
時變態百出 非口授不能盡也

out [▶ with the butt sticking out, the upper body will be disconnected with the lower body]. When you straighten the legs, you avoid the fault of having a wobbly stance. If you stand steadily in an open stance, you avoid the fault where the legs and body are floating. [▶ In the expression 不丁不八, the 丁 represents the feet being placed in a 'T' position with the front foot pointing towards the target, and the 八 represents the feet roughly parallel to each other thus the open stance 不丁不八 is somewhere in between.] When these faults are gone, then the whole body can start being "solid."

Regarding the arm and hand techniques at pre-draw, the root of the palm should hold firmly, the bow arm and elbow should be rotated and straight (you can start by pointing the bow arm towards the ground), the bow shoulder is rotated and settled down [▶ clockwise for a right-handed archer, counter-clockwise for a left-handed archer], the draw shoulder should be hunched up (to mitigate the tendency for the bow shoulder to hunch up), and the two fists should move away from each other evenly. At full draw, the bow-side/draw-side shoulders and bow-side/draw-side arms should be aligned properly. This is the ideal arm and hand technique. <See the illustrations in Book 2, Chapter 5.> So why is that? When you hold the root of the palm firmly, the web of the hand will not be tense. When you have extended the bow arm, it will be straight. When you have rotated the bow shoulder, the shoulder blade will be firmly settled all the way down. When you hunch the draw shoulder, there will be a triangle formed between your bow hand, bow shoulder, and draw shoulder (with the bow shoulder being the lowest point of the triangle).

With the bow shoulder pressed down firmly, the two fists can coordinate evenly in a push-pull motion, which will ensure the arrow flies flat. When you are at full draw and about to release, the bow-side and draw-side shoulders are properly aligned, and upon release the elbow drops down-and-back to allow the draw hand to escape backwards from the string cleanly. When these techniques are done correctly, the arm and hand technique will begin to be solid. When the body and arms are solid, you will be able to achieve full draw without shaking. Then you will be able to use your eyes to aim at the target steadily so that you can become more accurate.

If you only tell people to "grip the bow firmly" like in *New Book on Discipline and Effectiveness,* you will only mislead people. I have only talked about the general guidelines for shooting. If you encounter specific problems like your arrows veering left, right, high, or low, then there are too many potential causes. I have to teach you in person.

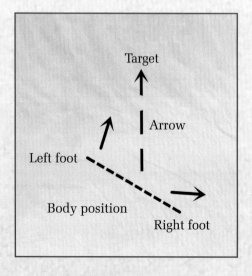

A diagram of foot and body position with respect to the direction of the target (for a right-handed archer). The exact angle depends on individual comfort and will vary from person to person. *Courtesy of Glenn Murray, Esq.*

2.4 *Wobbly Arrow Flight*

『If the arrow wobbles or flies slowly, it is always because the arrowhead is not touching the bow hand finger.』

When the arrowhead does not touch the bow hand finger, it is because you are not reaching full draw. As a result the arrow flies slowly and cannot reach far.

As for the arrow wobbling, there is more than one explanation: the arrow could be bent; some of the fletchings could be damaged or missing; the string could be hitting the sleeve, which disrupts the arrow's flight; the draw hand could be holding the string too tightly which results in a tense release; or your draw hand is pressing too hard on the nock end of the arrow. If you only think the arrow wobbles because you fail to reach full draw (with the end of the arrowhead touching the bow hand finger), that is wrong.

『凡矢搖而弱　皆因鏃不上指也』〈第四段〉

夫鏃不上指者　只因引弓不彀　發矢弱而不能及遠耳　若矢搖者　不止一端　或矢曲　或箭翎缺半邊　或因括袖激動箭鋒　或因後手羈弦太緊　發矢不鬆　逼箭之故　若概謂鏃不上指　則非矣

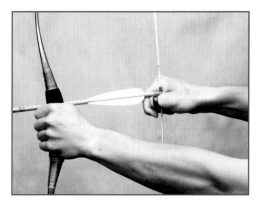 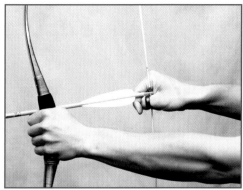

Left: hooking the index finger too deeply makes the draw hand crowd the arrow nock and will interfere with the cleanliness of the release. Right: using only the tip or distal joint of the index finger to cover the thumbnail is better for a clean release.
Courtesy of Glenn Murray, Esq.

2.5 *Estimating the Target and Remaining Calm*

『You should estimate/aim at the target when you are at full draw and about to release. Nowadays, people start aiming when they are past half draw, but what good is that? Instead you should concentrate/estimate most intensely at the moment you are about to release. Then, your mind can be clear and relaxed, and your arms and legs can be solid. When you can release, your arrows will fly straight and hit the target.』

『審者　審於弓滿發矢之際　今人多於大半矢之時審之　何益　必將滿臨發之際　尤加意于審　使精神和易　而手足安固　然後發矢必直而中的矣』〈第五段〉

審于臨發之際 直而可中的 此
審之善法 無容議矣〈審法詳於捷
徑門 茲不具〉若謂精神和易手足
安固亦由於審 則非矣 審者 以目
用事 僅可知矢之遠近大小而已 至
其形神實固 實固穀弓得法 乎之骨
節直 足之站立穩 腹挺胸欽所致 安
得謂神和形固 亦由于審乎

『射法中審字與大學中慮而後
能得之慮字同 君子於引滿之餘 發
矢之際 尤加審 而後中的可決 能
知審字工夫合于慮字工夫 玩之乃
得』〈第六段〉

大學慮字之義 戚南塘比之審字
同 以爲君子能慮而後能得所止 猶
射者能審而後中的可決 此說甚
美 施之用則疎 何也 大學慮字與
得字 義皆在心上做工夫 故慮而後
即能得 若射者審在目 托力在手者
也 目雖能審 毫髮不爽 若肩臂骨
節未直 主持不固 如何即能中的 故
審特射中之一事 安得謂能審者即
能中的乎 故曰 其說甚美 施其用
則疎

故習射者 手中射法無不備具 發
矢時 尤加詳審明察 方可中的 戚
公之言 蓋指射法熟習者云 然今人
不知習法 而專致力於審 必至敗
迴 何也 目力能審 錙銖不差 手不
合法 矢發必不準 以必不準發矢 將
發之際 合必準之目力 則未發之
時 矢鏃雖能對的 矢發出時 必不

Estimating and aiming before release is a good method, without a doubt. "The Shortcut" (Chapter 1.1) already talks about "estimation," so I will not repeat it here. However, *New Book* claiming that "your mind can be clear and relaxed, and your arms and legs can be solid" because of estimating the target is wrong. Estimation and aiming is only about using your eyes to judge the trajectory and landing point of the arrow. Having a calm mind and solid arms and legs depends entirely on having proper form, which allows you to hold full draw. You ensure that your joints are properly aligned, you stand stably, your belly is tucked in, and your torso is inclined forward. Only then you can you have a steady posture, which in turn allows you to take your time to aim at the target.

2.6 *Estimation and Deliberation (General Qi's Allusion to Confucius)*

『The term "estimation" in archery form is the same as "deliberation" in Confucius's *Great Learning* (大學). When gentlemen reach full draw and are about to release, they need to pay extra attention to estimation, which will allow them to hit the target. You have to think about the connection between "estimation" and "deliberation" to understand. 』

Qi Jiguang compares his concept of "estimation" with the gentleman's "deliberation" in *Great Learning*. Just like a gentleman has to deliberate carefully to achieve his goals, an archer needs to estimate and concentrate to achieve his goal of hitting the target. Although this expression is very pretty, it is hardly of any use. Why? *Great Learning* talks about how careful deliberation leads to resoluteness, both of which are in the mind. That is why careful deliberation can lead to achieving your goals. As for archery, estimation is in the eye, but pulling the bow and holding full draw is in the hands. Even if you can see the target clearly, if the joints of the shoulders and arms are even slightly misaligned, then you will not be able to support the bow steadily. How can you hit the target? Estimation is only one component of the shooting process: how can you say that estimation alone guarantees a hit? That is why I say Qi's expression is pretty, but hardly of any use.

Thus, good archers have to fully train their form. Then when they release, they can pay extra attention to aiming at the target clearly. Only then can they hit. However, I believe General Qi's words only apply to experienced archers. But people these days do not know how to practice properly, so they devote themselves to working on their estimation and aiming, only to achieve poor results. Why? Although you might be able to achieve unwavering concentration with your eyes, if your hands do not have the proper technique then your release will definitely be unsteady. As for the release being unsteady, you might have the proper focus with your eyes when you are just about to release. But before you to release, although the arrowhead might be pointing at the target, once the arrow starts flying, it definitely will not fly in the right direction. Your shooting will be very poor. For subpar archers, this is their most common mistake yet they do not realize it. That is why I write about this problem here to help resolve the confusion.

2.7 *Bow Hand Grip*

『The thumb should press the middle finger when holding the bow. This is the most ingenious of the old methods. You must absolutely use this method for holding the bow.』

The "thumb pressing the middle finger" refers to the Eagle Claw. For gripping the bow, you have to consider the bow's draw weight. You do not always have to use the Eagle Claw. Why? Light bows have little force, so the arrow will not fly far. In this case you want to use the Eagle Claw. Heavy bows have a lot of force, so the arrow should fly far. But in this case we are worried the arrow will fly too far and pass the target. That is why you want to use a Full Grip to hold the bow. If you use the Eagle Claw with a heavy bow, the arrow will fly too high and far, and it will be very difficult to be accurate. There is no single grip that works for every situation.

<I also talk about the method for gripping the bow in the middle of the discussion about "Hu" and "Han" style shooting (which can be found in Book 2, Chapter 3.1). I will not repeat the description here.>

2.8 *Why Advising Beginners to Overshoot Is Wrong*

『It is better to have the arrow pass high over the target than to have it fall short of the target.』

This statement is not entirely correct. In fact, it can be detrimental. Good archers have mastered every detail of their form, therefore they can hold their bows solidly and stand steadily. They take their time to estimate and aim at the target clearly, then they release. Their aim becomes one with their vision: even though they have not released, they are certain to hit the mark. They might miss in the first few shots, but they can adjust the following shots and hit. Again, why would you bother shooting high on purpose?

對的矣 此敗廻之大弊 拙射犯此弊者最多 而人莫之察也 故書之以示 明者見之 當爲解頤

『大指壓中指把弓 此至妙之古法也 決不可不從之而更從他法』〈第七段〉

大指壓中指 此鷹爪把弓之說也 大抵把弓 須看弓力軟勁 不必專用鷹爪 何也 軟弓力小 矢不能及遠 則用鷹爪把弓 勁弓力大 矢發必遠 恐太遠而益過的端 故必用滿把持弓 若弓勁而亦鷹爪 則矢插天而大 必難中的 豈至妙之法哉
〈持弓法詳于指迷集三卷 錄胡射漢射論中 茲不載〉

『凡發矢 寧高而過的 慎勿低而不及也』〈第八段〉

此說雖是 而未盡善也 夫善射者 百法閑習 持弓則固 步立則穩 審視詳明 然後發矢 大小左右了然在目 有不發 發必中的 即始發者 未必中的 而繼發者 自能斟酌得宜 又何必寧大無小乎
若射法習之未精 大小皆不能自

115

主 過低者固不中的 過高者又豈能
中節哉
　　戚公之論 特就初習射者云 然
非射家之正法

When your form is not mature, of course you will not be able to control the flight of your arrow. A shot that falls short certainly will not hit. But a shot that is too high will not hit either!

General Qi's advice is appropriate for novice archers, but this is not the right way to train in archery.

[▶ On the battlefield, you might only be able to see the front line of the enemy. For beginners, it is better to shoot high (instead of low) because it gives them a chance to hit the enemies behind the front line. The target audience for Qi Jiguang's training method is common soldiers, not elite officers.]

2.9 *Shooting Anxiety (Part 1)*

『 When shooting on the examination range, as a matter of duty you must be afraid to miss, and you cannot relax your willpower even in the slightest. Shooting in front of officials will be the same as your day-to-day practice: shoot slowly and gradually, make sure the back of the arrowhead reaches your bow hand finger before release. How can you miss? 』

『凡場中較射 要須業業恐不
中 決不可有一毫自放之意 都如無
監射官在上 與平日自射一般 慢慢
枝枝 知鏃過指 如何不中』〈第九
段〉

This refers to those are practicing on the examination field. You have to be relaxed, as if there was no official watching. This advice is on point.

However, "you must be afraid to miss" and "you cannot relax your willpower even in the slightest" are wrong. Why? When people are at the examination range, this is precisely the reason they miss. These people do not suffer from a lack of attentiveness. The problem is that they are over-attentive and lose their sense of normality. Their spirit gets all mixed up, and their breathing stops. In doing so, they fail to show their best.

此訓場中射者 都要意氣安閒 如
無監射官在上一般 言言切中

惟業業恐不中 不可有一毫自放
之意 此二句非是 何也 今人在場
中 不中之根正坐此病 每見場中射
者 不患其不業業 但患其用心太
過 業業失其常度 神昏氣沮 不及
展其所長耳

惟善射一志并慮 旁若無人 自
能登場與平日無異 意氣安舒 而舍
矢如破矣 又何事業業爲念 惟恐不
中爲

Good archers act as if no one is watching, so that there is no difference between exam vs. day-to-day shooting. Their temperament is relaxed, and they simply release the arrow and hit the target. Why do you want to add more anxiety to your shooting by "being afraid to miss"?

2.10 *Shooting Anxiety (Part 2)*

『 People who can hit the target do so at a calm and steady pace. They cannot achieve this by being abrupt and anxious. Those who are abrupt and anxious yet still hit the target are just plain lucky. 』

『凡中的之箭 可取必者 皆自
從容閒暇中能之 未有忙忽而可取
必者 忙忽而有中者 亦幸耳』〈第
十段〉

These various discussions about shooting in a relaxed state are a good thing. Everybody shooting today knows this piece of advice, but once they enter the examination range they become anxious. Their anxiety reaches a level that contorts their facial expression because they are not familiar with archery form, or the difference between good and bad shooting.

Thus, when you practice you should take your time to become familiar with the various aspects of your technique. That way when you finally do enter the arena, your familiarity lets you take control, thereby leading you naturally to shoot in a relaxed manner. If you are not familiar with your form yet want to be relaxed, you are doing nothing more than paying lip service: you might say you are relaxed, but your mind is not relaxed.

<See the detailed discussion about form in "The Shortcut" (Book 1).>

2.11 *Shooting Anxiety (Part 3)*

『If you have trouble hitting the target after 5–6 arrows, you have to calm down even more in order to concentrate. You cannot be anxious because of missing, or else the 7th, 8th, and 9th arrows will not hit their mark either.』

This expression about being in a state of relaxation is key to an archer's success. If you want to be relaxed, you must constantly practice your form until it becomes second nature. Only then will you be able to develop confidence. Thus, after shooting 5–6 arrows and not hitting, you can collect yourself and be able to hit the target again on the 7th, 8th, and 9th arrows.

The relaxation in an experienced archer reflects his diligent training and high skill level. He is definitely not your average archer. General Qi spent his entire life with all these soldiers, so he knew the difficulty of achieving a state of relaxation. Thus, if you want to achieve relaxation, you have to think about how to achieve it.

2.12 *Problems with the "Thrust Forward" and "Snap Back" Release*

『When shooting, the bow hand should be like pushing Mount Tai, and the draw hand should be like pulling a tiger's tail. The bow hand takes most of the effort, and the bow-side and draw-side arms are in a straight line. Draw the bow slowly, and then release rapidly. If you shoot too high, then you should adjust by aiming lower. <That is, if you shoot the arrow too high, then you want to lower the bow hand to lower the trajectory of the arrow.> If you shoot too low, then you want to aim higher. <If you

此等從容閑暇議論極是　然今人平時談射　孰不知閑暇爲美　一或登場　不覺心動神馳　五官無主者　以胸中射法利弊未析　手中把持未有定衡耳　若平時習射　手中百法閑熟　登場自有主持　而從容閑暇之規模自若也　苟不習于法　而徒慕安閑之度　口雖言之而神不與也
〈射法詳于捷徑門〉

『凡射至五六矢之外　猶未中的　更要從容審決　不可因不中而自忙　若忙則七八九矢更無中理也』〈第十一段〉

此說今人安閑乃射家之要訣　然欲安閑　必自平時熟習射法　而膽勇德度養之有素　方得于五六矢不中之後　悠然自得　需之七八九矢而復中　若而人者　今日之安閑　可卜他日之造詣　不可以常人目之　戚公老于兵間　故見及此　後之習射者　欲求安閑　必於所以安閑處三致思哉

『凡射　前手如推泰山　後手如握虎尾　一拳主定　前後正直　慢開弓　緊放箭　射大存于小　〈言射矢過大者　宜存壓其前手　則矢自小〉射小加於大　〈矢發小者　加舉其前手　則矢大〉務取水平　前手撇　後手絕』〈第十二段〉

117

shoot too low, then raise the bow hand to raise the trajectory of the arrow.> Release straight back from the arrow, thrusting forward-and-left with the bow hand [▶ so the bow tilts forward towards the target after release], and snapping backward with the draw hand. 』

According to the above passage, you have to push the bow with the bow hand and lightly pull the string with the draw hand. To release, the bow hand "thrusts forward" and the draw hand "snaps back." This method relies entirely on arm strength, and the idea is to coordinate the bow-side and draw-side hands. This is plausible. Meanwhile, the passage says you have to lower the bow hand to compensate for shooting to high, and you have to raise the bow hand to compensate for shooting too low. This is also plausible.

However, both of these ideas only talk about arm strength, and they say nothing about using shoulder and back strength. Arm strength is limited. You will not be able to hold full draw steadily with arm strength alone. As for the "thrust/snap" method of releasing, you will not be able to coordinate the bow-side and draw-side hands, and the arrow will go all over the place. If you lower your bow hand to compensate for shooting too high, then your bow shoulder will hunch up, and the draw shoulder will be lower than the bow shoulder. In this configuration, your joints are misaligned and you cannot hold full draw steadily. In the end you will not be able to shoot accurately.

That is why archers must learn to use their shoulder and back strength. When you are using shoulder and back strength, your bow-side and draw-side hands are well-aligned with your shoulders. Your bow shoulder sends the bow arm sloping upward to the bow hand, which is reaching out. The draw elbow starts high and then settles down, and then the draw hand releases straight backward. When you are drawing the bow, you must ensure you are still relying on back tension and coordinating your shoulder blades naturally as you aim at the target. You will definitely hit!

With this method, you do not have to consciously adjust your bow hand elevation: the arrow will naturally fly at the correct level. Nor do you have to "thrust forward" or "snap back": the arrow will not veer left or right, but simply fly straight.

<You can find more discussion about shoulder technique in "The Shortcut" (Book 1, Chapter 1), as well as Book 2 (this book), Chapter 5.>

此儿說 前作後遲 前順後絕 俱是用臂之力 期於前後手相應 此亦射家可行之說 又云 射過大者壓低前手 矢過小者加舉前手 亦是可行之法

但二說俱是用臂力 而不知用肩力 則前後手之力有盡 引弓彀時 發矢而用撇絕 豈矢必兩手 盡相應乎 兩手不相應 則發矢必有左右大小之偏 若射大存壓 低其前手 則前肩聳 後肩低 骨節不直 主持不定 矢發亦有左右大小之偏

故射者果得用肩之法 則彀時 前後手俱與肩平直如衡 前肩從下達上 送前掌直出 後肘從高瀉下 後手平脫 兩手分開時 矢之大小左右 俱在兩肩轉運之間 自然相應 發無不中矣 不必存小加大 而矢自無大小 不必左撇右絕 而矢自無東西之偏

<用肩法 捷徑門并指迷集五卷內 言之已詳>

Thrusting the bow hand forward and left during the release (and making the upper tip of the bow point towards the target) is an alternative technique that Gao Ying did not advocate.
Courtesy of Mike Loades.

2.13 *Draw Weight and Distance Training*

『You want to choose a bow of an appropriate draw weight when you shoot, and you first have to make sure you are able to hold it at full draw. First learn to shoot nearby targets, then learn to shoot faraway targets. These rules never change.』

When it comes to choosing a bow, you had better choose one with a draw weight that lets you save some strength, rather than a bow that is too heavy and that you cannot control. This rule will never change.

But the advice that says beginners should start with closeby targets and progress to faraway targets is nonsensical. When you follow the proper shooting technique, then regardless whether you shoot left/right/high/low, all you have to do is look at the target and control the bow. Then it does not matter whether you are shooting near or far. How can you not hit?

When you do not follow the proper shooting technique, then you might get lucky and hit some closeby targets. But if you move further away, the number of successful hits diminish. And if you move even further away, you will not be able to hit anything at all. This is not a surprise. These days people only talk about starting closeby and moving further away, but they do not spend much effort on improving their own technique. This is dumb. Mr. Tang Jingchuan's *Military Compilation* also gives the same piece of unhelpful advice. I do not know why.

Tang Jingchuan (唐荊川) was a general from the Ming Dynasty who lived 1507–1560 CE. He was known for his battles against the Wokou invaders. He died at sea from disease.

2.14 *Shooting Enemies at Close Range*

『For shooting the enemy, you must have unmovable courage, you must create a threatening situation (like a crossbow already held at full draw and ready to shoot at any time), and you must be abrupt and powerful (like a crossbow being released suddenly) [▶ these last two expressions are from Sun Zi's *Art of War*]. How can you miss this way? Here is the method: pull the bow but do not pull all the way, and do not release too early or frivolously. Use the Low Stance [▶ see Book 2, Chapter 3] and do not retreat. That is how you create a threatening situation. When the enemy comes within about 10 paces (17.5 yd, 16 m) or more, a single shot will definitely hit and definitely kill a man. This is how you make your shooting abrupt and powerful.

『凡射必力勝其弓 但先持滿射之 先近而後遠 此不易之法也』〈第十三段〉

射者寧使人力有餘 足以制其弓 無過用勁弓 而爲弓所制 古今不易之論

但學射而執自近及遠之說 此世俗不通之論也 夫射須求合法 則左右大小之分 目能見之 手能持之 可遠可近 無不中的矣 若不合法之射 近或可偶中 漸遠則中數亦漸寡 更遠則不中矣 此必然之理 今人不肯講究射之精義 而專講自近及遠之法 愚矣 唐荊川先生纂輯武編 亦同是說 何哉

『凡對敵射箭 只是膽大力定 勢險節短 則發無不中矣

對敵射法 將弓扯起 且勿盡滿 勿輕發 只用四平架手 立定不退 則勢自險矣 約近十數步 一發必能中 必能殺人 而後發矢 則節自短矣 馬上之賊 只當看大的射 不可射人 諺云：「射人先射馬 擒賊先擒首」是也』〈第十四段〉

此戚公親履戎伍 百戰破倭 故
臨陣能伸士卒立定 引弓持滿不
發 待賊近 方發矢殺賊 此有制之
兵 必勝而無敗者也 然必得智勇之
將 因能授任 練習士眾如一人 方
能臨敵致命

今用匹夫之勇 資郎紈袴爲將 練
習無制 望敵即奔 雖有射法 孰肯
持滿立定 射賊乎 故得智勇如戚公
者爲主師 必能選膽勇之人爲列
校 而收討賊之功 故曰:「有必勝
之將 無必勝之兵」今患無戚公
耳 寧患無列校 又寧患無兵乎

嗟嗟 今天下諸患 無任戚公者
耳 寧患無戚公

As for shooting mounted enemies, focus on the big target. Do not try to shoot the horseman. The old saying still holds: "Shoot the horse before you shoot the man, subdue the leader if you want to subdue the enemy."』

Qi Jiguang trained his own soldiers and led them to victories over the Wokou [▶ the "Japanese" pirates] in countless battles. On the battlefield, Qi gets his troops to stand their ground and face the enemy, drawing their bows fully (but not yet releasing), waiting until the enemy enters close range, and then shooting the arrow for a sure kill. Soldiers with such discipline will never be defeated. Only wise and brave generals are able to organize and train their troops to act as a single unit, which will be lethal to the enemy.

Nowadays, the generals are corrupt and useless. The soldiers lack proper training and discipline, and they will run away when they see the enemy. Although they might know how to shoot, no one is willing to reach full draw and stand their ground to wait for the enemy.

That is why you need wise and brave generals, such as General Qi Jiguang, to be in charge. They are able to select troops with real courage, so they are able to stay in formation and wait for the enemy. That is why they say: "A skilled general will have more impact than a group of skilled soldiers." If you do not have capable generals like Qi Jiguang, then you will not have capable officers, and you will not have capable soldiers.

Sigh... Today, the biggest problem in the country is that although we have qualified people like Qi Jiguang, the government never puts them in charge.

Qi Jiguang (戚繼光), who lived 1528–1588 CE, is a very famous and innovative general from the Ming Dynasty. At age 17, he inherited the commandership of the Dengzhou (登州) Garrison from his father (who had just passed away). However, he was far from complacent, as indicated by the defining poem he penned a year later saying "封侯非我意 但愿海波平" or "I am not after high titles; I only desire peace for the people." It was Qi's campaigns that finally defeated the Wokou (Japanese pirates and their Chinese collaborators) who were attacking the coasts of China.

His innovations included strict recruiting standards, training regimens, as well as battlefield tactics that emphasized teamwork and courage to overcome well-trained individual pirates. Qi gained a lot of recognition for his successes both against the Wokou invaders, as well as against the Mongols. However, due to the Ming government's distrust of Qi's influence and popularity, they eventually stripped him of his rank and he retired in humiliation.

『 For horses, you have to train and feed them daily so that they are able to respond to your orders: if you want them to jump, they will jump; if you they you want them to go, they will go; if you want them to stop, they will stop. They will not be afraid of their surroundings. While galloping their stride is not cut short: their front legs will reach forward together as far as their ears, and their rear legs will extend forward even more. This makes the horse quick and steady, allowing the mounted rider to use weapons. In warfare, a man's life depends on his horse having these qualities. Nomad horses have much, much more experience in warfare than Chinese horses. How can their temperament be so well-suited to the task? It is all due to proper care and training. 』

A war horse first needs to be well-fed and trained. You need to cover its eyes and ears so that it does not become startled. Train its gallop gradually, and take your time in training it to stop and go. The man and horse have to be very familiar with each other. Only then can you use the horse for war.

When the ancients go to war, even as a conflict grows more heated, those who can control the pace of war in an orderly manner owe it to the strength of their cavalry. The horse has to be trained constantly, otherwise how can you use it for war? Qi Jiguang says a man's life depends on his horse, so proper training is vital.

This has always been the right method. The military strategist Wu Qi [▶ who was at one time mayor of Xihe during the Warring States period around 400 BCE] said in his military classic *Wuzi*: "In difficult situations, it is better to expend labor from humans rather than horses." This is not because he loves horses and despises people. The reason is because he wants to save the horses' energy for the unpredictable situations in warfare. This shows the importance of the horse.

Unfortunately, today's government does not have a good system for breeding horses. They buy horses from civilians, but the quality of these horses is inconsistent. There are also so-called "foreign" horses in the marketplace, but these are fake labels. If war were to suddenly break out, I have no idea how we would be able to acquire good horses.

『凡馬 須要平日飼養 調度縱
蹲 聽令進止 觸物不驚 馳道不
削 前兩足從耳下齊出 後兩足向前
倍之 則疾且穩 而人可用器矣 故
馬者 戰陣時人命之所寄也 胡馬慣
戰數倍中國 豈特風氣使然 亦居常
調度之功也』〈第十五段〉

臨陣之馬 必先飼養 戢其耳
目 無令驚駭 習其馳逐 閑其進
止 人馬相親 然後可使 古人臨
陣 衝突長驅 疾徐不亂者 皆馬力
爲之 然非訓之平時 倉猝豈爲我
用 戚公以馬爲人之命 居常必先調
度 此不易之法 昔吳西河有云:「
日暮道遠 必數上下 寧勞于人 慎
無勞馬」非愛馬而輕人也 欲節其
力 以備卒然之用也 則馬之爲人命
可知 今國家之馬 養之于官者烏
有 取之民者無制 市之夷者 徒事
虛名 不適于用 吾不知 猝猝將何
所給也

『騎射須要開弓至九分滿 記
之 記之 即至七八分滿 亦難中
也』〈第十六段〉

騎射雖不比步射之遠 即近至尋
丈 亦須開弓至十分滿與步射同 方
可命中 何也 射之法 莫如牢固爲
主 固之道 莫如彀 惟彀而後 目力
可審 骨節可直 發矢方準 若開弓
不滿至十分 骨節未盡 體勢俱鬆 兼
之馬馳身驟 發矢必不齊 戚公云:
「七八分滿亦難中」愚謂 九分滿
亦未盡善 故制馬箭之式 比步箭應
長半寸許 射時極力引滿 鏃猶在弓
弨外半寸 則開弓時 方敢放膽控
弦 無不彀之患 制步箭 隨人臂之
短長爲之 〈詳擇物門〉

『騎射把箭 以三矢爲準 須以
箭二枝 連弓弨把定 又以一枝搭掛
弦中爲便 其有以箭插衣領內或插
腰間俱不便 決要從吾言』〈第十七
段〉

按戚公所言 特就武場應試者而
云 然故以一矢掛弦 二矢連弓弨握
之 非指對敵言也 若臨陣對賊 帶
箭不止三四矢 必須箭服弓室置之

2.16 *Draw Length for Horseback Archery*

『On horseback, draw the bow until 90% of full draw. Remember this! If you only draw to 70–80% of full draw, you will have a hard time hitting.』

The distances for horseback archery are not as far as for infantry archery, with the closest distance being about one zhang (3.5 yd, 3.2 m). But when you are shooting on horseback, you still want to reach 100% full draw like in infantry archery. Only then can you achieve a sure hit. Why?

Shooting has to be steady and solid. What better way to be solid than to reach full draw? Only when you have reached full draw can your eyes concentrate and your joints become aligned, thereby giving you a steady shot. If you do not reach 100% full draw, your joints are not correctly aligned, and your posture will be too loose: as you are shooting from horseback at full gallop, your draw length will become inconsistent. General Qi said: "it is hard to hit at 70–80% full draw." I even think that 90% full draw is not that good either.

That is why when you make arrows for horseback archery, they should be longer than your infantry arrows by about a half cun (0.63 in, 1.6 cm). Thus, when you reach full draw, the back of the arrowhead will still be in front of the handle by a half cun (0.63 in, 1.6 cm). So when you draw the bow, you can rest assured that you can take the string and pull all the way, and you will avoid the mistake of pulling less than full draw. When making infantry arrows, you must size them according to the length of your arms. [▶ Do not add the extra 1.6 cm for infantry arrows.] <Details are in "Choosing Equipment: Choosing Arrow Length," Book 1, Chapter 3.7.>

2.17 *Holding Arrows at the Bow Handle vs. the Hip Quiver*

『When you are on horseback, you should hold 3 arrows. You should hold two of them together with the handle, and have one arrow already nocked on the string for convenience. Do not stick arrows in your collar or at your waist; these methods are not advantageous. You should definitely follow my advice.』

General Qi's words here for holding the arrows is only useful in an examination setting. Having one arrow on the string and two gripped at the handle is not good advice for fighting on the battlefield! When you are at war with the enemy, you do not bring just 3 or 4 arrows. You need your arrow quiver and bow quiver at your waist, only then can you have access to many arrows: enough to shoot and kill any enemy you face. If you only have a few arrows, how can you drive back the multitude of bandits? If you hold two arrows at the handle, your grip of the bow is going to be unsteady, making it especially difficult to hit and kill the enemy. General Qian Shizhen's *Commentary on Archery* has a more detailed explanation of what I am saying.

When shooting during a military exam, you are only steady if you have one arrow already nocked and two arrows in your waist quiver. You need to practice getting used to this method. You can also follow Qi Jiguang's advice (with one arrow on the string and two at the handle). But doing something special for a military exam is not going to be practical [▶ e.g., on the battlefield]. This is a tough time for the country. As a man, you have to rise to the occasion. That is why you should treat the exam ground the same as the battlefield. Why bother with following the majority in taking the easy way out? That is why if you are not using the method of keeping your arrows in your waist quiver, you are going to suffer in battle.

2.18 *Reaching Full Draw on Horseback*

『 When you teach mounted archery, tell them: "You should ride like the wind, and your vision should be like lightning. Reach full draw and release quickly." 』

Mounted archers have to shoot quickly: that is the only way they can hit. That is why Qi uses metaphors like "you should ride like the wind," "your vision should be like lightning," and "release quickly." People know how to do these three things. The only thing people have trouble with is reaching full draw. Why? In mounted archery, arrows must release quickly and the targets are close. But if you follow through with this idea, then some archers will skip full draw and simply draw-and-release. That is why Qi Jiguang emphasized the importance of reaching full draw: you cannot draw the bow carelessly or else your joints will be misaligned and you will have the problem of failing to reach full draw. This is the true method of shooting. Everybody knows that there is nothing better than reaching full draw on horseback. However, not everybody knows the right technique, so most of them fail to reach full draw on horseback.

How do you reach full draw? It is the same for both mounted and infantry archery. You want the shoulder and arm joints to be well-aligned. When the joints are aligned, you are using your skeletal frame to support the weight of your bow, rather than pure muscle power. You do not have to try hard yet you will already reach full draw! Thus, people who can master infantry archery techniques will not have any problem reaching full draw on horseback.

腰間 方可容百枝 乃能射敵殺賊 若止三四枝 何以卻眾寇 若以二矢握之弓弸 則握弓必不固 亦難命中殺敵 吾邑參戎公錢三持射評言之詳矣

若論武場應試 以一矢掛弦 二矢置腰間出之爲穩 然須平時演熟 方用得此法 不然則戚公所云一矢掛弦 二矢握之弓弸 亦無不可 但此特應試 非實用也 多難之秋 丈夫作事 應試時即當爲實用之地 何可自同于眾人 故騎射矢 不置腰間必然有失

『凡教騎射 必勢如追風 目如流電 滿開弓 急放箭』〈第十八段〉

騎射者 必發矢捷疾 方能中的 故曰「如追風」「如流電」又云「急放箭」此三語人人能之 惟滿開弓之法 人多不能 何也 騎射出矢速 對的近 使存苟且之意 孰肯恣力引滿 如對敵乎 故戚公云 滿開弓者 戒人勿蹈不滿之病也 此射家之正法 然騎射莫妙于彀 人皆知之 卒莫能彀者 未知所以彀法耳 彀法云何 騎射與步射同 肩臂骨節平直而已 惟骨節直 引弓只用骨力 不用筋力 弓不期彀而自彀矣 故工於步射者 未有騎射而不彀者也

『凡騎射 或對賊 或對的 搭箭
時 目止視賊 視的 不可看手 搭箭
只宜信手搭之』〈第十九段〉

搭箭若用目視 則發矢不捷 射
的 則騎馳過的而不及中 射賊 則
賊知避遠而不能中 惟一心視的與
賊 信手搭箭射之 則神注而發矢迅
速矣 然須平居演武 百倍其功 乃
能信手搭箭 而無逼箭墮矢之患 信
手搭箭者 馬箭式須用一扣 切勿用
兩扣者 忙促時若用兩扣 必然有
失 〈兩扣者即俗號四扣齒箭也〉善
騎射者 熟習久試 當自知之

2.19 *Importance of Nocking the Arrow without Looking at the Hands*

『While shooting on horseback (whether towards the enemy or towards a target), when you nock the arrow you should focus your attention on the enemy or the target: you should not look at your hands. When you nock the arrow, you should rely only on your hands.』

If you have to look at your hands while nocking the arrow, you will not be able to shoot quickly. If you try to shoot a target at full gallop, you will ride past the target and will not be able to hit it. If you try to shoot at an enemy, the enemy would have time to hide, making himself hard to hit. Instead, you must focus your vision and treat the target like the enemy. Trust your hands to nock the arrow so you can focus your willpower on the target and release the arrow more rapidly.

For military training, this is a skill you absolutely must master. You need to be able to nock the arrow without looking and avoid dropping it or pushing it too hard. For the people who nock without looking, their arrows should only have one nock slot. By no means should you use the double-nocked arrows [▶ nock slots cut in a "+" pattern]. If you are in a rush and using double-nocked arrows, you are bound to make mistakes <these double-nocked arrows are sometimes called "four-tooth arrows">. Those who shoot well on horseback can definitely understand what I mean.

3.1 *Bow Hand and Draw Hand Techniques*

『In archery, there is the "Han Method" and the "Hu Method." In the Han Method, the bow hand uses the Eagle Claw, and the draw hand uses a single finger to hook the thumb. This method emphasizes finesse. In the Hu method, the bow hand holds a Full Grip, and two fingers hook over the draw hand thumb. This method emphasizes strength.』

Wu Bei Yao Lue says the Han method involves holding the bow with the Eagle Claw and using a single finger to hook the draw hand thumb, while the Hu method involves using the Full Grip to hold the bow and two fingers to hook the draw hand thumb. But it does not discuss this in relation to the strength of the bow at all: it only discusses the Han/Hu dichotomy of bow hand and draw hand technique.

Before you select a bow hand technique, you have to know the strength of your bow. Light bows require the Eagle Claw, and heavy bows require the Full Grip. Why? People who are not strong use light bows, so it is difficult for the arrow to reach far. That is when the Eagle Claw is suitable. If you use the Eagle Claw, the root of the palm is firm and the web of the hand is relaxed: that way the arrow will go high and travel far. Folks who are strong use heavy bows, so the arrow will definitely shoot far. That is why you use the Full Grip to mitigate this tendency. If you use the Full Grip, both the root of the palm and the web of the hand hold firmly: this will help the arrow fly level [▶ with a heavy bow]. Thus if you use a light bow, use the Eagle Claw. If you use a heavy bow, use the Full Grip.

As for which draw hand technique to use, the choice does not depend on the strength of the bow. You should always use the double-hook technique [▶ index and middle fingers over the thumb]. Why? The double-hook is strong, whereas the single-hook [▶ index finger over the thumb] is weak. There are those who think that single-hook should be used with light bows because they think the release for single-hook is quick, whereas the release for double-hook is sluggish. What you should do is if you draw with double-hook, the middle finger should tuck in tightly and never open, whereas only the index finger and thumb should open up after the release. That will make the release as clean and crisp as if you were using single-hook technique.

<More details in "Common Mistakes: Pulling a Heavy Bow Too Early" in Book 1, Chapter 2.4. You should take a look at it.>

[▶ Regarding the utility of double-hook and single-hook, we have already commented about this before in "Recommended Draw Hand Technique" in Book 1, Chapter 2.4. We believe the hooking technique is a preference, and you do not have to stick to a single method. Good or bad is always based on practice.]

武經射學正宗指迷集 卷三

錄《武備要略》射法 共計六段

『 夫射有漢射 有胡射 漢射者 左手鷹爪持弓 右手單搭扣弦 惟務巧勝 胡射者 左手滿把持弓 右手雙搭扣弦 惟以力勝』〈第一段〉

要略云：「漢射用鷹爪持弓者 用單搭 胡射用滿把持弓者 用雙搭」是不論弓力之強弱 而概以漢射胡射論持弓搭箭矣 不知持弓之法 須視弓之軟勁 軟弓宜鷹爪 勁弓宜滿把 何也 力弱之人 弓用軟 矢難遠到 故用鷹爪助其勢 以鷹爪持弓者 掌根實 虎口鬆 矢發插天而大 力大之人 弓用勁 矢發必遠 故用滿把殺其勢 以滿把持弓者 掌根雖實虎口亦緊 發矢平疾 此用軟弓者 利用鷹爪 用勁弓者 宜滿把也 若搭弦法 無論弓之軟勁 皆宜雙搭 何也 以雙搭力全 單搭力弱耳 凡軟弓用單搭者 以單搭脫弦快捷 雙搭脫弦遲滯耳 若雙搭脫弦時 以中指收緊勿開 只用食指大指開脫 則脫弦鬆快 反過於單搭矣

〈其法詳於 辨惑門早射勁弓章內 宜參考之〉

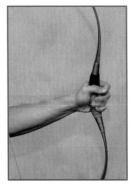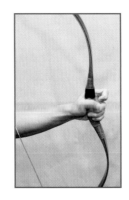

From left to right: Big Eagle Claw (Variation 1), Big Eagle Claw (Variation 2), Little Eagle Claw, Full Grip. *Courtesy of Glenn Murray, Esq.*

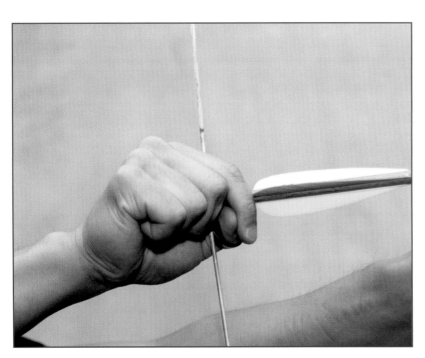

Left: single-hook draw hand technique. Right: double-hook draw hand technique. *Courtesy of Glenn Murray, Esq.*

『For your stance, you want an open stance (between a 90-degree foot placement and a parallel foot placement). If you want to shift the aim of your arrow, shift your back foot. For shooting right, move your back foot to the left. For shooting left, move your back foot to the right. This is the key to hitting the target.』

Regarding the merits of the open stance, because the two feet are not placed side-by-side, your body has stability. You also avoid the problem of squatting down in a horse stance. Thus, the open stance is the right way to stand.

Wu Bei Yao Lue also says that if you want to shift the aim of your arrow, shift your back foot. If you want to shoot right, the front foot is fixed, so you should move the back foot to the left. If you want to shoot left, the front foot is fixed, so you should move the back foot to the right. This is the correct way to shift your footwork.

But there are those who take this idea too far and think that if their arrows veer to the right, then they should shift their back foot to the right [▶ to provide a leftward correction]. Or if their arrows veer to the left, they should shift their back foot left [▶ to provide a rightward correction]. This is a misguided way of thinking. Why? If arrows veer off course, then the problem can be traced to (1) the archer's method of aiming and looking at the target, or (2) whether the shoulders, arms, fists, waist, and spine all coordinate with each other. [▶ Additionally, a sloppy release can cause wobbling.] This has nothing to do with the feet!

As for an overall description of the footwork, if you want to shoot South, your stance should be towards the Northwest. If you want to shoot West, your stance should orient towards the Northeast. The same reasoning follows for shooting to the North and to the East. [▶ Your body is facing 45-degrees to the target.] But the key to stance is stability. You need to be stable like an immovable mountain: why do you want to constantly shift your feet back and forth? If the arrow is flying off course, you do not have to move your feet to correct the direction of the arrow.

When General Qian Shizhen (the famous general from my home town) encounters people who advocate constantly shifting their feet, Qian responds "When you are shooting from a horse, how can you shift your feet?" So constantly shifting your feet is a pretty ridiculous idea. The problem is not the changing of the feet. The problem is people who ignore the importance of proper form and prefer the easy method (like shifting the feet to improve accuracy). But if you have not yet reached a comfortable stance and the body is not in the right position towards the target, then you can adjust your feet a little.

『其足法無過丁字不成 八字不就 隨箭改移 只在後足 射右改左 射左改右 乃射中中的之竅也』〈第二段〉

按立足法 不丁不八者 既不並足立 而失之體浮 又不蹲倒作坐馬之態 此立法之善者也 又云立足法 隨箭改移 只在後足 射右邊 前足跟立定不易 只將後足移在左邊 若射左邊 前足跟亦立定不易 只將後足移在右邊 此亦改移之善法 乃世俗又有執射偏于右者 使後足還右 射偏于左者 使後足還左說者 此不通之論也 何也 制發矢偏斜之弊 只在目力審視詳明 及肩臂腰膂轉運之間耳 與足何與 而必藉後足改移乎 假如望南射者 體勢向西北立 望西射者 體勢向東北立 向北向東射 體勢可以例推

凡立法以穩便爲主 足立定向如山不移 何必屑屑改移其足 謂矢發之偏斜 分毫必藉於足 過矣

吾邑參戎公 錢三持 見人改足之說 曉之曰：「假令騎射 足亦可移乎」則改足之說 謬甚可知矣

非改足之謬也 世人不思請求射法爲必中計 而專恃改足以求中 乃不可耳 若足立未穩 體勢與的 未甚相對合宜 後足少移 亦無不可

『要略曰：考之射家有三勢 曰
大架子 曰中平架子 曰小架子 大
架子者 直身並足而立 左手直如
箭 右手平如衡 弓稍直豎 拉滿弦
挨右腮旁 鏃引至左手中指之末 左
手虎口緊 手頸一直 弓稍前指認定
的心 右手微仰掌 往後一拖 胸骨
開背肉緊 矢去疾速而不滯 雖文而
不雄 利於官場』〈第三段〉

按要略大架子之病有六：一在
直身 二在並足 三在弓稍直豎 四
在虎口緊 五在弓稍前指 六在後手
往後一拖 何也 射法身勢全在站立
安穩 而後審固諸法 皆從此出 若
兩足並緊而立 站無勢 全體皆浮 當
風靜之日 發矢可準 一值當風飈衝
突 體浮搖動 發矢必偏斜矣

若直身與直豎弓稍者 引弓不得
勢 何以能彀 今人多坐此病 夫彀
弓之本 全在前肩向前番下 前肩既
番 前臂方可番直向地 肩臂盡番 虎
口自斜 弓稍不得不斜矣 弓斜則胸
必欽 而身又安能直乎 故引弓必欲
彀者 直弓直身之說 不可行也

至于後手一拖之說 益又不宜 引
弓彀時 臂力已竭 況持弓直豎之
人 前肩未番 肩力未奮 惟恃前臂
撐持 若後手往後一拖 矢必偏於右
矣 縱使前臂能撐 亦屬勉強 安得
從容中的乎

兼之虎口又緊 發矢時 弓稍前
指的心 則矢不能及遠 彼謂利於官

3.3 *Faults of the High Stance*

『 *Wu Bei Yao Lue* wrote the following. There are three primary forms for archers: the High Stance, the Middle Stance, and the Low Stance.

The High Stance is as follows: the body and legs are straight, and the feet are close together. The bow hand should stick out straight as an arrow, and the draw hand should be level as a balance. Hold the bow vertically [▶ i.e., do not cant]. When you reach full draw, the string should be near the side of your cheek, and you should pull until the back of the arrowhead touches the end of your bow hand's middle finger. The web of the bow hand should be tight so that your wrist is thrusting forward and leftward on release, which will cause the upper tip of the bow to point forward towards the target; at the same time, the draw hand's palm faces forward slightly, and it will snap back on release. The chest should open up and the back should squeeze tight. This way, the arrow will fly quickly without any sluggishness. The appearance is refined/soft and shows less fighting intent, which makes it appropriate for examinations. 』

There are six problems with the High Stance: (1) the body is straight, (2) the feet are close together, (3) the bow is held vertically, (4) the web of the bow hand is tight, (5) the upper tip of the bow thrusts forward and leftward after release, and (6) the draw hand snaps back. Why are these problems?

The key to a good posture is stability, which allows you to execute all the elements of your form properly. Standing with your legs straight and your feet close together is like having no stance: your body is simply floating. You might be able to shoot accurately under normal wind conditions. But if the wind suddenly gets stronger, you are going to be thrown off balance and your arrows will fly off course.

Keeping your body straight and holding your bow vertically is an improper way to draw the bow. How can you hold full draw steadily? These days, a lot of people have this problem. The key to achieving full draw is rotating the bow shoulder blade clockwise [▶ for a right-handed archer] so that it is settled all the way down. When you have rotated the bow shoulder blade, the bow arm will rotate in the same direction. When the shoulder and arm rotate and settle, the web of the hand (虎口) will be canted (斜). Thus, the bow has to be canted! Canting means the chest has to be inclined. So how can the body be upright and vertical? Therefore, if you want to hold full draw steadily, keeping the bow and body vertical is inadequate.

As for snapping the draw hand backwards, it is okay but also impractical. When you have reached full draw, your arm strength should already be at its limit. The people who hold the bow vertically [▶ no canting] and stand straight [▶ no incline] are not rotating their bow shoulder blade. As a result, they will not be using shoulder power and back tension to hold full draw. Instead, they rely too heavily on the muscles of the bow arm. If the draw hand snaps back, the arrow will definitely skew to the right. And even if your bow arm is strong enough to hold full draw, it will do so barely. How will you be able to take your time and hit the target?

The High Stance features holding the body and bow upright and vertical. This tense posture may look proper, but it will decrease the effective draw weight that you are able to pull. *Courtesy of Chang Pengfei and Glenn Murray, Esq.*

For comparison, here is the naturally canted body and bow position that Gao Ying advocated. *Courtesy of Chang Pengfei and Glenn Murray, Esq.*

場 謬矣 又謂文而不雄 不雄則是
文 亦何所用之 大抵握弓虎口緊
者 矢出多傷于小 若勁弓又當別
論 終不若不用虎口 惟以肩力送前
掌 直出之為愈也

又有用虎口踰緊 而反能及遠
者 必後手低於前手耳 但能低者 前
肩必聳 發矢全憑兩臂撐持 臂力有
盡 弓必不能愨 此又不可不知

『中平架子者 左足直 右足微
彎 左手如推泰山 右手如握虎尾 弓
稍微斜 拉滿弦挨右腮下 鏃至左手
中指之末 左手虎口緊 認定的心 一
撒 右手抑掌往後一絕 胸骨開 背
肉緊 矢去平而疾 文而且雄 利于
戰陣』〈第四段〉

按要略中平架子之病有五：一
在右足微彎 二在右手拉弦 挨右腮
下 三在虎口緊 四五在前手一撒 後
手一絕而已 五病中 惟拉弦挨右腮
下 為害最大 餘無大害也 何也 持
弓在手 何藉于足 而取必于右足微
彎乎 若發矢時 前手虎口緊 恐矢
傷于小 不能及遠 前手撒 矢多偏
左 後手絕 矢多偏右 惟兩手相

If you both hold the web of the bow hand tight and thrust the upper tip of the bow to tilt forwards towards the target, then you will not be able to shoot the arrow far. They say the High Stance is suitable for the military exam. How absurd! Moreover, they say "the appearance is refined/soft and shows less fighting intent." Of course, if you lack fighting intent you will become soft! A "refined" technique is impractical.

Most people who hold the bow with the web of the hand tight are not able to shoot the arrow far. Of course, if you are using a heavy bow that is a different case [▶ see Book 2, Chapter 3.1]. In general, it is better to relax the web of the bow hand, and make sure you are using proper shoulder position to send the palm of your bow hand straight forward. This is the best way to go.

There are those who are able to shoot the arrow far despite keeping the web of their bow hand tight, but they achieve this by anchoring their draw hand lower than their bow hand. The people who do this will inevitably suffer from hunching their bow shoulder. As a result, they rely entirely on arm strength to pull the bow. But the strength of the arm muscles is limited, so they will not be able to hold full draw steadily. You should be aware of this.

3.4 Faults of the Middle Stance

『The Middle Stance is as follows: your front leg is straight and your back leg is slightly bent. Your bow hand is like pushing Mount Tai, and your draw hand is like pulling a tiger's tail [▶ lightly and cautiously]. Your bow is slightly canted, and at full draw the string is under your right cheek [▶ if you are right-handed]. You should pull until the back of the arrowhead touches the tip of your middle finger, and the web of your bow hand should be tight. Upon release, thrust the web of your bow hand forward to make the upper tip of the bow point towards the target, and the right hand palm should face forward while the right hand snaps back. The chest should open up and the back should squeeze. The arrow will fly fast and level. The Middle Stance is both refined and shows fighting intent. It is suitable for warfare.』

The Middle Stance has five problems: (1) the back leg is bent slightly, (2) the draw hand anchors under the draw-side cheek, (3) the web of the bow hand is tight, (4) and (5) are that the bow hand thrusts and draw hand snaps.

The most severe of these five problems is anchoring the draw hand under the cheek (the other faults are not as severe as this one). But why are the other problems are not as severe? Regarding (1), holding the bow is an action performed directly by the arms (not the legs), so bending the back leg is irrelevant. Regarding (3), if the web of the bow hand is tight, the arrow will fly low and you will not be able to shoot far. For (4) and (5), if the bow hand thrusts forward, then the arrow will skew to the left.

And if you snap back with the draw hand, the arrow will skew to the right. With this release technique, the arrow only flies correctly when both hands coordinate perfectly. But if the straightness of the arrow is sensitive to small deviations in the in the thrust/snap coordination, then how can you say this is completely balanced? Your arrows will skew every which way. But these are not the most serious problems [▶ because they do not lead to injury].

The most serious problem is anchoring under the draw-side cheek. The key to full draw is in rolling and settling the bow shoulder. As you are about to reach full draw, the bow-side and draw-side hands and arms should be higher than the bow shoulder. At full draw just before you release, you will feel the bow shoulder sending the bow arm sloping upward to the hand, with the bow-hand palm reaching forward. Only then will the arrow fly far. It is like how an inchworm has to bend first before it can extend. At the beginning of the draw, when the bow shoulder is lower than the arms, is like the inchworm bending to store energy. From full draw to the release, when the bow shoulder sends the bow-hand palm forward, is like the inchworm extending to crawl forward. With this method, the draw hand has to anchor above the draw-side cheek, close to the ear. This will let you settle the bow shoulder all the way down.

If you want to anchor below the draw-side cheek, then the draw hand will be too low, which forces your bow shoulder to hunch up. Once you reach full draw, the bow shoulder will not have any strength to stabilize the bow [▶ as you are only using your arm strength]. Once the draw hand releases, the arrow is going to skew to the right. This is no way to reach full draw. That is why I say anchoring under the draw-side cheek is the biggest fault.

People who anchor above the cheek settle their bow shoulder all the way down. They are able to entirely use their two shoulder blades [▶ and back tension] to shoot. The shoulder blades coordinate together so that you can balance the force of the draw. However, if your draw hand anchors below the cheek, then you have to rely entirely on your arms to open up. When you are only using your arms and not your shoulders and back to release, the hands will operate out of sync, and the thrust and snap will lack coordination. Those who understand the problems of anchoring below cheek level will deeply appreciate the merits of anchoring above cheek level.

應 矢出方準 然撇絕之間 兩手各
分一路 豈能盡勻 矢不能不少偏
耳 故曰:「四病俱無大患也」
　　惟拉弦挨右腮下 爲患最大者 以
彀弓之根本 全在前肩下捲 故方引
弓時 前後拳臂勢 反高于前肩 及
引弓既彀 發矢時 將前肩從下達
上 送前掌直出 矢方超揚 夫尺蠖
之屈 以求伸也 引弓之初 前肩反
低于前後拳臂者 正尺蠖之屈也 及
弓彀時 而發矢 前肩送前拳直出
者 正尺蠖之求伸也 此法後手拉
弦 必須在右腮之上 與耳齊 則前
肩方得下捲 若拉弦在右腮之下 後
手太低 前肩必聳 引弓將彀 前肩
無力撐持 右手又往後一拖 矢必偏
右 且引弓亦必不能彀 故曰:「拉
弦挨右腮下者 爲病最大也」
　　弦挨右腮上者 前肩低 出矢皆
從兩肩 并力運開 則兩肩合爲一
氣 故分開之力始勻 乃若弦挨右腮
下 則全憑兩臂分開 發矢用臂而不
用肩 兩手各自爲氣 撇絕必不相
應 故深知弦挨右腮下之病者 方能
深知弦挨右腮上之妙也

Wu Bei Yao Lue's **Middle Stance.**
Courtesy of Glenn Murray, Esq.

131

From left to right: anchoring at shoulder level, anchoring below shoulder level, anchoring at chest level, and anchoring at mouth level. *Courtesy of Glenn Murray, Esq., and Mike Loades.*

3.5.1 *Faults of the Low Stance (Horse Stance)*

『The Low Stance is as follows: you bend both legs, you hold the bow as if you are embracing a crescent moon, and the arrow is nocked like a hanging scale [▶ nocked in the middle of the string]. The bow hand holds the bow and the draw hand anchors at the draw-side nipple. At full draw, the back of the arrowhead reaches the tip of the bow hand's middle finger, the web of the bow hand is tight, and the bow hand points to the center of the target. The palm of the draw hand faces forward a little bit and then it snaps back. Both arms open up during the release, causing the chest to open and the back to squeeze tight. The arrow will fly flat, fast, and penetrate powerfully. This stance has fighting intent and is very powerful. It is good for infantry and horseback archery, as well as pulling heavy bows. When it comes to understanding the essence of shooting, this is the quintessential form.』

The Low Stance's description, which says "you bend both legs, you hold the bow as if you are embracing a crescent moon, and the arrow is nocked like a hanging scale," describes a stance without substance. These descriptions have nothing to do with archery, so we will not talk about them.

The part that says "the draw hand anchors at the draw-side nipple" is really bad for the draw. The part that says "the web of the bow hand is tight" and "both arms open up" is really bad for the release. Why is that?

『小架子者 兩足俱彎 出弓如懷中吐月 架箭如弦上縣衡 左手臥弓 右手摸奶 拉滿 鏃上左手中指末 左手虎口緊 對的心 右手抑掌一齊分撒 臂膊俱合 胸骨自開 背肉自緊 矢去水平而疾者 又能穿札 雄而有威 步騎俱利 能開勁弓 最得射中之奧矣』〈第五段〉

按小架子云「兩足俱彎 弓如懷中吐月 箭如弦上縣衡」諸語皆是虛架子 與射無益 不必論矣
其云「右手摸奶」是開弓時之一大病 又云「虎口緊 臂膊俱合〈兩臂一齊撒開 臂膊從背後俱合也〉者」 是發矢時之二大病也 何

132

The foundation for shooting is reaching full draw. The basis for full draw is in the proper alignment of the bow shoulder joint. If your draw hand anchors at your nipple, then it anchors too low. This will cause the bow hand to be held low, in turn causing the bow shoulder to hunch up. Your joints are misaligned, so drawing and releasing relies entirely on the muscle strength of the arms to open up. But arm strength has its limits. From outward appearances, the draw and release might seem coordinated, but there is actually no stability. You will not even reach full draw before you release. Being unable to reach full draw, when combined with the web of the bow hand being held tightly, will prevent the arrow from traveling far.

That is why "both arms open up during the release, causing the chest to open and the back to squeeze tight," "you can pull a heavy bow," and "the arrow will fly fast and flat" are all nonsense!

I have seen a lot of famous archers who might be able to reach full draw in the beginning with this kind of method. But then after 4–5 years, or after decades, or after reaching old age, they all end up with the problem of failing to reach full draw. These people do not know why they lose the ability to reach full draw. Yet in every single case, it is because they make the mistake of anchoring at the nipple! The problem of anchoring at the nipple persists. People today do not realize its faults, thinking it is a great method for shooting. This method keeps getting recorded in training manuals and keeps getting passed down. People believe in it, and it gets into their bones. How pathetic!

If you want to know more about the faults with anchoring at the nipple, and want to know the proper method for reaching full draw, take a look at some of these previous passages in detail: the previous sections about the Middle Stance in Book 2, Chapter 3.4; "The Tale of the Bowyer's Wife (弓工妻)" in Book 2, Chapter 1.4; and "The Shortcut" in Book 1, Chapter 1. Wise people should adopt these methods.

也 開弓以必彀爲主 而彀弓之本 又
在前肩骨節平直 若右手摸奶 過於
低下 則前肩必聳 前手亦低 肩骨
不直 發矢必恃兩臂 一齊分撒 臂
力有限 兩臂外貌雖見分撒 內剛不
足 必不及彀而分撒矣 弓既未彀而
虎口緊 發矢必不及遠 如是而欲兩
臂膊俱從背後合 胸骨開背肉緊 開
勁弓而出矢水平 徒虛語耳 穎見名
射多矣 始初引弓雖滿 後四五年 或
數十年 或垂老之年 坐不滿之病
者 百人而百 然終莫知所以不滿之
故者 亦百人而百 則皆摸奶之病誤
之也 摸奶之害一至此 今人不察 以
爲妙法 紀藉載之 世家習之 後學
者戶誦而印心 入於骨髓 可痛也 夫
故欲去摸奶之病 而求彀弓之法
者 前中平架子中 及弓工妻章內捷
徑門言之詳矣 智者採焉

Wu Bei Yao Lue's Low Stance (Horse Stance). *Courtesy of Glenn Murray, Esq.*

『諸家射法 無過此三者之勢 站
立不同 射法亦異 惟身法 內志
正 外體直 無殊傳也 謹識之 以爲
學者勞』〈第五段（分段）〉

按武備要略云「三勢站立不
同 射法各異」今觀三架子勢 果有
或直身 或灣足 或蹲倒之不同 彼
云站立不同 此誠然矣 三勢皆是前
肩聳起 前後兩臂皆低 則骨節不直
之病 實同一轍 安得云射法各異
乎 又云「身法內志正外體直 無殊
傳也」則不免言是而行非矣 何
也 三勢骨節皆不直 引弓一彀 臂
力將竭 前拳必然顫動 非外體直
矣 手既顫動 審視必不能詳明 何
以正內志乎

由此觀之 三勢皆坐不彀之病 當
爲世戒 何足爲好學者之勞耶

『身法有六忌：忌頭縮 忌身
脛 忌前倒 忌後仰 忌臀露 忌腰
彎 六忌明而立身之法善矣』〈第六
段〉

按法 頭不宜縮 又不宜太仰 犯
卻垂之病 胸欲欽 則無前突之病 大
約兩足必須直立而脛其腹 則前
倒 後仰 臀露 腰灣之病俱可免
矣 身法之弊 大約俱在初學時習

3.5.2 *Summary of* Wu Bei Yao Lue's *Three Stances*

『All archery techniques can be categorized into these three stances. The stances are different, so the techniques are different. What they have in common is that the inner intent is focused, and the outer body is steady and straight. Once students have this in mind, they are on the path to success.』

Wu Bei Yao Lue says "the three stances are different, so the three techniques are different." When you take a look at the differences among the three stances, some of them require you to straighten your body, others will require you to bend your legs, others require you to crouch down entirely. When it says "the stances are different," that is pretty obvious.

But what the three stances have in common are that the bow shoulder is hunched up and the bow-side/draw-side arms are lower than the shoulders, thereby leading to the problem where the joints are misaligned. They all have the same problem. How can you say they are different?

The passage also says "what they have in common is that the inner intent is focused, and the outer body is steady and straight." This is just lip service. Why? In all three stances the joints are misaligned. Once you reach full draw, your arm strength becomes exhausted, and the bow hand shakes. Of course the outer body is neither steady nor straight! When the bow hand is shaking, you cannot concentrate on the target at all. So how can your inner intent be focused?

According to these observations, we can see these three stances suffer from the problem of failing to reach full draw steadily. You should avoid this. How can this be the right path to success?

3.6 *Faults in Shooting Posture*

『There are six common shooting faults: (1) the neck sinking into the shoulders, (2) the chest sticking out and being too straight, (3) the body falling forward, (4) the body leaning too far backward, (5) the butt sticking out, and (6) the waist bending. If you can remedy these six faults, then your body position will be correct.』

For proper technique, the neck should not sink into the shoulders, but the neck should not look up either, otherwise you violate the advice that the head should to be slightly tilted. The chest should be inclined so as to avoid the fault of sticking the chest out. Overall, if you straighten your legs and tuck in your belly, then you will avoid the faults of falling forward/backward, sticking the butt out, and bending the waist. These problems always emerge in the early stages of learning, and they are difficult to correct. Only if a beginner is modest (i.e., enjoys asking questions and receiving advice) can he quickly correct these problems immediately as they emerge. If you can follow and keep the proper form, then after practicing for a while, you can definitely avoid all these faults.

Sigh... A lot of problems today happen because people are not cautious when they start out. Later it becomes too late to repent. If you know the essence of archery, you can improve your character. Then you are in a position to talk about the Way of Archery.

成　後卒難改　惟始初虛心好問　聞
病即速變　得法則固守　熟習之後　動
中繩墨　終身可寡過矣
　　嗟嗟　天下事　皆因始之不慎　後
悔無及　故知射之精義　可以進德　可
與語道矣

A Comparison of Body Postures

From left to right: tilting the hips sideways, neck and torso too scrunched, neck and torso too upright and vertical, and neck and torso with comfortable inclination. *Courtesy of Mike Loades, Glenn Murray, Esq., and Chang Pengfei.*

雜錄射法遺言　共計十六段

『莫患弓軟　服嘗自遠　莫患力
贏　緩引自任（任　滿也）』〈第一
段〉

勁弓方可遠到　軟弓豈能及遠　即
服習之久　人弓相親　大小如意　矢
發可中近的耳　若射遠　則弓力有
限　非插天而大　則不能到　何云「
服當自遠」乎

軟弓必欲遠到　亦有一法　大約
弓之上手宜微軟　下手宜微勁　此弓
之常式也　若以下手之微勁者　以火
揉之　倒作上手　軟弓亦可及遠　但
軟弓及遠　矢必插天而大　終難中
的　僅可偶用　非可爲訓也

若力弱之人　欲彀勁弓　必熟肩
臂平直之法　方能引弓使滿　茍不得
法　骨節不直　而妄欲彀弓　急引固
不滿　緩引亦不能滿　何云「緩引自
任」乎

『法曰：鏃不上指　必無中理　指
不知鏃　同於無目』〈第二段〉

按鏃不上中指之末者　特引弓不
彀耳　而必其無中理者　甚言不彀之
害　以警世必欲其彀也　然人卒不肯

Book 2, Chapter 4: Last Words on Miscellaneous Archery Methods

4.1 *Draw Weight*

『Do not worry that your bow is too soft: if you can control it, you can make it shoot far. Do not worry if your bow is too heavy: if you draw slowly and gradually, you will be able to reach full draw.』

A strong bow can shoot far. How can a soft bow shoot far? You might be able to fully control a soft bow (to the point that man and bow are connected) and maintain accuracy for close-distance targets. However, once you switch to shooting at long distance targets, the physical limitations of the bow will force you to aim up into the sky for the arrow to reach the target. Otherwise, how can you shoot long distances accurately with a soft bow?

If you have to shoot far away with a soft bow, there is a method. For standard bows, the upper limb is slightly weaker and the lower limb is slightly stronger. You can apply heat to the lower limb and massage it, then flip the bow upside-down so that what used to be the lower limb is now the upper limb. That is how you make a soft bow shoot far. But under these circumstances, the arrow will definitely fly at a high angle, and it will still be hard to hit the target. You cannot use this on a regular basis, as you do not have any control over the bow.

Folks with less strength who want to draw a heavy bow must familiarize themselves with the method of keeping their shoulders and arms aligned. Only then can they reach full draw steadily. If they do not apply this method, the joints will be misaligned, which is not good for reaching full draw. You will not reach full draw steadily regardless whether you pull briskly or pull slowly. So how can someone say "if you draw slowly and gradually, you will be able to reach full draw."

4.2 *Draw Length Indicator (Wang Ju)*

『Wang Ju's Archery Method says: If the back of the arrowhead does not touch the bow hand finger, there is no way the arrow will hit. If the finger does not touch the arrowhead, it is like shooting blind.』

"The back of the arrowhead does not touch the tip of the middle finger" means you are not reaching full draw. "There is no way the arrow will hit" is the result of failing to reach full draw. Thus Wang Ju makes it clear that full draw is crucial.

However, there are people who absolutely refuse to learn full draw. These people think that if you have a consistent draw length, then you can still hit the target. But if you do not reach full draw, the arrowhead is about a half cun (0.63 in, 1.6 cm) in front of the handle. We can say for sure you are failing to reach full draw. If you perform every single shot like this, you can still make shooting consistent and still hit. However, if you hit but do not reach full draw, your arrows will lack impetus. If you do not reach full draw, the joints are not properly aligned. Instead, you rely on arm muscle power to pull the bow. After a while of shooting, your arm muscles will fatigue. Day after day your lose the ability to reach full draw. At the beginning you can have a consistent draw length even though you fail to reach full draw, but eventually you lose that consistent draw length as well! If you cannot reach full draw consistently, how can the arrows fly consistently? That is why Wang Ju says: "If the back of the arrowhead does not touch the bow hand finger, there is no way the arrow will hit." [▶ This passage discusses the merits of full draw, rather than specifically emphasizing the merits of touching the arrowhead. Gao Ying likes the idea that "touching the arrowhead" encourages an archer to reach full draw. However, in the following passage Gao discusses why touching the arrowhead is not necessary by describing an alternative technique.]

Now the expression "if the finger does not touch the arrowhead, it is like shooting blind" means that you cannot see the arrowhead, so you use your bow hand fingers instead of your eyes. But when you are shooting a faraway target, your eyes look past the right edge of the bow as you sight along the arrow shaft through the arrowhead through to the target. You do not need to substitute your finger for your eyes in this case.

However, if you are shooting at target within 20 paces (about 35 yd, 32 m), you are looking over the left edge of the bow and you will not be able to see the arrowhead. [▶ In Gao Ying's technique, the bow is canted so that the left edge of the bow will be above the right edge of the bow for a right-handed archer.] In this case, you still do not need to use your finger as a draw length indicator. Why? The archer's arm span dictates the size of the arrow: taller people will use longer arrows, shorter people will use shorter arrows. In either case, the fact your joints are properly aligned will let you know you are at full draw. Why do you have to rely on the finger to touch the arrowhead?

Sometimes on the battlefield you will only have shorter arrows available: then you will definitely have to rely on your finger to touch the back of the arrowhead (so you do not overdraw). But this is a special situation, and is not for orthodox shooting.

學彀者 以不彀之人 發矢能齊 亦
能中的耳 假如引弓不彀者 箭鏃在
弓弝外半寸許 是爲不彀 若箭箭皆
然 則發矢亦齊 所以能中 但不能
彀者 矢發多傷於小 而中的者少
耳 且不彀之射 骨未盡而直 惟恃
筋力引弓 久後筋力少疲 引弓日漸
不彀 始雖不彀而能齊 後漸不齊
矣 彀弓既不能齊 矢出又安能齊
乎 故曰「鏃不上指 發無中理」也
　夫云「指不知鏃 同於無目」
者 是目不能視 而寄目于指 豈知
射遠之法 目視在弓右 自箭桿至鏃
以達于的 一目可睹 何必寄目於
指 惟射近二十步之內者 視在弓
左 目不見鏃 然亦不必藉力於指 何
也 用箭必量臂之長短 故長人用長
箭 短人用短箭 各以骨節盡處爲
彀 又何藉指之知鏃乎 或者臨敵矢
竭 倉猝而用短箭 不得不寄目於指
耳 然亦特論其變 非論射法之常也

『法曰：前手攢緊 不由不狠』〈
第三段〉

發矢之狠 由於引弓之彀 引弓
之彀 由於骨節之直 故竭周身之
力 以彀弓 盡弓之力 以遣箭 方得
平狠 若只謂前手攢緊而狠 何也 如
使前手虎口緊 則矢發必小 不能及
遠 若五指一齊攢緊 只是把握之固
而已 矢何由狠乎 意者 引弓極彀
時 前手攢緊撇出 乃為狠耳 然撇
法 矢多偏於左 不若以前肩下捲 彀
弓之際 以肩力達之前掌 直托而
出 矢可平衡至的 乃為狠之正法 而
無勉強之艱難

〈彀法詳 捷徑門 并後 或問八
章內 宜合看〉

『法曰：息氣開弓 怒氣放箭』〈
第四段〉

夫謂息氣開弓者 以射為動事
也 若又以粗浮之氣開弓 恐欲速而
未能彀 故以息氣開之 則沈潛握
固 緩引自滿耳 放箭以怒氣者 以
為息氣之後 繼以怒氣 是果銳發於
恬澹之中 靜而能斷 發必中節耳 此
有得於射中之一見者 乃有此議論
也

孰知又有不必然之道乎 夫開弓
猛事也 以強勁之弓 游優息氣以引

4.3 Why Gripping the Bow Tightly Is Wrong (The Archery Method)

『The Archery Method says: "The bow hand should grip tightly, which will make the arrow fly fiercely."』

The arrow flies fiercely because you reach full draw. You reach full draw because your joints are properly aligned. Thus, if you pay attention to how you allocate your strength, you will reach full draw. With the bow's strength at its limit, the arrow will fly level and with ferocity.

As for holding the bow hand tightly to make the arrow fly fiercely, what good is this? You will end up holding the web of your bow hand tightly, and the arrow will not fly far. If you hold the five bow hand fingers tightly, you are only holding the handle solidly. How can the arrow fly fiercely? When some people reach full draw, they will hold tightly and thrust forward the bow hand, thinking that will achieve the required "ferocity." With the "thrust forward" method, most of your arrows will veer to the left.

But nothing beats settling down the bow shoulder blade. When you have reached full draw, your shoulder strength supports the bow hand palm, which is sticking straight out. This way, the arrow will fly level and straight towards the target. This is the proper method for having a fierce shot without overexerting yourself. <For further reading, please see "Full Draw" from "The Shortcut" (Book 1, Chapter 1.2), as well as "Miscellaneous Questions," Question 8 (Book 2, Chapter 4.7.8).>

4.4 Timing of the Draw (The Archery Method)

『The Archery Method says: "Draw gradually with tranquility. Release suddenly with anger."』

There are those who think you should draw gradually with tranquility because they consider archery a very solemn practice. If you are too abrupt while drawing the bow, you risk being hasty and failing to reach full draw. That is why you draw gradually, so you can achieve a steady grip and reach full draw automatically. Releasing suddenly with anger comes naturally after drawing gradually with tranquility. If you release sharply from this state of relaxation, you will be able to hit with no problem. This is only one theory about how to hit the target, and there are a lot of other theories out there.

However, the above description is not necessarily the right way! Drawing the bow is a vigorous activity. If you are pulling a heavy bow and you draw gradually with tranquility, you will lose your breath and have no strength left. How can you reach full draw this way? Moreover, the archer who wants to hit a small target beyond a hundred paces must have fine-grain control. If you release suddenly with anger, you will shake abruptly. How can you hit a small target from afar?

I have pondered this point thoroughly. From the moment the archer draws to the moment he releases relies on one mouthful of air. By the time he exhales, there is no time to take another inhale. Drawing the bow should be brisk (pulling slowly will delay your timing, causing you to tire prematurely). The moment before release should be slow (rushing the release will make the process too hasty). That is why nothing beats concentrating your strength and drawing briskly: you will reach full draw right away. This way, you still have energy to spare and your strength is sharp. Right after reaching full draw, you have time to balance the force of the draw among your joints. Then you will be able to release steadily in a state of peace so you can hit. Once again, when you reach full draw briskly in the beginning, you will have a lot of energy to spare, which will make your release easy, in-control, and error-free. For this reason we say: "draw briskly with anger, release steadily with tranquility." This is a fundamental truth.

If you are relaxed at the start of your draw, you will waste your energy and it will be hard to reach full draw. If you tense yourself on release, you will be anxious and hasty. As a result, the arrow will not be steady. Wise people will understand.

4.5 *Number of Days to Learn Archery*

『People have a saying: "100 days to learn the crossbow, 1,000 days to learn the bow, and 10,000 days to learn the pellet bow."』

This quote discusses how learning the crossbow is easier than the bow, and how learning the bow is easier than the pellet bow. Everybody thinks archery is easier than pellet bow shooting. That is why beginners think they can learn how to shoot a bow and arrow without proper instruction, and they are in a rush to shoot outdoors for military practice. When you are a beginner, your muscles are strong and your strength is sharp, your willpower is focused and you have no fear or apprehension. Within 100 days, you get used to pulling to full draw and can also hit the target. You think archery is easy: you think you have skill and arc superior to others.

If you shoot without proper technique, the joints will be misaligned, the shoulders will hunch up with the arms dropping, and the chest, hips, and butt will be sticking out. If you are only using muscle strength to pull the bow, it is easy for your power to diminish. Within 4–5 years, the hands will tremble and day-by-day you lose the ability to reach full draw. At first you will be short of full draw by roughly a half cun (0.63 in, 1.6 cm), but before long you will be 2–3 cun (2.5–3.8 in, 6.4–9.6 cm) short.

之 氣衰則力必索 如何能彀 且射
者中微於百步之外 以粗而實精者
也 若以怒氣發之 必且震蕩激烈 何
以中微於遠

　穎嘗思之 射者自開弓 以至于
發矢 只恃一口氣 呼而不及吸者
也 始之開弓當急 而緩則過遲而氣
散 既而發矢當徐 而疾則過逼而氣
促 故開弓者 莫若并氣悉力 以怒
氣開之 一引便彀 則氣有餘而力
銳 一彀而相機導竅 甘以發之 則
氣和平而中節 且始之彀弓既速 則
氣有餘 而後之發矢從容 有斟酌而
無差忒 故曰：「怒氣開弓 息氣放
箭」方是不易之論 若息氣開弓於
前 則蹈氣散之失 而弓難彀 怒氣
發矢於後 又太急而氣促 矢亦不
準 惟智者審之

　　『人有云：百弩千弓萬彈』〈第
五段〉

　是以學弩易於射 學射易於彈之
說也 人皆以射易於彈 故初習之人
謂射不必學法 遽往郊野演武 初射
時 筋強力銳 心志專一 不懼不
憚 蕩蕩無所顧慮 百日之間 機勢
一熟 引弓可彀 便能中的 自以爲
射法果易 而資稟之 果能過人矣

　抑孰知 無法之射 骨節未直 肩
聳臂垂 胸脡臀骯 專以筋力引弓 其
強易弱 不四五年 引弓手顫 日漸
不滿 始之未彀者半寸許 未幾而二
三寸矣 數年而後 益不能彀 無一
矢至的 即終身習之 不得其門而入
者 比比也 寧可千日計效乎 此病

舉目皆然 辨惑門具之詳矣 此穎之
親試而且親見者 此病犯過者 聞言
始信 不曾犯過 而初蹈此病者 聞
言不信也

『唐荊川先生武編云：發矢
法 弓前稍畫地 後稍合右膊 後手
心微向上絕出』〈第六段〉

出箭而前手撇 尚恐矢偏左 後
手絕 尚恐矢偏右 今按此法發矢
時 弓前稍畫地 後稍合右膊 則比
之撇絕 其勢又震動十倍 是粗浮搖
蕩之甚者也 豈能中的

故欲中微于百步之外 非沈毅審
固者不能 古云「後手發矢 前手不
知」方能中微及遠 此千古不易之
正法 豈粗浮者所及哉

彼畫地合膊之說 外觀雖美 求
之實用則疎 年少初學者 見其綽躍
可愛 鮮不為其所誤

細觀唐先生荊川所纂輯 非迂則
晦 其間有數行明白可行者 皆出自
古語 已為紀效新書所錄出 其餘
者 想為好事者附謂云爾

After several years, you lose more of your ability to reach full draw, and there will not be a single arrow that reaches the target. There are a lot of people who practice like this for a lifetime but never enter the proper gate. How can they hope to obtain archery skill in "1,000 days"? This problem is obvious, and I already have a detailed discussion in "Common Mistakes" (Book 1, Chapter 2). These discussions are based on my personal experiences and observations. Most people will not understand until they themselves have committed this mistake. People who have never had this problem, or have just started to develop this problem, will never believe what I say.

4.6 Criticism of Tang Jingchuan's Release Technique

『Tang Jingchuan's *Military Compilation* said: "Upon release, the upper tip of the bow paints the ground, and the lower tip of the bow moves towards the draw-side upper arm. The draw hand snaps back with the palm upturned slightly."』

When you release the arrow and the bow hand "thrusts forward and to the left," the arrow will veer leftward [▶ for a right-handed archer]. If the draw hand "snaps back," the arrow will veer rightward. Now if you use the method where the "upper tip of the bow paints the ground, the lower tip of the bow moves to the draw-side upper arm" [▶ i.e., spinning the bow in the bow hand until the upper tip points towards the target], then you will have 10 times more shaking than the "thrust-snap" method. This is an extremely crude and unsteady way of shooting. How can you hit anything?

If you want to shoot with precision beyond 100 paces (175 yd, 160 m), your technique must have an all-encompassing firmness and concentration. The old saying "the draw hand releases the arrow and the bow hand does not react" is exactly the way to shoot long distances with precision. For thousands of years this has been the tried and true method. How can you achieve the same result when your technique is crude and unsteady?

As for the "painting the ground" description: although the external appearance is pretty, this technique lacks utility. Youngsters love this flowery style of release, but they fail to recognize its faults.

If you take a closer look, Mr. Tang Jingchuan's compilation is pretty obtuse. The only passages in Tang's work that make sense all come from old writing, and Qi Jiguang's *New Book on Discipline and Effectiveness* already records them all. The other passages in Tang's book look like they came from the imagination of an amateur.

Tang Jingchuan's method of spinning the bow after release ("painting the ground") and snapping the draw hand back with the palm upturned. Gao Ying strongly disagreed with this release method.
Courtesy of Mike Loades.

4.7 Miscellaneous Questions and Answers

4.7.1 Confucius's Philosophy on Archery

Question: The Great Sage Confucius rightly said that practicing archery could help people develop "discipline and studiousness, as well as devotion, respect, loyalty, and honor." He also said "Archery can bolster military strength, and develop societal order." Even now you still think archery embodies Confucius's philosophy about "self-discipline leads to family harmony, which leads to national stability, which leads to world peace." Why?

Answer: The "Way (Dao)" encompasses everything from heaven to earth, from past to present. Archery is absolutely a part of the Way. People today only pay attention to studying archery, but do not think deeply about archery's underlying meaning. If you only think of archery as a means of training the body, then your experiences, aspirations, and tastes will become no different from ordinary people.

The Way of Archery is the following. When you are about to draw the bow, your body has to be steady. When you start drawing, you pull with vigor to reach full draw. When you are at full draw, your mind is steady as you harness your strength. When you are about to release the arrow, your estimation becomes sharper, your eyes focus more intensely, your strength exerts more powerfully, you hold full draw vigorously, and you harness the strength of your spirit. The arrowhead draws closer to the grip without stopping, and the shoulders coordinate to balance the force. After releasing the arrow, your spirit is calm and settled, and your body and bow do not move intentionally. This is what they mean when they say "the draw hand releases, and the bow hand does not react." Being solemn and deliberate from start to finish is the true Way of Archery.

We can draw parallels between the Way of Archery and other aspects of the Way (Dao). When you are about to shoot and want to settle your body, you are following

或問十發

〈一〉或曰：孔子 大聖也 於射之義 謂「其有修身好學 孝弟忠信之道」又謂「其可以戰勝無敵 可以臨民順治」今先生又推孔子之意 謂修齊治平之道 總不出此 何也

曰：道者 上天下地而無不包 往古來今而無不貫 射而進於道 無施不可矣 今人但知習射 而不深惟其道 所以終身習之 識不加廣 而志趣猶夫人耳

請以射之道繹之 當其持弓之初 必先穩立 安其體 其開弓也 猛勵迅疾 期其彀 及既彀也 固氣并力持其盈 矢之將發也 詳審慮精 目愈注 力愈奮 怒張之 氣愈歛而愈雄 鏃浸進而不已 肩旋運而徐分 矢發之後 氣定神完 形體凝然不動 是謂「後手發矢 前手不知」謹初慮終而得射之正道

廣其道而推之 夫射之始而安其體者 壯固根本之道也 既而猛力彀弓者 勵精克治之道也 又既而并氣持盈者 非翼翼小心 勤身修行 保

業持安之道乎 及其發矢 形神愈
銳 怒氣愈微者 又非就業以善後 無
怠無荒 兼剛柔強弱 而時出之道
耶 矢發之後 形氣安閑者 即雍容
和平 以養清靜恬熙之道 何以踰
此 由此觀射 則於孔子六言 與修
齊平治之道 果相通矣

今人習射未彀而即發者 固不足
道 其有將彀即脫 無暇堅持周謀
者 是爲謹始怠終 行衰於末路 功
隳於垂成 以此推之 修身治民 爲
將爲君之道 胥失之矣

射之所包至廣 故於射學之終 而
極論之 此天造地設之理 非勉強湊
泊成章也

〈二〉或曰：射者 乘機發捷 以
殪敵於目睫者也 今觀射法 一矢之
中轉折多方 則學射者 必欲盡習于
法 發捷之頃 不其艱沮遲留而碍機
勢乎

曰：不然 射法雖繁 得勢則
捷 譬之破竹 數節後迎刃而解 無
復著手處者 得勢故也 故學法者 熟
習之久 巧妙自生 舍矢如破矣 何
患轉折之多方 假使學法之人與不
學法者 分曹角射 得法之射 手一
開弓而即彀弓 既彀而能持 體固神
完 蓄猛銳之全力 而甘以出之 故
其出也 中微及遠 得勢得機 習之

---

the Way of establishing a solid root. When you pull the bow vigorously to reach full draw, you are following the Way of being motivated and disciplined. When you gather your mind and strength to hold full draw steadily, then you are following the Way of diligence and self-improvement. When you release, if your mind and form are sharp, then you can achieve internal peace without any anger: you are following the Way of pursuing perfection, staying motivated, being simultaneously hard and soft, and catching the right moment! After the arrow releases, if you keep your form and spirit calm and collected, then you are following the Way of tranquility. Thus, if you observe these principles while you shoot, then what you are practicing is connected with Confucius's philosophy of "self-discipline leads to family harmony, which leads to national stability, which leads to world peace."

People who fail to reach full draw and release hastily are not worth mentioning here. I want to warn the people who can reach full draw but release in a hurry: you begin carefully but end carelessly. Like walking aimlessly towards the end of the road, all your previous hard work goes to waste. If you fail halfway through, how can you hope to follow the Way of discipline, governing the people, being a general, or being a ruler?

The Way of Archery has many dimensions. This is why I mention this to students at the end of their learning process. This is the natural Way, not just something I made up.

4.7.2 *Familiarity and Catching the Moment*

Question: Archers need to shoot quickly to exterminate enemies on sight. These days when people observe your shooting technique, they can see there are many steps involved. It seems that you have to dedicate a lot of effort to execute the steps for such a deliberate technique, so how can you shoot quickly enough to catch the moment?

Answer: I disagree. Although proper form seems complicated, once you master it you can be quick. Just like splitting bamboo: splitting the first several segments is difficult, but then it takes very little effort to split the remaining segments because of your inertia. Thus, when you study proper form and dedicate yourself to long-term practice, you will pick up the nuances naturally and be able to hit the target. Do you still think these "complicated" steps will slow you down?

Suppose you have a competition between archers with technique versus archers without technique. For the archers with technique, reaching full draw is effortless. Once they reach full draw, they are able to hold it steadily and concentrate completely. They can pick the exact moment they want to release, and they are able to hit small, faraway targets. That is the way to do it. The more they practice, the more their technique matures (acquires flavor). Each day, they practice diligently and enjoy it. <The enjoyment does not stem from just hitting the target. What they enjoy is the process of exploring and understanding the core principles of archery. Once they understand the principles, they are on the Way. Once they get to know the Way, their interest in archery grows and their enjoyment of it is neverending.>

As for the archers without technique: they will release the string just before they reach full draw. They have a very hurried and obscene way of shooting. They lack situational awareness. Their shoulders are hunched, their body is misaligned, and their timing is all off. Although they are in the prime of their youth, they are already mentally and physically exhausted!

This is the difference between having technique and not having technique. Why would you avoid learning technique? In the beginning, learning technique is very challenging, whereas shooting without technique is very easy. Mediocre people take the easy path and are afraid of challenges. Although wise people do not fear the challenge, they might have trouble finding the right Way. It is for wise people that I write this book.

4.7.3 *Why the Beginning Cannot Be Simplified*

Question: A simple archery form is the best. But with your current form you say that the bow/draw shoulders and arms have to be well-aligned. With the beginning exercises you recommend, you say the soreness will last a month or so. Even young people will still need 20 days for the soreness to stop. [▶ See Book 1, Chapter 2.1 for a discussion of exercises.] Why are you making things so hard? Should you simplify things so more people are able to learn?

Answer: I disagree. People might think I make things hard when I teach them, but that is because I teach them something that will make their lives easier down the road. <"The Shortcut" in Book 1, Chapter 1 already has a detailed discussion on the hard versus easy way.> Let us use the analogy of a crossbow. Hitting the target with a crossbow is easy because the stock of the crossbow is straight. A straight stock makes it easy to reach full draw without shaking, thereby making the release consistent. People's arms and shoulders are just like the crossbow's stock, so how can they not be straight? If your arms and shoulders are not straight and well-aligned, then you are really walking down the wrong path. Even if you practice a lifetime, you will not be able to enter the correct gate. <See "The Shortcut" in Book 1, Chapter 1 for a detailed discussion on how to enter the gate.>

滋久 愈增多味 日新其好學 無已
之心而樂生矣 〈樂非止于射也 樂
其理也 理明而道存 其人之志趣愈
達 而樂射不倦〉其不學法者 將彀
即脫 促急猥瑣 魂神範匜 肩聳身
歆 機勢俱失 即少壯之年 意氣消
沮 而倦億衰歇之念生矣 此得法與
不得法之分也 法何可不學也 第學
法者 始習甚難 不學法者 始射甚
易 庸人樂從其易 而憚其所難 智
者雖不憚其難 而苦于無所適從
也 此穎射學之所由作也

〈三〉或曰：射法以簡便爲高 今
先生射法 必欲前後肩臂平直 骨節
瘦痛月餘方止 年少手柔者 亦須二
十餘日始安 不亦難乎 何不少貶爲
可幾及也

曰：不然 予之教人以難 乃其
所以易也 〈難易之說捷徑門詳矣
〉 請以弩喻 弩之所以易於取中
者 以弩身直也 直則持滿不動 故
發矢必準 人之肩臂 猶弩身也 可
無直乎 此而不直 正所謂舍正路而
不由 終身習射不得其門而入也 〈
入門之法詳于捷徑門〉 然平直之
本 全在前肩 故令下捲而肩窩前
向 又恐前肩過突 而括臂之病起 令
拳臂前靝 〈音竅〉 與目齊 肩窩前

向〈肩上小潭曰窩〉勿復退縮 而愈捲愈下以欲之〈此有口訣 筆不能盡〉則括臂之患消 後肩反聳 前肩反低 方爲平直〈此法詳于辨惑門引弓篇〉與弩身等 則持弓自然 滿固不搖 而射法盡矣 是爲一勞永佚 何惜兩月之艱辛 不以破終身之迷也

　若不求合法 只求簡便 今人不習法 而射者比比 簡便執一焉 終身習之 茫無所得 簡便安在哉 子欲予少貶以便拙射 誤矣

　〈四〉或曰：既云「兩肩平直」矣 又云「後肩聳起 反高于前肩」何耶

　曰：以前肩易聳 後肩易低 故引弓未彀時 使前肩反低 及發矢時 兩肩一齊并力 平平運開 始得平直如衡 而弓不求彀 而彀自至矣〈此段宜與 辨惑門引弓篇 合看爲美〉

The basis for properly aligning your joints is all in the bow shoulder. That is why you rotate and settle down the bow shoulder blade. But if you do this, there is the possibility that your bow shoulder might stick forward and your bow arm will become "exposed" [▶ meaning the bow fist is angled behind the body, causing the bow shoulder to bulge forward horizontally]. Thus, you must also make the bow fist and arm slope upward and forward to eye level and make the top of the bow shoulder rotate forward. You must not let this shoulder position falter. The more you rotate and settle down the shoulder blade, the more solid it will be. <Explaining this in person is easier, as it is difficult to relay this in writing.> This is how you eliminate problems with the "exposed arm." When you hunch the draw shoulder and lower the bow shoulder, then your joints will be well-aligned! <See the discussion in "Common Mistakes: Pulling the Bow Carelessly" in Book 1, Chapter 2.1.> This is exactly like a crossbow: you will be able to support the bow naturally and reach full draw without shaking. That is the epitome of good shooting technique! A moment of toil yields a lifetime of ease. Beginning with two months of hardship doing the right thing sure beats a lifetime of being misguided!

If you do not seek proper form, you are looking for the easy way out. There are a lot of people who do not practice with any technique, and they only think about the easy way. Practice that way for a lifetime and nothing good will come of it. How is that easy? You want to simplify my methods, but doing so will only cause people to shoot poorly. That would be a mistake!

4.7.4 *Shoulder Alignment*

Question: You said "the two shoulders should be well-aligned" yet you also say "the draw shoulder should be hunched higher than the bow shoulder." Which is it?

Answer: It is easy to make the mistake of hunching the bow shoulder and dropping the draw shoulder. That is why before you reach full draw, the bow shoulder should be lowered. When you are about to release, the shoulders have to exert their strength in a balanced way as they spread open. Then they begin to be well-aligned, and you can reach full draw naturally without even trying. <Read this section along with the articles about pulling the bow in "Common Mistakes" (Book 1, Chapter 2). It will be a good thing.>

4.7.5 *Dropping the Draw Elbow During Release*

Question: You said "the two arms should be straight and well-aligned." But during the release, why do you want to drop the draw elbow slightly?

Answer: When you have drawn the bow to your fullest extent, the shoulders are already well-aligned. The two fists are coordinated, with the bow fist at eye level and the draw fist at ear level. But if you do not drop the draw elbow a little bit during release, then the draw arm cannot move back any further, and the draw hand will not be able to release straight back. That is why you let the draw elbow drop down-and-back during release, which causes the palm of the draw hand to face forward towards the bow hand, resulting in a clean loose. This is exactly the method where "the draw hand releases and the bow hand does not react."

There are people today who drop the draw-side elbow before reaching full draw. They are trying to imitate "dropping the elbow," but they do not have a deep understanding of its actual meaning.

An example of lowering the draw elbow too early (i.e., before the release rather than during the release).
Courtesy of Mike Loades.

4.7.6 *Keeping the Draw Hand Level During Release*

Question: You are afraid the draw hand will have a dirty release, so you advocate dropping the elbow down-and-back during release. The draw-side fist keeps level with the ear and does not drop. Why do you only let the draw-side elbow drop?

Answer: The draw-side and bow-side fists move away from each other evenly in a straight and level line. None of the fists should drop! If the draw fist drops, then it will cause the bow fist to drop. If the fists drop, then the bow shoulder will hunch, causing your joints to be loose. You will not hit the target.

When you release, the draw hand should move directly away from the bow hand in a straight line, which will cause the draw hand palm to face forward [▶ to the bow hand] and open lightly. The draw hand does not drop at all!

〈五〉或曰：既云「兩臂平直」矣 發矢時 後肘稍垂者 何也

曰：引弓滿極之時 兩肩既平 兩拳又平 前拳與目齊 後拳與耳齊 若後肘不稍稍下垂 則後臂更無退步 後拳如何發矢 故後肘下垂 則手心向前 發矢得勢 即所謂「後手發矢 前手不知」之法也

今人又有引弓未彀 後肘便垂 是徒慕下垂之名 而不深惟其義者矣

〈六〉或曰：恐後拳發矢無勢 後肘下垂 以張其勢是矣 後拳如何獨與耳齊 不肯下垂以便其勢 只令後肘獨垂乎

曰：後拳與前拳 如衡之相對 豈得獨垂乎 使後拳一垂 必牽動前拳俱垂矣 兩拳既垂 前肩復聳 骨節俱鬆 發矢必不準 此發矢時 後拳只宜與前拳相對平腕 令手心向前輕開 毫不得下垂耳

〈七〉或曰：既云「兩拳平對」
矣 何前拳與目齊 後拳稍低與耳根
齊 何也

曰：此法但指武場中射的於八
十步者然耳 亦指軟弓射遠 故前拳
稍高 矢可遠到 若勁弓射近 後手
反高 尚恐矢益過的端 斟酌在人 不
可執一〈審法詳捷徑門〉

〈八〉或曰：人言「胸前肉開 背
後肉緊」之法者 眾矣 然卒未見其
人者 何也

曰：人但聞其言 未繹其奧耳 夫
兩臂之力根於肩 前肩之力根於
背 後肩之力根於胸 彀極發矢之
時 須用背骨〈俗云「飯超骨」〉并
力向前番下 送前肩從下達上 而前
拳之出矢 始平而疾 胸前之骨豎
起 送後臂從高瀉下〈向背後瀉〉而
後拳之脫弦 始輕而勻 如此則胸前
肉不期開而自開 背肉不期緊而自
緊矣〈前捷徑門審彀勻輕注之法 皆
托根于此〉今人不知此法 如武備
要略云 中平架及小架子俱用「前
手撒 後手絕 兩手一齊分撒」為「
胸前肉開 背後肉緊」非也 何也 射
貴剛中 剛蘊於內 而柔出之 則發
矢猛屬 而能中節 若以撒絕為彀 則
銳氣盡發於外 內剛不足 用臂而不

Question: You said "the two fists should be level and coordinated." But then you say the bow hand should be at eye level and the draw hand should be a little lower than earlobe level. Why?

Answer: The latter method is appropriate for (a) military exam shooting where the goal is to shoot a target 80 paces (1 pace = 1.75 yards or 1.6 meters) away or (b) making a light poundage bow shoot far. That is why the bow hand has to be slightly higher so that the arrow can reach a long distance target. But if you are shooting a heavy bow at a short distance, the draw hand has to be higher because you do not want the arrow to fly over the top of the target. You as an individual have to decide what works for you regarding the level of your fists. There is no single answer. <See the section on "Estimation" in "The Shortcut," Book 1, Chapter 1.1.>

4.7.8 *Core vs. Peripheral Muscles*

Question: People say "open the chest muscles and squeeze the back muscles." But in the end you do not see people doing that. Why?

Answer: Although people hear these words, they do not grasp the underlying meaning. Your arm strength comes from the shoulders. Your bow shoulder strength comes from the back, and your draw shoulder strength comes from the chest. When you have reached full draw and are about to release, you are relying on your bow shoulder blade <or *fanchaogu* 飯超骨>. [▶ *Fanchaogu* "飯超骨" is Gao Ying's term for shoulder blade. This happens to be the same term used for shoulder blade in modern-day Suzhou, which borders Gao Ying's hometown.] You need to really press and settle down the bow shoulder, which sends the bow arm sloping upward from the shoulder up to the bow fist. As the arrow passes the bow hand, it can fly efficiently.

You need to lift your draw-side chest muscle to make the draw elbow drop from level to a slightly lower position <with the elbow moving down and towards your back>, and the draw fist will release straight back from the string. This makes the draw and release both light and balanced.

Overall, you are not expecting to open the front chest muscles, but they open up naturally. You are not expecting to squeeze the back muscles, but they squeeze naturally. <This forms the basis for the Five-Step Method from "The Shortcut" in Book 1, Chapter 1.>

Today, people do not understand this technique. Like the *Wu Bei Yao Lue* descriptions of the Middle Stance and the Low Stance, they prefer to intentionally "thrust forward" the bow hand and "snap back" the draw hand, separating the hands simultaneously to release. They say this is their interpretation of "open the chest muscles and squeeze the back muscles." They are wrong. Why? The key to archery is hitting the target with power. You must make your core [▶ back] strong and your periphery [▶ arms] finessed [▶ do not interrupt the natural action of the bow, string, and arrow]. This lets the arrow fly fiercely and lets you score many hits.

If after reaching full draw you want to "thrust forward" the bow hand and "snap back" the draw hand to release, then your release involves extraneous peripheral motions. Your core strength lacks stability, as you are using your arms rather than your shoulders to release. There is no way you can reach full draw properly. When you actively separate the hands, your body shakes, and you will not be able to hit. You might be able to score hits in practice, but when you are in a high pressure situation then you definitely will not score. I make these observations based on my personal experience with these techniques, which is why I have recorded them in this book to warn future readers.

4.7.9 *The Written Word Is Not Enough*

Question: *An Orthodox Introduction to Martial Archery* (Book 1) only talks about shooting technique, and *An Orthodox Guide to Martial Archery* (Book 2) talks about the pros and cons of various methods. But why do you not discuss any details about problems that occur during shooting?

Answer: When some people face the target, they only think about hitting the target [▶ instead of proper form], and various problems emerge that are difficult for me to anticipate. A disease requires the right medicine, so I have to diagnose the archer in person. This is not something I can write on paper ahead of time. It is easy for a good doctor to cure a disease, but the doctor cannot prepare medicine for a patient that is not yet sick. Now you want me to write about all these problems in the book, but that is just like preparing medicine for a disease that is not there!

用肩 弓必不觳 兩手分撒 身勢搖
動 矢必不準 即或中的居常乃爾 若
臨利害之場 必多喪失 此皆穎之所
屢試而歷覽者 故書之以示知者

〈九〉 或曰：先生射學入門 僅
言射法已耳 指迷集條著諸法之利
弊已耳 至對的發矢時之病 何一言
不及也

曰：凡人對的時 存一求中之
心 百病俱生 不可名狀 因病而
藥 必須目睹而口授 不能預擬而筆
也 假如良醫之治疾 手到病除 然
不能未病而投之劑也 今子欲以病
筆之書 無乃未病而藥歟

<十> 或曰：先生所云尺蠖勢 引
弓時 先將前肩下捲 以蓄其屈曲之
勢 弓將彀時 兩臂從高壓下 俟臂
平直 則矢隨出 弓必彀而矢疾 故
名 "尺蠖勢" 今觀要略所云 三架
子勢 俱是引弓時 先將前肩聳起 兩
臂下垂 亦蓄其屈曲之勢 及弓將
彀 兩臂托直求伸 以出矢 亦是先
曲後伸之意 云何弓多不彀乎

曰：此理易曉 人未之察耳 大
抵自上而下者 其勢順 自下而上
者 其勢逆 尺蠖勢 先下前肩 彀時
兩臂從上壓下 以求伸 其勢順 故
彀弓易 若三架子勢 先聳前肩 兩
臂從下托起 以求直 則彀弓難 但
聳肩易 下肩工夫難 故人樂從其易
耳 嗟嗟 天下事焉有易而能精者
乎 故技而能精者 其始必先有所甚
難也 而况射之道至大 非可一藝目
乎

武經射學正宗指迷集 卷五
引弓撒放圖 凡九圖共十段

<第一> 引弓體勢圖說

射之法 莫先於彀 彀之托根 全
在前肩下捲 爲尺蠖屈曲之勢 而下
屈之勢 又須預蓄於開弓搭箭之初 <
弓既開之後 兩臂爲弓所束 前肩不
能復下 故云：「預蓄于開弓之
初」> 故開弓之初 先下前肩 使肩
窩前向 後手扣弦 將肘向上緊提 前

Question: In your Inchworm Method, you settle down the bow shoulder blade before the draw, using this coiled position to store energy. When you are about to reach full draw, your two arms start from a high position and press down until they have become level and well aligned. You can control the moment you want to release. You are able to reach full draw steadily and the arrow flies quickly. That is why it is called the Inchworm Method.

By contrast, the three stances described in *Wu Bei Yao Lue* all have you hunching the bow shoulder and lowering the two arms before the draw. This is also a coiled position for storing energy. When you reach full draw, the two arms separate from each other in a straight line to release. This also complies with the idea that you can bend first to achieve straightness. How is it that most people cannot reach full draw this way?

Answer: The explanation is pretty simple. Having the arm go from up to down is more natural than having the arm go from down to up. The Inchworm Method requires you to first rotate the bow shoulder downward, and while reaching full draw the arms start up and press down to extend. This technique is more natural, which is why it is easy to reach full draw. If you are doing any of the three *Wu Bei Yao Lue* stances, the bow shoulder hunches up first, and then the two arms start low before extending straight away from each other. It is harder to reach full draw this way.

But hunching the bow shoulder is easy, whereas lowering the bow shoulder is hard. That is why people blithely follow what they think is easy. Alas! With anything you do in this world, how can you do your best by choosing the easy path? That is why skillful archers (or those looking to improve) are willing to put in the difficult effort in the beginning! The Way of Archery is very deep. You cannot underestimate it.

Book 2, **Chapter 5:** Illustrations of the Draw and Release

5.1 *Overview of the Illustrations for Draw Technique and Posture*

When learning archery technique, you must first learn to reach full draw. The basis of reaching full draw is in rotating your bow shoulder blade clockwise and keeping it settled down. Just like an inchworm curls to store energy, settling down the bow shoulder will store the energy you need before you start to draw. <When you have drawn the bow, your two arms are already occupied with supporting the draw weight, and it is not possible to lower the bow shoulder at this moment. That is why I say "store the energy before the draw."> Thus, at pre-draw you should lower your bow shoulder blade and make the top of the shoulder face forward [▶ as discussed in previous chapters]. The draw hand hooks the string as you draw a little bit by pointing the draw elbow up and away from the bow. Meanwhile, the bow hand palm secures the handle and the bow arm extends straight pointing down and forward [▶ though it is angled a little bit in front of your torso].

The two hands work together to draw the bow. When you have drawn the bow about two chi (25 in, 64 cm), the bow fist should lift up <at the same time, the bow shoulder should stay down, and the bow arm will slope upwards a bit: hence, you only lift the bow fist>. Meanwhile your draw fist will pull the string towards full draw.

At this moment, the bow shoulder will press down while the draw shoulder hunches up. The bow shoulder sends the bow arm sloping upward to the bow hand, while the bow palm reaches out. Because you lowered the bow shoulder, you are able to extend and let the bow-side and draw-side shoulders and arms become properly aligned. <By "properly aligned," what I mean is that the bow shoulder should be settled down and rotate clockwise while the bow arm slopes upward. This way the arrow will fly fiercely. The bow shoulder will have a tendency to straighten out because of the stored energy, but before it straightens you have already released the arrow cleanly. That is why it flies fiercely. If you straighten the shoulders before you release the arrow, you have already missed the right moment for the release, which at that point will be dirty. How can the arrow fly fiercely this way?>

You bend like an inchworm because you want to extend yourself. You do not expect to reach full draw, but you reach full draw anyway.

By contrast, the three stances of *Wu Bei Yao Lue* have the bow shoulder hunched up before the draw. After pulling to full draw, the arms are already cramped by the bow. How can the bow shoulder settle down? How can the joints be well-aligned? How can you reach full draw steadily? If you wanted to draw the bow fully, you need to do everything properly before you start to draw.

However, hearing with your ears is not like seeing with your eyes, so teaching people with words is not as effective as showing them illustrations. I will first show diagrams of the three stances from *Wu Bei Yao Lue* followed by diagrams explaining the Inchworm Method. You can review the choices and decide.

The High Stance, Middle Stance, and Horse (Low) Stance: I have seen these three stances used all over the country. *Wu Bei Yao Lue* describes these stances because they have been around a long time. These stances did not originate with *Wu Bei Yao Lue*! That is why I show those illustrations so that archers can discuss the faults. Capable archers cannot avoid identifying these faults.

掌托實弓心 前臂番直向地 兩手一齊撐開 約二尺許 然後前拳翕<音"竅">起 <前肩下實不起 只將前臂斜起 故曰翕> 與後拳齊力引滿 此時前肩反低 後肩反高 急將前肩從下達上 送前掌托出 則前肩下屈之勢 至此方伸 與前後肩臂平直如衡 <雖曰如衡 到底前肩之勢須下曲達上 則出箭方狠 前肩將直 即出矢方爲出得其機 故狠 若肩直過而後出矢 銳氣已盡 出不得機勢 何能狠> 猶尺蠖之屈 而求伸 弓不期彀而彀矣

不然開弓搭箭時 如武備要略所載 三等架子者 先將前肩聳起 引滿之後 兩臂已爲弓所局 前肩如何而下 骨節如何能直 引弓如何能彀乎 故欲彀弓者 盡先於開弓時 體勢求之哉

然耳聞不若目觀 以言教人不如以形示人 穎先以要略三架子勢圖之於先 而創尺蠖勢圖之於後 兩圖並陳 使智者並觀而審所擇焉

大架子 中平架子 坐馬架 三勢 予觀大江南北及九邊射者 俱不出此 故武備要略錄之 此勢從來已久 而非自要略始也 故表而出之 使知射家之流弊 賢者不能免也

<第二>《武備要略》搭箭開弓圖

如此勢引弓搭箭 前肩預聳 前後手預低 骨節不直 引弓惟恃筋力撐開 未彀時 前肩不得番直推出 後手不得從高瀉下之勢 用一分力 方能開弓一分 如平地拽石 步步費力 引弓將彀 臂力已竭 前拳顫動 不能撐持 後手不能凝定斟酌 急忙吐出 如何能彀 必須如後面尺蠖勢 引弓先下前肩 前拳對的直推 後臂從高壓下 則彀弓得勢 比前聳肩者 十倍之易 既彀之後 蓄全力以發矢 斟酌如意矣

5.2 Wu Bei Yao Lue — *Pre-Draw Illustration*

In this pre-draw diagram, the bow shoulder is already hunched up, and both hands are already too low. The joints are not properly aligned. Only muscle power is available to draw the bow. Before reaching full draw, the bow shoulder will not be able to properly support the bow arm, and the draw arm cannot press down from a high position. You exert more force as you pull further: like dragging a stone on the ground, you gradually waste your strength. When you are almost at full draw, your arm strength is almost gone. The bow hand is shaking and cannot support the bow, the draw hand cannot keep things under control, and you are anxious to spit the arrow out. Is this any way to reach full draw?

You should follow the Inchworm Method discussed later, where at pre-draw you settle down the bow shoulder blade and you send the bow hand straight towards the target. Then as you reach full draw, the draw arm presses down from a high position. That is the way to reach full draw, which is 10 times easier than if you were to let the bow shoulder hunch up. When you have reached full draw, you will have energy left so you can control when you want to release the arrow.

Pre-draw position for *Wu Bei Yao Lue*. *Old illustration from the edition of Gao Ying's manual compiled by Jiang Qilong and edited by Ogyuu Sorai (published in Kyoto, Japan, 1780). Live photo courtesy of Glenn Murray, Esq.*

5.3 Wu Bei Yao Lue — *High Stance Illustration*

In this High Stance, you see the bow shoulder is almost straight and well-aligned, which is a little better than the case of the Middle Stance. But in the end, the bow and draw hands are still lower than the shoulders, causing the bow shoulder to hunch up. When the archer has reached full draw, the draw arm is closed tight and cannot move back any further: this causes the problem where the draw hand kicks out away from the body during the release. To compensate for the draw hand kicking out away from the body, the archer instead "snaps back" the draw hand during the release: however, this causes the arrow to skew to the right. Because the bow shoulder is hunched, at full draw he is not able to use the bow shoulder to send the bow hand towards the target at all. If he tries to force the bow shoulder to extend, the bow arm will inevitably perform the "thrust forward" motion that causes the arrow to skew to the left. After a while of shooting, his muscle strength will dry up and he will gradually draw shorter. He begins to fall short of full draw by barely a cun (1.3 in, 3.2 cm), but within five years it will become 2–3 cun (2.5–3.8 in, 6.4–9.6 cm) short. At this point, even if he practices all day, not a single arrow will hit the target. Everyone knows that he is failing to reach full draw, but no one realizes that is because he is letting the bow shoulder hunch up!

〈第三〉《武備要略》大架子圖

此大架子 前肩稍平直 比之中平架子稍善 畢竟前後手低 而前肩聳起 引弓彀時 後臂肘膊合緊 更無退步 則後臂有吐出之病 恐其吐也 後手往後一拖 矢必偏右 前肩聳起 弓將彀時 肩力更不能向前推出一分 強欲推出 必然一撇 矢必偏左 久射之後 筋力一竭 矢漸不彀 始之不彀者 僅寸許 不五年而寸許者 漸至二三寸矣 此時終日習射 無一矢至的 人皆知不彀之病使然 孰知肩聳之流弊乎

***Wu Bei Yao Lue*'s High Stance.** *Old illustration from the edition of Gao Ying's manual compiled by Jiang Qilong and edited by Ogyuu Sorai (published in Kyoto, Japan, 1780). Live photo courtesy of Glenn Murray, Esq.*

〈第四〉《武備要略》中平架勢圖

按中平架子 前肩獨聳 前後手皆低 比大架子尤甚 引弓前後肩臂骨節 不能平直 肩力無所用 全靠而臂撑持 雖大力之人 引弓 然時而臂必然顫動 弱弓且然 況無力之人引勁弓乎

又況前拳既低 矢出必不能遠到 恐不能及遠也 臨發時 將前拳一擎而出 則矢雖見遠到 然大小之間 必無定準 穎見拙射犯此病者屢矣 雖言之諄諄 奈聽者之默默乎

5.4 Wu Bei Yao Lue — *Middle Stance Illustration*

In the Middle Stance the bow shoulder is hunching up noticeably and the hands are absolutely lower than the shoulders. It is even more problematic than the High Stance. While pulling the bow the shoulders and arms are misaligned, and no shoulder or back tension is being used. Everything rests on the strength of the two arms. Although an archer might have a lot of strength, the moment he reaches full draw he will start to shake even with a weak bow using this method. Think how much worse it would be if a weak archer uses this method to pull a strong bow!

Moreover, because the bow hand is low, the archer cannot hit faraway targets. To compensate, he suddenly jerks the bow hand up and forward before release. Although it looks like he is able to shoot far, he is not able to control the elevation of his arrow and will be inaccurate. I see a lot of people making this mistake. Even though I point out their mistakes over and over again, they still do not have a clue what is happening.

Wu Bei Yao Lue's **Middle Stance.**
Old illustration from the edition of Gao Ying's manual compiled by Jiang Qilong and edited by Ogyuu Sorai (published in Kyoto, Japan, 1780). Live photo courtesy of Glenn Murray, Esq.

5.5 Wu Bei Yao Lue — *Low Stance (Horse Stance) Illustration*

This diagram shows the "Touching Nipple" stance. The shoulders are very high, the arms are low, and the joints are misaligned. It is even worse than the High Stance and Middle Stance. You might be strong, but you will not be able to use your strength with this stance. You might shoot accurately in the first three or four rounds, but after a while your accuracy will disappear by the fifth and sixth rounds. Especially in a high-pressure situation, your heart will be unsettled and both your arms will start shaking. As a result, you will have no control over where your arrows go. Before you reach old age, you will not be able to reach full draw. About 90% of people have this problem, but none of them realize the root of the issue is that their joints are misaligned.

There are people who want to learn how to extend the joints, but they study half way and give up. Then there are those who are reluctant to learn anything and instead criticize the method for aligning the joints. That attitude is even worse. That is why they say: "It is possible to discuss things with wise people. There is no point wasting words on numbskulls."

〈第五〉《武備要略》小架子坐
馬勢圖

　按此圖乃摸奶之勢　前後肩俱
高　兩臂低　骨節不平直　甚於大
架　中平架　有力無所用之　日日三
四迴　射矢猶準　五六迴後　射無定
準　一臨利害之場　中心無主　兩臂
筋疲顫動　矢不知偏於何所矣　年未
及衰　必犯不轂之病　今人坐此弊者
十之九　而未悟其爲骨節不直之故
者　種種也

　又有學伸骨　而不得其竅　半塗
而廢者有之　又有己不能學而沮他
人之學　且謂直骨節之無是理　則誤
甚矣　故曰：「可爲智者道　難爲俗
人言也」

Wu Bei Yao Lue's Low Stance.
Old illustration from the edition of Gao Ying's manual compiled by Jiang Qilong and edited by Ogyuu Sorai (published in Kyoto, Japan, 1780). Live photo courtesy of Glenn Murray, Esq.

<第六>《武備要略》撒放勢圖

如此之勢發矢 前手如托泰山 後
手如抱嬰孩 即此謂也 但前手撒後
手絕 外貌殊見雄猛 然氣焰俱現於
外 巧力不從肩出 矢發氣淨身動 何
能及遠中微 且骨節不直 引弓必不
能彀 而能爲怒張之氣 觀美亦何益
乎

何如尺蠖勢—前肩低而前後臂
俱高 發矢時 前肩從下達上 送前
拳直出 後臂從高瀉下 愈瀉愈彀 矢
皆從肩內推出 捷疾而身色不動 內
剛外恬 賢於此勢遠矣

The "thrust forward" and "snap back" release advocated by *Wu Bei Yao Lue*. Gao Ying strongly disapproved of this method.
Old illustration from the edition of Gao Ying's manual compiled by Jiang Qilong and edited by Ogyuu Sorai (published in Kyoto, Japan, 1780). Live photo courtesy of Glenn Murray, Esq.

以上文武備要略引弓撒放圖 以
下皆指迷集引弓撒放圖

5.6 Wu Bei Yao Lue — *Release Illustration*

This diagram allegedly portrays the release according to the principle: "The bow hand is liking pushing Mount Tai. The draw hand pulls the string as if carrying an infant." However, the bow hand is thrusting forward-and-left and the draw hand is snapping back. The outward appearance looks very heroic, but it is just pompous movement in the periphery of your body. The strength does not come from the shoulders, and the arrows will fly erratically because the body moves during the release. How can you hit a faraway target? Your joints are misaligned, so it is impossible to reach full draw and you become very uptight. You might look nice, but your form is useless!

By contrast, in the Inchworm Method the bow shoulder is low and the bow-side and draw-side arms are high. When it comes time to release, the bow shoulder is sending the bow arm sloping up to the bow fist, which is reaching out. The draw arm settles down from a high position: the more it settles the more you reach full draw. The release relies on your back and shoulders, the arrow will fly quickly, and your body will not shake. Your core is solid and your periphery is finessed. This is so much better than that *Wu Bei Yao Lue* style.

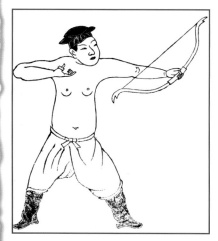 

Above I have discussed the diagrams for *Wu Bei Yao Lue*. Below, I discuss the diagrams for *An Orthodox Guide*'s method for drawing and releasing.

The inchworm must bend itself before it can straighten and move forward. Before drawing the bow, you must lower the bow shoulder and extend the bow arm forward and down. You lift the draw elbow, pointing it up and back as you take hold of the string. The bow shoulder is fixed and should not move while you raise your bow arm. At the same time, you start opening the bow with your two hands, with the bow fist raised to eye level and the draw fist at cheek level. Before you know it, the bow is at full draw! At this moment the bow shoulder is still low but the bow and draw arms are high. The bow shoulder sends the bow arm sloping upwards toward the bow hand, providing a stable base for the bow hand palm to point forward. Meanwhile the draw arm settles down from a high position, and the draw hand pulls straight back. You do not expect to reach full draw, but you automatically reach full draw anyway! The repeating crossbow (*Zhuge Nu*) pulls the string the same way: the crossbow's lever starts high and then presses down while the stock of the crossbow is straight and motionless. Without laboring, the crossbow reaches full draw.

Nowadays, people forget how to reach full draw. They first hunch up the bow shoulder and rely entirely on arm strength to open the bow. By the time they reach full draw, their arm strength is exhausted and they let the arrow go right away. They have no time to relax and focus on the target. How can they be accurate?

If you use the Inchworm Method to draw the bow, all you have to do is pull the string back and you are already at full draw. Once you are at full draw, you keep pressing the bow shoulder down, which acts as an anchor for supporting your bow fist as you raise your bow arm. You have strength to spare. The draw fist pulls away, coordinating with the bow hand to open the bow. Meanwhile the two shoulder blades coordinate using back tension to handle the force, incorporating lightness and balance to release the arrow. You will be able to make the arrow travel in any direction you wish. Hitting the target will become easy! <For discussion on lightness and balance, please see "The Shortcut" in Book 1, Chapter 1.>

〈第七〉《指迷集》尺蠖勢開弓圖

尺蠖惟屈 所以能伸 開弓將前肩先下 前臂番直向地 後肘朝上 扣弦提起 前肩下定不動 只將前臂舉起 兩拳一齊撐開 前拳與目齊 後拳與腮齊 而弓已彀矣 此時前肩尚低 前後臂俱高 前肩從下達上 送前掌托出 後臂從高瀉下 而後拳平引 則弓不期彀而自彀矣 如諸葛弩之控弦 只以後機從高壓下 弩身直挺 按定不動 故不勞力而弩自彀 今人不知彀法 引弓先聳前肩 專恃臂力撐開 故弓一彀 臂力已竭 隨即吐出 不能從容審的 如何發矢必準

若用尺蠖勢彀弓 後手向上一提便彀 既彀之後 前肩從下按實 則前拳直撐 力量有餘 後拳平引 與前拳相對 以張其勢 兩肩并實運開 輕勻以發矢 大小左右隨意所指 何難於中的乎哉 〈輕勻法詳捷徑門〉

Inchworm Method Pre-Draw. *Old illustration from the edition of Gao Ying's manual compiled by Jiang Qilong and edited by Ogyuu Sorai (published in Kyoto, Japan, 1780). Live photos courtesy of Chang Pengfei.*

Inchworm Method Mid-Draw.
Courtesy of Chang Pengfei.

5.8 An Orthodox Guide — *Inchworm Method Pulling to Full Draw Illustration*

When you are at full draw, the bow shoulder should be pressing down and rotated clockwise [▶ for a right-handed archer], providing a solid base to send the bow-hand palm out to support the bow handle. When you are about to reach full draw, the bow fist should be raised to nose level, and the draw hand should be at ear level. When you are at full draw, the bow fist will point towards the target, and the draw fist will gradually settle down to cheek level. At this moment, the bow shoulder is lower than the bow-side and draw-side fists and arms, so the joints are almost properly aligned. Just as your arm strength is about to be exhausted, you let your shoulders take over to open the bow. The arrowhead will move ever closer to the middle of the bow handle, and then the two arms will be properly aligned. This is full draw!

You are ready to release, but your draw hand cannot move backwards. That is why you have to drop the draw elbow down-and-back a bit during release. Then you will be able to apply lightness and balance to release the draw hand straight backwards. The diagram for this is in the next section.

〈第八〉《指迷集》尺蠖勢引弓將彀圖

引弓將彀時 前肩愈按實下捲 送前掌根托實弓心 大抵引弓初滿時 前拳覠起與鼻齊 後拳與耳齊 弓極彀時 前拳撑實對的 後拳漸低與腮齊 此時前肩尚低于前後拳臂 則骨節猶未平直也 然臂力將盡 以肩力繼之 兩肩并力瀉開 矢鏃已至弓弝中間浸進 則兩臂平直 彀極矣

將發矢時 後拳無退步 故後肘宜漸垂 輕勻以脫出 後肘垂圖在後

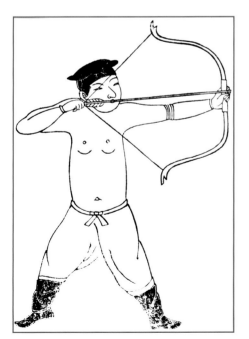

Inchworm Method Nearing Full Draw.
Old illustration from the edition of Gao Ying's manual compiled by Jiang Qilong and edited by Ogyuu Sorai (published in Kyoto, Japan, 1780). Live photos courtesy of Chang Pengfei.

157

<第九>《指迷集》尺蠖勢引弓彀極 矢臨發圖

弓極彀時 後臂骨節已盡 後肘與膊合緊 發矢時後肘不垂 後拳更無退步 故以肘稍垂<矢發時亦可垂 若未發時 肘不宜垂> 後拳切勿下垂 只宜平脫

今人學尺蠖勢者 始初亦知下前肩矣 至弓彀發矢時 後肘稍垂 後拳亦從之而垂 引弓非不彀也 但後拳垂 前拳亦爲後拳所牽而垂 前拳既垂 前肩復聳矣 孰知前拳若垂 發矢必不及遠 前肩復聳 則前臂主持不定 矢出亦不準 而始初下前肩之功 俱不效 所以學尺蠖勢者 未見其美也

故學尺蠖勢 而先下前肩者 當極彀時 發矢必將後拳守定 與前拳相對勿垂 只將後肘垂 而前肩從下送前拳 從上達出 弓愈滿 前肩愈下 後肩愈聳 兩肩繃開 鏃至弓弝中間浸進 兩拳相對平脫 此時前肩之下屈者方伸 後肘之勢將垂 而矢正從此出 是得機于此 得勢于此 而尺蠖之法 方見全美 而收其效

使前肩未盡伸而矢即出 則失之早 前肩已伸而矢不出 則失之遲 後肘不垂而矢出 則氣未足而出無勢 後肘既垂而後出矢則氣竭 出亦無勢 是前肩後肘之間 遲速失宜 出矢皆不可言得機勢 惟前肩下極方伸 後肘平極將垂 矢正從此發 飽滿充足 不先不後 方爲得機得勢 嗟嗟 非沈雄之士 安能至此哉

夫射法只有三大端—始而引弓之速彀也 既而持盈之堅固也 終而發矢之得機勢也 非從尺蠖勢者 不能到此妙境也 <尺蠖勢妙境在此數行 智者勿輕也>

5.9 An Orthodox Guide — *Inchworm Method Full Draw the Moment Before Release Illustration*

When you are at full draw, your joints have reached their limit [▶ your shoulder and back muscles are in place, without overextending or underextending yourself]. Your draw elbow is closed firmly (the draw-side forearm is touching the upper arm). If you neglect to drop your draw elbow by the time you release, your draw fist will not be able to exit straight backwards. That is why you have to drop your draw elbow a little bit. <You should only drop the elbow during the release. You should not drop your elbow before the release.> The draw fist should not drop: it should only move straight back.

People who learn the Inchworm Method today already know that lowering the bow shoulder is important. But when they reach full draw and are ready to release, they drop the draw elbow and then inadvertently drop the draw hand as well. They have no problem reaching full draw, but when they drop the draw hand then the bow hand might also drop in response. When the bow hand has dropped, the bow shoulder will react by hunching up! They did not realize that dropping the bow fist would prevent their arrows from going far and would cause their bow shoulder to hunch up. As a result, their bow arm will not be able to support the bow steadily, and their arrows will not fly accurately. All that work they put into lowering their bow shoulder is wasted. That is the reason why some people learning the Inchworm Method have not had success.

When you learn the Inchworm Method, you know to lower your bow shoulder. But when you are at full draw, your draw fist should hold steadily at the same level as your bow fist. Your draw fist should not drop (only the draw elbow will drop later during the release process), and allow your bow shoulder to send your bow fist sloping up and out. As you approach full draw, you will feel that the bow shoulder is getting lower, that the draw shoulder is staying high, and the two shoulder blades are squeezing together to open the bow. The arrowhead will draw ever closer to the handle, and the two fists will coordinate so that you can release the draw hand straight backwards. At this critical moment in time, the bow shoulder (from its lowered and bent position) is about to extend and the draw elbow is about to drop. Then when you release your arrow will fly true, you will have achieved the right timing, and you will have performed the right movements. At this point you are executing the Inchworm Method to perfection and making use of its full potential.

If you have not extended your bow shoulder and the arrow is already gone, then you have released too early. If you have already extended your bow shoulder but have not yet let go, then you are releasing too late. If you do not drop the draw-side elbow but let the arrow go, your release will be dirty. If you drop the elbow before letting go of the arrow, you will exhaust your strength and your release will also be dirty. All of these are not efficient.

When it comes to the positioning of the bow shoulder and draw-side elbow, if you time your movements incorrectly then your arrows will not fly well. Only when your lowered bow shoulder is about to extend, only when your draw-side elbow is about to drop, will you be able to have a clean release. Everything has the right timing: neither early nor late. Only then will everything be in order. Alas! Only people with resolve can reach this point!

In archery, there are only three main steps. First, you must pull briskly to full draw. Second, you must hold full draw steadily. Third, you must release at the right moment. People who are proficient in the Inchworm Method know that these three steps are extremely important.

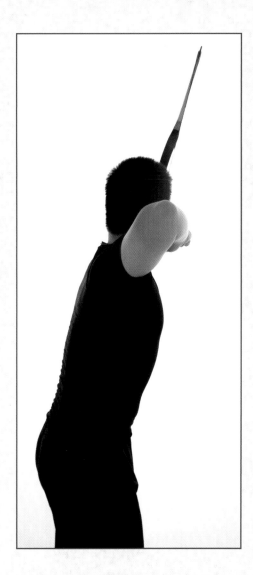

Inchworm Method Full Draw.
Old illustration from the edition of Gao Ying's manual compiled by Jiang Qilong and edited by Ogyuu Sorai (published in Kyoto, Japan, 1780). Live photos courtesy of Chang Pengfei.

〈第十〉《指迷集》尺蠖勢撒放圖

發矢法不專用臂 專托力於肩 直推而出 不撇不絕 前肩從下送前掌根直托 而前虎口自然不緊 彀極肘垂 而矢即發 掌必自然向前 極勻平脫 體勢反覺朝後 聲色不動 出矢自雄 正所謂「後手發矢 前手不知」者也 較之要略所載撒放勢 專以撇絕發矢 銳氣盡露於外 彀弓沈雄之實則不足 手動身搖 矢發偏斜者 異矣

5.10 An Orthodox Guide — *Inchworm Method Release Illustration*

You should not rely on your arms to release. You should rely on your shoulders to extend the bow hand forward and release the draw hand backwards. Do not "thrust forward" the bow hand or "snap back" the draw hand. The bow shoulder will send the bow arm sloping up towards the bow hand palm, whose root is holding solidly (which will make the web of the bow hand relax automatically). At full draw the elbow is about to drop. Just after you have released, the draw hand palm will naturally face forward, as you have released it backwards in a light and balanced manner. You are applying full back tension. You avoid any unnecessary emotions and movements. Your arrow will fly sharply. You are the embodiment of the expression "the draw hand releases, and the bow hand does not react."

By contrast the stances depicted in *Wu Bei Yao Lue*, which advocate "thrusting forward" and "snapping back" to loose the arrow, only provide the superficial appearance of sharpness. Their full draw lacks stability: the hands release and the body shakes. The arrows will fly erratically.

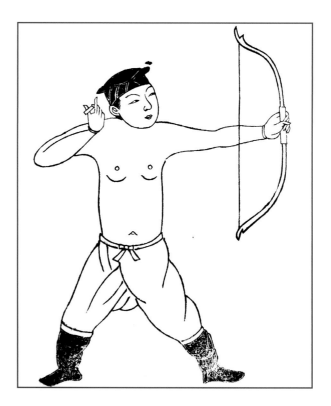

Inchworm Method Post-Release.
Old illustration from the edition of Gao Ying's manual compiled by Jiang Qilong and edited by Ogyuu Sorai (published in Kyoto, Japan, 1780). Live photos courtesy of Chang Pengfei.

眉山蘇氏云「有意而言　意盡而
言止者　天下之至言也」故意盡則
無以言爲矣　夫射一技耳　習之者不
過　一派弛爲止矣　何射學而累數千
言不止也　無乃意盡而言不止耶　而
非也　射雖一技乎　而其道至大　大
道至一也　而害道之說則至紛　惟其
道紛然雜出　則一言一行之偏　皆足
爲道之蠹　而道始不明於天下　無惑
乎　今之射者　雖有良材美質　童而
習之　白首而茫無所得　皆雜亂之
說　錮之也　此予所以不能無言而
言　所以屢遷變易　而不能自己也　言
雖屢遷　而總之發明變幻　驅除異
說　使天下群然　以歸於正道　猶禹
之治水　疏瀹決排　無非盡驅之海　孟
氏之闢邪放淫　無非羽翼聖教　則予
之數千言不止者　即琉瀹闢放之意
也　烏可已也

乃今之論射者　輒曰：「射之
道　始而開弓　不過兩手平直如衡而
已　既而發矢　不過兩臂輕勻而已　終
爲中的　又不過審視詳明而已」則
射之道　兩言盡之　奚以多言爲也　不
知所以如衡　所以輕勻　所以精詳而
明辨者　其間先後疾徐　合宜中節之
道　則不可勝窮也　而天下邪僻迂疏
之說　足以蠹我宜節之道者　又不可
勝窮也　夫邪正不兩立　利害不同
途　今欲盡舉射中之法　安得不搜射
中之弊而詳示其端　則予之書不爲
無意　而有意之言　是爲至言　以至
言告天下　天下必有以誠應者　故是
書也　不籍貴人言　以弁其首　亦不
假文士之筆　以飾其辭　而直書其所
自信者　示人以明白詳顯之辭　發射
中隱微之祕　昭如日星　辨於眉列　使

Conclusion to Book 2

Su Shi [▶ this is Su Dongpo, the famous Song Dynasty official/scholar/gastronome] once said: "You only speak with meaning. Once you have fully conveyed your meaning, you stop speaking. This is the best way to speak." Thus when you have conveyed your meaning clearly, you do not need to spend additional words to elaborate. Archery is only a skill: nothing more than drawing and releasing. But why, after I have written these two books on archery with thousands of words, do I feel like it is not enough? Is this a case where I keep talking even after I have fully expressed my meaning? In fact, this is not the case.

Although archery is just a skill, the Way of Archery is deep with only one destination. The other ways will lead you astray. That is why it only takes a tiny mistake to lead you to the harmful path. If you begin archery without being aware of the Way, how do you avoid mistakes? Today's archers have good equipment and physical conditioning. They start practicing when they are young, but they achieve nothing even when their hairs turn gray. This is all the fault of people believing in bad advice.

That is why I cannot write once and be done with it. That is also why I repeat myself and rephrase the same content in my books. Although the words are repetitive, rephrasing the concepts helps eliminate misunderstanding and allows the readers to go back to the right Way of Archery.

It is like when Yu the Great [▶ the legendary founder of the Xia Dynasty, 2070–1600 BCE] controlled the floods, endlessly dredging the river beds to allow the water to flow to the sea. It is also like when Mencius would continuously defend the original principles of Confucius and refute the half-baked theories of the time. That is why I have written so much: I cannot stop dredging the river beds and refuting the half-baked theories.

Today people talk about archery and say: "The Way of Archery begins with opening the bow, which is nothing more than the two hands moving in a straight line. Then you release the arrow, which is nothing more than the two arms applying lightness and balance. Finally you hit the target, which is nothing more than focusing the vision clearly." That is the Way of Archery in simple terms. Why do you need to spend more words on it?

If you do not know how to move the hands in a straight line, apply lightness and balance, and focus the vision clearly, then the sequence and tempo of the Way of Archery will be very hard to figure out. Meanwhile, all the world's half-baked theories distract us from understanding the Way. Right and wrong cannot coexist: they are totally opposite. When trying to promote proper shooting technique, how can you avoid describing shooting faults in detail?

Thus my book is not void of meaning: it contains meaningful passages which can be "best words" too. That is why I believe that if I convey these "best words" to the world, there will be honest people who will be able to connect with me. That is why I did not need any famous people to write a foreword for this book, and I did not need any fancy words to make the passages look good. I am just writing this book based on my personal experience, using detailed and accessible words to show people the hidden secrets of archery as clear as the sun and the stars. I hope this book will help future educated gentlemen to understand the true principles and that it will still be accessible to non-scholars. I do not want to follow the example of scholars who use arcane and flowery vocabulary to dress an article that is vague. When you want to learn the details of how to keep the body straight or the secret of how to hit a faraway target, you will learn nothing from them. Their fancy words are no help!

These two books are the accumulation of my 40 years archery experience. Everything I learned came from archery experts all around the country, and the result is the natural way of shooting. I did not make up anything and I did not hide anything. I have showed everything I know, so that future generations can study it.

If you cannot be a general or minister who protects the country, then you should be a good doctor to cure the ailments of the country. Today I am very old, and the country is suffering a lot [▶ due to internal rebellions and the Manchurian invasions]. I cannot share the emperor's burden of dealing with this suffering. I really feel useless and ashamed, and after I die nobody will know my name. That is why I gathered all the secrets of archery and compiled them into a book as a way to help the country, even if it seems like a tiny contribution.

The volume named *An Orthodox Introduction* (Book 1) discusses "The Shortcut" of the archery learning process, showing people the steps of how to enter the Way of Archery. The volume named *An Orthodox Guide* (Book 2) identifies the pros and cons of various old and contemporary archery methods, preventing people from taking the wrong path. All my stored experience and deep thoughts are just waiting for the right reader.

I know that I sound prideful and arrogant in my writing. I cannot deny it. So there will always be people criticizing me. Those who agree with me are humble and studious: they will not be confused by bad shooting techniques because they only listen to logic. All those who criticize me are arrogant people who have practiced for many years: they hold on stubbornly to the first thing they learned. Arrogant people will only veer further and further off course, and their faults will grow with age. People who are humble and open-minded will travel on the Way, and they will improve in a short time.

Alas! If I can help these studious and open-minded people step on the Way of Archery, then I am willing to put up with all the criticism!
— Chongzhen Era, Ding Chou Year, Second Month, Sixteenth Day
(1637 CE, March 12th): Gao Ying

後世博雅君子見之知其爲理之正 厚重少文者讀之 亦能曉暢而通其意 曾不效世儒之篡輯 文非不古 意非不幻 而皆粉飾於虛張容貌之粗 而於志正體直之由 中微及遠之根竅 杳無所得 則奚取於文辭之古也

射學兩集 乃予四十餘年射癖所鍾 要皆考集四方射家之精意 出於天成自然之節 非有勉強矯拂之偏 一朝盡吐 傳之其人者 亦嘗竊計之矣

丈夫不能爲將相 以安邦 亦當爲良醫 以濟世 今穎年幾古稀 丁國家多難之秋 不能爲聖天子 分一職之任 以佐時艱 而恥生無益於時 死無聞於後 爲陶土行之所羞也 故舉射學之奧 集之編 聊以爲當事者 驅除一臂之助 其名之入門云者 縷指射中之捷徑 開示人以入道之階梯也 名之爲指迷云者 辨古今射法之利弊 杜人妄趨之徑竇也 儲之歲年 擴之胸臆 以俟君子 自知僭妄之愆 無所可逃 然罪我者恒於斯 知我者必虛心好學之士 未爲拙射所惑 而惟理自聽者也 罪我者 必多聞自是之老 積學滋久 而以先入之言爲主者也 自是者愈趨愈遠 弊與歲增 虛心者率由正道 功可日計

嗟嗟 若使中道之道 得行於好學虛懷之士 則穎雖以僭妄 獲罪所忻願也

—崇禎丁丑仲春
既望 高穎 識

163

Appendix

Equipment and Practice Notes
for Today's Archer

Choosing Bows

The appropriate bow for practicing Chinese archery (or any kind of Asian archery) is a bare bow with a simple handle. There are no aiming sights, stabilizers, arrow shelves, or arrow rests.

Traditionally, Chinese archers used everything from wooden longbows to bamboo bows (including the sinew-backed variety) to horn composite bows. Gao Ying was especially familiar with horn composite bows, which were made with horn on the belly (the side facing towards the archer), bamboo or wood in the core, sinew on the back (the side facing away from the archer), and bound together with glue (such as fish glue or hide glue). Nowadays there are excellent craftsmen who can make a horn bow for you, but bear in mind that horn bows are for serious archers who know how to care for their equipment properly.

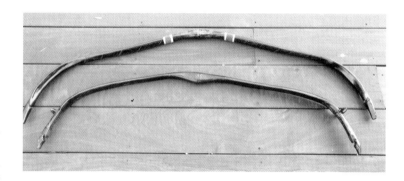

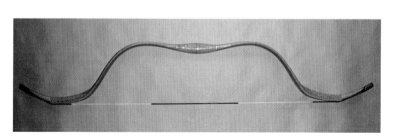

An Indo-Persian horn bow made by Lukas Novotny. Similarly shaped horn bows had existed in the Ming Dynasty in China, as depicted in old paintings. *Courtesy of Lukas Novotny of Saluki Bow Company.*

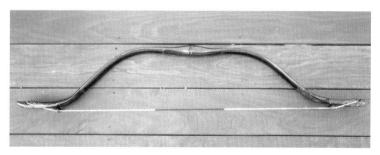

Asiatic horn bows made by Jaap Koppedrayer in the unbraced and braced configurations. Similarly shaped horn bows had existed in the Ming Dynasty in China. *Courtesy of Jaap Koppedrayer of Yumi Archery.*

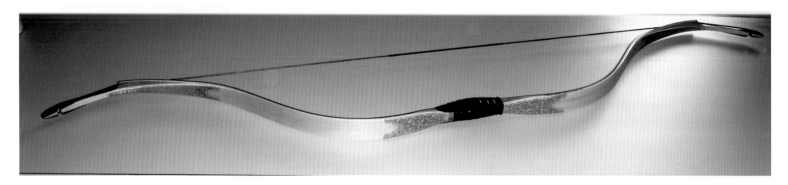

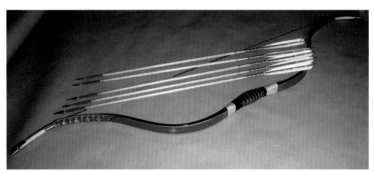

Examples of Crimean-Tatar bows with hybrid materials made by Lukas Novotny. Similarly shaped bows of the *xiaoshaogong* (小稍弓) genre existed in the Ming Dynasty in China. Wooden arrows are shown in the second picture. *Courtesy of Lukas Novotny of Saluki Bow Company.*

Gao talks about the structure of horn bows in Book 1, Chapter 3. Many of the general ideas can also apply to choosing Asian-style bows that contain modern materials (such as fiberglass laminations on the belly and back). Generally, Asian-style bows made with modern materials are appropriate for beginners because they are easier to maintain, less expensive, and less sensitive to weather conditions than traditional horn bows.

Examples of bamboo-fiberglass laminated bows. The first is a Ming Dynasty style bow made by Gui Shunxing (Mariner). The second is made in the style of a Tang/Song Dynasty non-contact recurve bow (with the tips swept towards the archer at rest). *Courtesy of Mike Loades.*

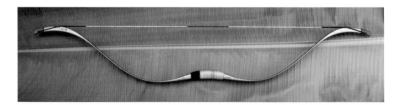

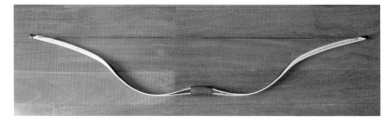

Checking and Tuning the Bow

Checking Straightness

There are many methods for stringing the Asian-style bow, so we are not going to discuss them here. It is best to consult the maker of the bow or to meet with an experienced archer in person for advice on how to string it.

Regardless of your stringing method, it is extremely important that you check the straightness of your bow after stringing it. You want to make sure the string is perfectly aligned with the tips and the handle. The string should essentially bisect the bow into two even halves (unless the bow is specifically designed so that the string is biased to one side, but again you have to check with the maker).

Checking Brace Height and Tiller

The appropriate brace height for a bow (the distance between the handle and the string) will depend on the size and style of the bow. Gao Ying gave guidelines for brace height and discussed the relative pros and cons of a high vs. a low brace height in Book 1, Chapter 3.6. However, rather than following his guidelines for which brace height is a function of the archer's finger length, we recommend contacting the maker of your bow for the recommended brace height.

In most bows, the tiller (i.e., the relative strength of the top and bottom limbs) is such that the bottom limb is slightly stronger than the upper limb. The brace height of the upper limb (measuring the distance between the middle of the upper limb and string) will be slightly higher than the brace height of the lower limb. "Slightly" is the key, because if the upper limb's brace height is dramatically higher than the lower limb, or if the lower limb's brace height is higher than the upper limb's, then the bow might be broken. Please consult the bow maker on what the appropriate tiller for the bow should be.

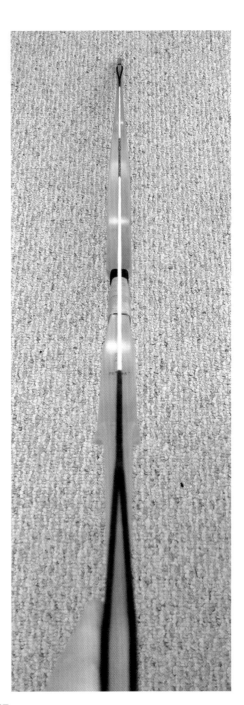

One method for checking the bow for straightness is to view the bow from the belly side while placing one of the tips on the ground and holding the other tip in your hand. You want to observe whether the string bisects the body of the bow evenly from tip to tip.

The bow square is a tool you can use to check the brace height as well as the nock point indicator height for your bow. Treat the "0" marking of the bow square as you would the bottom edge of your arrow and place the bow square in the same location you would rest the arrow. In this example, the brace height of the bow is 6.75" and the nocking point height is 0.625". The suitable brace height and nocking point height will vary based on the type of bow you are using.

Tuning the Nocking Points

The location of the nock point indicator (under which you nock the arrow) is important. As a rule of thumb, you want the nock point indicator as close to level as possible so that the arrow does not scratch your bow hand on the way out. If the indicator is too low, your arrows are going to scratch your hand. If the indicator is too high, the arrow can fly erratically and you will overstress and break the upper limb. Getting the nocking point level wrong can give beginners a tremendous amount of frustration.

Use a bow square and align the level-marker (where it reads "0") to where the bottom edge of where the arrow would rest. For example, if there is a clearly marked arrow pass area, then align the level-marker to the bottom edge of the arrow pass. If there is no clearly marked arrow pass area, then take note of where you rest your thumb when you grip the handle and align the level-marker with the top edge of your thumb.

Typically, we set the nocking point at 0.5–0.625" above level. Some people set the nock lower. Very rarely do you set it higher. It is best to experiment with a set of temporary nocking points before tying a permanent nocking point.

Tuning How the Arrow Nock Fits onto the String

The center serving of the string makes direct contact with the arrow's nock. Because the string is pushing the nock to accelerate the arrow, the thickness of the center serving in relation to the nock plays a crucial role. If the serving is too thick the nock will hold onto the string too tightly, which can result in a dirty, oscillating release, as well as long-term damage to the string itself. If the serving is too thin the arrow will not hold onto the string at all, resulting in a greater chance of the arrow falling off the string accidentally while shooting, which in turn could result in a dry-fire that damages the bow.

Ideally, you want the string to be barely thick enough so that the arrow can hold onto the string. At the same time, if you were to nock an arrow on the string with the bow and arrow pointed towards the ground, you should be able to make the nocked arrow (which is currently holding onto the string) fall off the string by giving the string a quick tap with two fingers (do not tap the nock itself).

Adjusting the thickness of the center serving or adjusting the width of your arrows' nocks can help you achieve a good nock/string fit. *The Traditional Archer's Handbook: A Practical Guide* by Hilary Greenland (Bristol, England: Sylvan Archery, 2001) has some great tips on nock fit and other aspects of traditional archery.

> ### *How to Calculate Arrow Mass Ratio*
>
> Arrow Mass Ratio = (Arrow mass in grains) /
> (Bow's draw weight with specified arrow)
>
> You can measure the mass of the arrow by using a scale whose units are in grains, grams, or fractions of an ounce. Be sure to do the appropriate units conversion from grams-to-grains or from ounces-to-grains.

Choosing Arrows

As Gao Ying mentioned in Book 1, Chapter 3.12, Chinese archers back in the day used both bamboo arrows and wooden arrows. In modern times, arrows with shafts made of bamboo, wood, carbon, and aluminum are available. As for fletchings, we highly recommend using feathers instead of plastic vanes.

The spine of the arrow describes the tendency for the arrow to bend around the handle during the shot. Gao Ying understood the practical effect spine would have on the flight of an arrow (see the relevant sections about arrows in Book 1, Chapter 3): lighter bows should be used with lighter, more flexible arrows, and heavier bows should be used with heavier, less flexible arrows. However, Chinese archers back then did not have a quantitative system for describing spine. Modern people understand the science behind arrow spine and can quantify it. You can use spine reference charts to give you guidance, but ultimately the appropriate spine of an arrow depends on the individual preferences of the archer (trial and error might be needed). In general, a clean, straight release will allow you to use a wider range of arrow spines with your bow.

For beginners who are unsure about their draw length, we recommend using arrows that are slightly longer rather than arrows that are too short. It is easier to cut an arrow to fit your draw later than to buy a new arrow that is longer. Moreover, some beginners have a tendency to overdraw, so it is safer to have slightly longer arrows.

Finally, but most importantly, is the mass of the arrow to use with modern bows. Gao Ying recommends an arrow mass that by modern standards is considered very light: a 5.25 grains-per-pound (gpp) ratio of arrow mass over bow draw weight. However, our guideline is to use an arrow with a mass of 8–10 gpp, but you should consult the recommended arrow-mass-to-bow-draw-weight guidelines provided by the bow makers and the arrow makers. Some bows with massive tips (such as Qing Dynasty Manchurian bows) might require even heavier arrows at closer to 12–15 gpp for a pleasant shooting experience.

Choosing Thumb Rings

A good, comfortable thumb ring is a necessity for the Chinese style of shooting. You can make your own thumb ring, or you can buy one. There are a couple factors to consider in choosing one.

Shape
There are a wide variety of ring shapes available. *Kay's Thumbring Book* (Milverton, Ontario: Blue Vase Press, 2002) provides a nice introduction to the different styles of thumb ring. Gao Ying discussed a few different styles of ring in Book 1, Chapter 3.11, and ultimately he recommended using a lipped ring with a guard. Although we are not 100% certain what Gao's Four Victory Ring looked like, we believe the rings with guards have the same function: no leather lining is necessary.

Size
Getting a properly fitting thumb ring is the most important point to get right. If the eye of the ring (the hole through which you insert your thumb) is too small, then you will have blood vessels bursting in your thumb during shooting. If the eye is too big, the ring might slip off during shooting, impede the release, or pinch your thumb in some other unforeseen way.

Beginners might consider getting a set of cheap plastic rings to find the proper size before upgrading to rings made with horn or some other material.

Effects on the Thumb
When using a properly shaped and fitted ring, you will not injure your thumb. You are not expected to develop crazy, unsightly calluses in the process of practicing with a thumb ring. If you

Example of a lipped ring with a guard.

are developing calluses or your thumb is uncomfortable, then you should consider changing the ring or adjusting your technique.

Over a long time frame, your thumb will grow in size from regular practice, and that is normal so long as there are no injuries to your thumb.

During a single practice session your thumb might actually get smaller due to compression by the surrounding ring. Sweat might also cause the ring to be more slippery. You might consider removing the ring temporarily between rounds to dry the thumb or let the thumb skin recover to its normal size.

Practice Preparations and Precautions

Warm-Up
Archery is an activity that requires using your muscles. A nice warm up can help prevent sports injury. Exercises that warm up the muscles around the shoulder blade will help you with lowering your bow-side shoulder blade during the draw. Exercises that warm up the back muscles (trapezius, rhomboids, lats) will help since those are the muscles that are supposed to engage the most when pulling a bow. Please consult a local coach or experienced archer for recommended exercises.

Equipment
Always inspect your bows and arrows before practice and during practice regularly to check for cracks or potential damage. You do not want an arrow (or parts of an arrow) ending up in the wrong place due to faulty equipment.

Gaozhen Practice
Practicing indoors at very close distance (~3 meters) in front of the gaozhen is the foundation for learning Gao Ying's technique (please see Book 1, Chapters 2.2 and 2.3). We repeat our caution from those sections here.

Traditional gaozhen were made from straw. However, modern synthetic targets may contain materials that could cause the arrow to bounce back towards the archer if (a) the target is too hard, (b) the bow is too soft, or (c) you have an unlucky release. We urge the readers to wear safety glasses in cases where there is a non-zero risk that the arrow will bounce back and hit your face.

Once you have established a safe setup for your gaozhen, choose a very small spot on the face of the gaozhen (or even draw a small mark or X) to focus your aim during form practice. With each shot, you are looking to (1) make sure your arrow lands straight (without the tail veering left or right) and (2) make sure it lands at or close to the small target marks you made. Point (1) is especially important, because it will tell you whether something is wrong with your release (such as the draw hand flicking out sideways away from your body, which is the most common culprit) or that the spine of your arrow is mismatched with your bow.

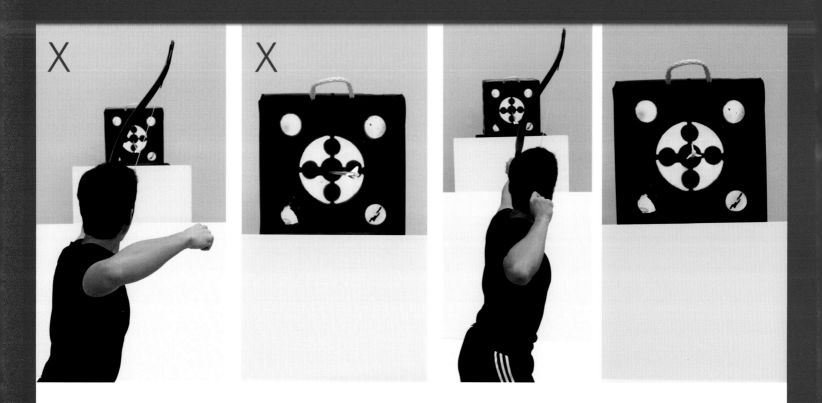

What to look for when practicing at the gaozhen. From left to right: (a) A sloppy, sideways release causes the arrow to land with the tail in a crooked position. (b) The result of a sloppy release from the archer's point of view. (c) A release where the draw hand exits straight back will mitigate oscillation at close range and allow the tail of the arrow to land straight. (d) The result of a clean release from the archer's point of view.

Further Reading

Axford, Ray. *Archery Anatomy: An Introduction to Techniques for Improved Performance* (London: Souvenir Press, 1995).

Greenland, Hilary. *The Traditional Archer's Handbook: A Practical Guide* (Bristol, England: Sylvan Archery, 2001).

Koppedrayer, Kay. *Kay's Thumbring Book* (Milverton, Ontario: Blue Vase Press, 2002).

Selby, Stephen. *Archery Traditions of Asia* (Hong Kong: Hong Kong Museum of Coastal Defence, 2003).

———. *Chinese Archery* (Hong Kong: Hong Kong University Press, 2000).

Index

For more information, please visit **www.thewayofarchery.com**